# Stop Investing Like They Tell You
### (Expanded Edition)

# STOP
## INVESTING
## LIKE THEY TELL YOU

DISCOVER AND OVERCOME
**THE 16 MAINSTREAM MYTHS**
KEEPING YOU FROM TRUE FINANCIAL FREEDOM

## STEPHEN SPICER, CFP®

NEW YORK

LONDON • NASHVILLE • MELBOURNE • VANCOUVER

# Stop Investing Like They Tell You (Expanded Edition)

## Discover and Overcome the 16 Myths

Published in New York, New York, by Morgan James Publishing. Morgan James is a trademark of Morgan James, LLC. www.MorganJamesPublishing.com

Proudly distributed by Ingram Publisher Services.

**Morgan James BOGO™**

A **FREE** ebook edition is available for you or a friend with the purchase of this print book.

CLEARLY SIGN YOUR NAME ABOVE

**Instructions to claim your free ebook edition:**
1. Visit MorganJamesBOGO.com
2. Sign your name CLEARLY in the space above
3. Complete the form and submit a photo of this entire page
4. You or your friend can download the ebook to your preferred device

ISBN 9781631956317 paperback
ISBN 9781631956324 ebook
Library of Congress Control Number: 2021938511

**Cover Design by:**
Megan Dillon
megan@creativeninjadesigns.com

**Interior Design by:**
Chris Treccani
www.3dogcreative.net

**Photography by:**
Jillian Farnsworth Photography
www.jillianfarnsworth.com

**Illustrations by:**
Daffa Amroe
Instagram: @damrubasah

Morgan James is a proud partner of Habitat for Humanity Peninsula and Greater Williamsburg. Partners in building since 2006.

Get involved today! Visit MorganJamesPublishing.com/giving-back

For Jessica
&
Grey, Lyle, Cass, and Rosie

# Table of Contents

"Doubt is not a pleasant condition, but certainty is absurd."
**—Voltaire**

# Introduction

I am not a doomsayer. Although it may sound this way at first, I have no wish to be alarmist.

I am merely an advocate for prudent asset stewardship. More than a decade in the investment and financial planning industry has left me concerned for the investments of my family, friends, and fellow humans—I'm talking about the vast majority of investors and billions of dollars in the market.

See, I told you I'd come off as an extremist doomsayer ... but bear with me, and you'll see I'm not.

First, you must know it's not your fault that you and your investment dollars are at risk; it's the poor advice you've received. It's the poor advice everyone receives: the investment paradigms commonly taught in schools and preached over the airwaves, and whose proponents include more than one Nobel laureate.

See? Not your fault. It's hard to argue with such a compelling force. Who would be crazy enough to question the dogmas preached by such highly esteemed authorities?

## Who Am I?

My name is Stephen Spicer. I have dedicated my career to helping people understand this potentially ruinous reality. And, after realizing that merely spotlighting all the flaws wasn't enough, I became obsessed with finding the absolute best solutions.

Why am I putting up such a fuss? It can't actually be *that* bad ... can it?

It's tempting to think that. I wanted to think that; it would make my life substantially easier. I could follow the cookie-cutter solutions to which most people subscribe, continue to market my services in the same way as other advisors, and do very well for myself and my family. In fact, I was on that path and making good money. Proceeding with that course would have been *much* less stressful.

There was just one problem (at least, it started as one problem): I kept discovering issues with the traditional investment paradigm—potentially devastating flaws in the logic. As I made these discoveries, I adjusted the investments I managed, only to find another flaw.

After years of searching for better solutions to each of these problems, I reached a point where I felt my investments could **better withstand the unpredictable yet *inevitable* market chaos and stress** without compromising the growth of a traditional portfolio.

I sighed a breath of relief ...

... and then looked around and realized almost nobody else had adapted. Nobody else was dedicating any time to challenging the traditional investment paradigms. They all just continued to argue about the same old *inconsequential* issues: which stocks will perform better tomorrow, the exact implication of a particular word uttered by the Fed Chair, or the residual repercussions of Donald Trump's most recent tweetstorm.

## A Galilean Task

In the early 17th century, the majority of educated people subscribed to the Aristotelian view that the Earth was the center of the universe. Galileo Galilei's research suggested otherwise. His writings on the subject of heliocentrism—the astronomical model where the Earth and planets revolve around the Sun—was met with harsh criticism from other scholars (read: "experts") of the time.

In 1615, Galileo's views on this issue were submitted to the Roman Inquisition, which *officially* declared the theory to be "foolish and absurd."[1] Ultimately, it was Galileo's pursuit of truth on this matter that led to him being sentenced to house arrest for the final *decade* of his life.

Challenging prevailing wisdom is no easy task. And, although I think an understanding of the movement of heavenly bodies is important, the concepts I am speaking out against will play a much more meaningful role in the quality of life of tens of millions.

---

1 Finocchiaro, M. "West Chester University–History of Astronomy; Lecture notes: Texts from *The Galileo Affair: A Documentary History*." West Chester University. https://web.archive. org/web/20070930013053/http://astro.wcupa.edu/mgagne/ess362/resources/finocchiaro. html#conreport.

At the same time, you won't need a grasp of astrophysics (or complex financial topics, for that matter) to understand—just **an ability to consider things logically and with an open mind.**

Understanding the resistance faced by Galileo, and the many others who have challenged a traditional way of doing things, will help provide you with context for some of the feelings you may experience throughout this book.

> "The most difficult subjects can be explained to the most slow-witted man if he has not formed any idea of them already; but the simplest thing cannot be made clear to the most intelligent man if he is firmly persuaded that he knows already, without a shadow of a doubt, what is laid before him."
> **—Leo Tolstoy**

## Agree?

I've spoken with many people for whom this book gave life to concerns they were suppressing. For them, this study has been the beginning of a financial planning journey that has resulted in a much happier, lower stress, financial life.

## Disagree?

There are also those who vehemently disagree—they stick to their academic-endorsed guns. That's totally okay and to be expected (think: Galileo and the Roman Inquisition—there was a strong authoritative opposition even when, as we now know, Galileo was entirely correct). For those who can't see it any other way and find fault in my research and logic, I welcome a healthy debate. I know that through civil discourse I will continue to put myself in an ever-improving position to find the absolute truth and couple it with the absolute best solutions.

You see, I'm not done; I'm not sure I ever will be. I don't claim to have all the answers already. As you make your way through this text, you'll discover that I've clearly cataloged the biggest problems with the way everyone tells you to invest. The solutions,[2] on the other hand, are merely the best I've found thus far for myself and my clients.[3]

## Somewhere in Between?

For everyone else:

- Those who deep down—whether they outwardly admit it yet or not—know something just isn't quite right.
- Those who long for an investment strategy that doesn't take years off their life due to stress.
- Those who are open-minded and willing to hear, learn, and consider counterpoints to some of the most widely held beliefs about investing.

More than anyone else, this book is for you!

## The Myths

I've spoken with many of you. The challenge for me is: you come from all walks of life.

- From financial advisors thrilled to finally hear another professional clearly articulate the problems they themselves were struggling with as they tried to help their clients …
- All the way to concerned "lay" investors with their life savings on the line, vigilantly just trying to find hope in this foreign-to-them world of investments.

It's for this reason the book is structured the way that it is.

- Myths 1–10 build on each other to destroy the prevailing stock-and-bond, buy-and-hold investment model that is taught by everyone from university professors to YouTube "gurus."
- Myths 11–12 evaluate the quality of the "expert" advice available to you within the industry and offer recommendations as to how to best navigate all the voices screaming for your attention.

---

2   Explored in Myths 15 & 16.
3   Don't get me wrong: they're great! But I will never stop researching in an attempt to optimize them even further.

- Myths 13–14 challenge the industry's recommendations regarding retirement planning and propose a more sensible approach.
- Myths 15–16 explore the best alternative strategies[4] you could incorporate in order to overcome these potentially ruinous investment flaws, empowering you to better protect and grow your hard-earned assets.

### Footnotes and Additional Guidance

As these myths build upon each other, we'll journey as deep as needed into the world of finance in order for you to fully understand the problems and potential solutions available to you. There are a handful of very basic concepts (e.g., stocks, bonds, Modern Portfolio Theory, etc.) with which every reader should be familiar.

To that end, I've created several supplemental video and text resources[5] to guide you along the way—from explaining some of those relatively basic financial concepts to diving deeper into some more-advanced side topics only briefly mentioned in this text to providing you with our most up-to-date research and potential solutions.

You'll find direct links for those resources along with other helpful insights[6] in the detailed footnotes throughout the text; skipping them entirely would be ill-advised.

## Who Is This Book For?

This book is for anybody with money invested in the market who cannot afford to lose a substantial portion (say, more than 50%) of their portfolio's value for an extended period (like, decades).

The investment reality I'll bring to your attention can be as harsh and unsettling as the childhood discovery that Santa isn't real ... except with your life savings at risk.

There it is again—that doomsayer rhetoric! I promise that by the end of this you'll see where I'm coming from. My logic is simple and sound. My concerns are real. In fact, I'm confident that by just a chapter or two in—if you're not there

---

4   That we have discovered to date.
5   You'll find them housed in our **regularly updated companion course: https://**
    **SpicerCapital.com/Go.**
6   Not to mention the occasional pithy sidebar ...

already—you'll begin to question your own portfolio makeup and crave better solutions, just as I did.

## What Will You Gain by Reading This Book?

Don't worry. The goal of this book is not to leave you feeling anxious and helpless.

In addition to openly presenting some specific potential solutions for you and your life savings,[7] as best I can, I'll help you reframe your understanding of investing for your long-term goals. You'll discover what **true financial freedom** could look like (hint: it doesn't involve crossing your fingers and hoping the stock market does well!).

My purpose is to start you on your path to a much more confident, stress-free financial future.

## Who Should Not Read This Book?

But hold up ... Before you proceed with this book, I feel compelled to include a word of caution.

You see, most people want things to be easy. That's a message that sells. That's the reason the mainstream advice—the advice which we'll be disproving throughout this text—is repeated over and over again. That message of "set it and forget it" is simple, and simple is comforting. People want it to be true. Unfortunately, the traditional investment paradigm is fundamentally flawed—a fact that, if you do decide to continue reading, will soon become abundantly clear. Naturally, as you discover this reality—especially if you have a significant portion of your assets exposed to the market in this way—you will become more stressed. You'll come to realize that your hard-earned money is at risk. You'll want to do something about it; you'll want to find a better way.

But unfortunately, the potential solutions discussed at the end of this book are *not* simple. Yes, they are the best solutions I've found to these problems, but even the simplest of them is nowhere near as "easy" as that traditional buy-and-hold strategy. Now, there will be some readers interested in this type of thing—with the personality, experience, and willingness to spend however many hours it may take for them to figure out how to implement these alternative strategies. But for most individuals, "do it yourself" will be out of reach, and the help of a

---

7   The solutions I'm using for myself and my clients.

qualified professional will be required. That is not what most people will want to hear; that is a message that will frustrate many.

And make no mistake, after reading through these myths, you *will* hunger for something better. And if you're expecting easy solutions to replace the flawed mainstream ones you have today, you *will* be frustrated.

So, to avoid that stress and frustration, it may be easier for you to just stay in the dark on all this … I won't blame you. I understand. And, if this is where we part ways, I wish you all the best. I hope things do just happen to work out for you in spite of everything. Good luck!

For everyone else: you've been warned; now let's get started!

# MYTH 1

---

## "The Stock Market Averages 12% Per Year"

Do you hate extreme temperatures—numbing cold and scorching heat? I do. If I were looking for a new place to live or a nice vacation destination, I'd want to avoid those extremes. At first blush, I might be attracted to a city boasting an average annual temperature of 65 degrees Fahrenheit. Sounds nice.

In reality, however, that singular summary data point is not helpful. If the city in question frequently gets as freezing cold as 20 degrees below zero and at other times as blistering hot as 120 degrees, I wouldn't find it quite so appealing a destination.

A city could experience those extremes and still average out to an apparently comfortable temperature. A single number is almost never enough to adequately convey the information you need to know to make an informed decision.

Or what about this one: you learn that scientists have created a pill to increase life expectancy. It's been used by hundreds of thousands of people all over the world over the last couple of decades. On average, the pill has been increasing lifespan by 4 years!

Would you take it?

Would it change your mind to learn that the worst impact of the drug could be a loss of 14 years of life with a maximum gain of only 8 years?

The details matter.

Summary statistics almost never convey the entire story.

> "There are three kinds of lies: lies, damned lies, and statistics."
> **—Popularized by Mark Twain**

Making life-impacting decisions based on statistics alone—no matter how accurate—is a dangerous practice. You often need more information coupled with logic and critical thought to fully understand the implications and ultimately formulate your own educated conclusion.

## Investment Return Statistics

So, what about with your own investments? How do you expect your market investments to perform over the years? C'mon, if you had to throw out a number here on the spot, what would it be? What are you anticipating? What rule-of-thumb percentage do you have in your head?

Some readers will have no idea. If you fall into that category, don't feel bad. In fact, most people—even otherwise extremely intelligent people—who have money invested in the stock market (often just automatically through their company's retirement plan) have no idea what rate of return they should expect.[8]

They're just all-in on the market because of yet another investing myth: that this is all just part of adulting.[9]

So, if a number did pop into your head when I asked those questions, what is it?

Don't worry. I'm not going to judge you. If it ends up being way wrong, so what. That's what we're here for—to correct these misconceptions, giving you a more accurate understanding of what the financial future

may hold. Besides, that number is probably one you've heard touted by some advisors or other financial "experts" anyway—so, even if you are way off … it's not your fault.

So, what is it? 10%? I hear that a lot.

Twelve percent, maybe? There are, after all, several notable financial personalities aggressively defending this one with some pretty convincing data. Realizing an annualized 12% return would be great, right?!

Or maybe your advisor has offered the "conservative" 8%? Good for her!

Which is it? Which of these percentages should you reasonably depend on as the projected average annual return that your investment portfolio will realize

---

8    If this describes you, you're probably especially going to want the companion resources at https://**SpicerCapital.com/Go**. And don't worry: by the end of this book, you're going to know what you need to know to **achieve true financial freedom** for yourself and your family. No more just praying the stock market does well enough so you can retire earlier! Also, by the way, congratulations on actively taking steps to better your financial future—on reaching beyond your comfort zone. I'm glad you're here; I'm excited to help!

9    In reality, there are better alternatives—even if most advisors and pundits don't talk about them. We'll explore some in later myths.

as you prepare for or enter retirement? And what does that really mean for how much you will actually have when you want or need it?

Now, keep that percentage in your head as we break down this misunderstanding (and, at times, misrepresentation) of the facts. You see, all of these figures—12%, 10%, 8%—could be "proven" using historical stock market returns, yet none of them is correct. This, of course, just adds to the confusion.

### The Reality

Even if we were able to come up with a reasonable percentage here, the reality is so much more complicated. Approaching your financial future with a simple rule-of-thumb expectation like this could leave you devastated, just as it has countless disciplined savers in the past.

The reality for most investors will likely be much lower than these figures. *Your* reality, in fact, could even be a shockingly dreadful *negative* average annual return for the decade and a half leading up to your retirement.[10]

Let's dig into this so that you can have a much clearer idea of what to expect.

## Source of the Myth

At the beginning of my career as a financial advisor more than a decade ago, I would assure clients that, historically speaking,[11] they could expect the stock market to average somewhere around 8–10% per year throughout their investing lives.[12]

To "prove" this, I'd just cite the historical returns of the stock market. Let's do that, shall we?

---

10  You'll learn exactly why and how as we explore these first few myths.

11  Such a tricky qualifier: "historically speaking." Although an accurate descriptor of the information that follows, it carries with it an unwarranted amount of believability and weight (more on this later). When I hear it now from someone, I think "no future guarantee and this person is just relieving themselves of all personal liability…" If things don't go as suggested, it's easy enough to just blame the numbers—blame history—it's not their fault! When you hear this caveat, don't let it influence your decision more than it should.

12  I'd go on to suggest, then, that a conservative expectation for their entire portfolio, between now and the time they retire, might be around 5–6% (with the stock market portion of that portfolio averaging the aforementioned low-end estimate of 8%).

## The Market

First off, we should probably define "the market" as there are, in fact, many markets in the world of investments. In most cases—in most finance-themed conversations where "the market" is mentioned—people are referring specifically to the *stock*[13] market.

## The S&P 500

The S&P 500 is the benchmark by which most investors measure. Made up of the 500 largest US companies—representing roughly 80%[14] of the total US stock market—this index[15] is one of the most representative of the US (and world, for that matter) economy in general.

Originally consisting of 90 of the largest companies in the United States, Standard & Poor's started tracking this index back in 1926. In 1957, it was expanded to the 500-company composite we recognize today.

Here's the year-by-year return breakdown.

### Table 1
### S&P 500 Historical Annual Returns

| | | | | | | | | | |
|---|---|---|---|---|---|---|---|---|---|
| 1926 11.62% | 1936 33.92% | 1946 -8.07% | 1956 6.56% | 1966 -10.06% | 1976 23.84% | 1986 18.67% | 1996 22.96% | 2006 15.79% | 2016 11.96% |
| 1927 37.49% | 1937 -35.03% | 1947 5.71% | 1957 -10.78% | 1967 23.98% | 1977 -7.18% | 1987 5.25% | 1997 33.36% | 2007 5.49% | 2017 21.83% |
| 1928 43.61% | 1938 31.12% | 1948 5.50% | 1958 43.36% | 1968 11.06% | 1978 6.56% | 1988 16.61% | 1998 28.58% | 2008 -37.00% | 2018 -4.38% |
| 1929 -8.42% | 1939 -0.41% | 1949 18.79% | 1959 11.96% | 1969 -8.50% | 1979 18.44% | 1989 31.69% | 1999 21.04% | 2009 26.46% | 2019 31.49% |
| 1930 -24.90% | 1940 -9.78% | 1950 31.71% | 1960 0.47% | 1970 4.01% | 1980 32.42% | 1990 -3.10% | 2000 -9.10% | 2010 15.06% | 2020 18.40% |
| 1931 -43.34% | 1941 -11.59% | 1951 24.02% | 1961 26.89% | 1971 14.31% | 1981 -4.91% | 1991 30.47% | 2001 -11.89% | 2011 2.11% | |
| 1932 -8.19% | 1942 20.34% | 1952 18.37% | 1962 -8.73% | 1972 18.98% | 1982 21.55% | 1992 7.62% | 2002 -22.10% | 2012 16.00% | |
| 1933 53.99% | 1943 25.90% | 1953 -0.99% | 1963 22.80% | 1973 -14.66% | 1983 22.56% | 1993 10.08% | 2003 28.68% | 2013 32.39% | |
| 1934 -1.44% | 1944 19.75% | 1954 52.62% | 1964 16.48% | 1974 -26.47% | 1984 6.27% | 1994 1.32% | 2004 10.88% | 2014 13.69% | |
| 1935 47.67% | 1945 36.44% | 1955 31.56% | 1965 12.45% | 1975 37.20% | 1985 31.73% | 1995 37.58% | 2005 4.91% | 2015 1.38% | |

To calculate a simple average, we just need to add all these returns together and then divide by the number of years (95). This calculation reveals that from 1926 through the end of 2020, the S&P 500 has averaged a 12.1% annual return.

Boom!

---

13   A stock represents actual ownership of a small fraction of a corporation. For a comprehensive video and text explanation review the companion resources at https://SpicerCapital.com/Go.

14   https://us.spindices.com/indices/equity/sp-500.

15   An index tracks a group of investments as opposed to just one individual stock. There are several popular indices. For a more thorough exploration of the most common explore the companion resources at https://SpicerCapital.com/Go.

There you have it. Case closed! Twelve percent per year is what you should expect in the market. And look at my-old-financial-planner-self from earlier taking care of you by presenting such a conservative bar for your expectations—with my 6%, 8%, or even 10% projections.

It's true: the simple average of the market's annual returns comes out to 12.1%!

An advisor trying to bring his point home might continue with, "And sure, everyone knows that the stock market falls sometimes. Right? But until 2008, it had never realized a negative annual return over any 10-year period, and even then, that was only a 1% average annual loss."[16] They could continue, "And when averaged with the decade prior, you would have realized a respectable 8% annualized return. Pretty great how that works out, right?!"[17]

I started my career with one of the largest financial planning firms in the country. I was trained to show people that over any 15-year period, the stock market has *never* lost money! (Over the last 95 years at least.)[18]

## Figure 1
## S&P 500 15-Year Annualized Returns

*Note:* Average annual returns for the 15-year periods ending in 1941 (1926–1941) through 2020.

Before the crash in 2008, one could have created compelling marketing material making a similar claim except for every 10-year period. Note how easy it is

---

16  It was actually –1.4%, but –1% sounds so much better and is still accurate without even stretching beyond traditional rounding conventions …

17  Although mathematically correct, this fact probably did little to comfort those expecting to retire around 2008.

18  That's without factoring for any fees (more on them in Myth 2). When you account for the average advisory fee, you'd have to extend the time period to 20 years for this statement to still be true.

to manipulate statistics: when the 10-year data are no longer helpful to prove a point, a slight adjustment can be made in order to continue selling the same story.

All these numbers are true. And if my goal was to just convince you that you should invest in the market and let it ride no matter what—that buy-and-hold strategy (which we'll debunk soon[19])—these data present a compelling case. It especially does so for the everyday investors who are not really interested in, and don't have the time to, thoroughly read between the lines. They just want someone they can trust to help them know what meaningful action they should take today in order to most efficiently achieve their goals as soon and as *safely* as possible.

## Industry Use of This Myth

These are the facts taught in universities and industry certification courses. They're the facts shared by financial professionals. They're the facts regurgitated by pundits and other finance personalities.

Those figures lead you to conservatively expect at least a 10% return on your market investment dollars over time. Right? It almost makes you think an 8% assumption would be playing it *super* safe. Don't you think? But more than anything, it can make you feel like "where else can I so easily get such a high consistent return?!"

I DON'T KNOW WHERE ELSE YOU CAN SO EASILY GET SUCH A CONSISTENT HIGH RETURN...

LIKE 12%, YOU KNOW?

That's how the data are used—and they're used masterfully.

When presented with the data of such high average annual returns, it almost seems foolish to not invest in stocks. Almost seems like you kind of have to—I mean, you're so far from your money goals and where else could you expect such quick growth?

When you see those charts of the market never losing money over the long run, well … it almost feels like a sort of guarantee. The safe long-term bet. A sure thing even.

This information is used to convince you that you'd be silly to not keep your money invested in the market, no matter what—no matter how chaotic the price movements may be.

---

19   Both Myths 9 & 10 will expose the flaws with that stock-and-bond, buy-and-hold strategy.

## Conflicted Interest

Why would anyone care whether or not you're invested in the market?

Before we explore the reality of these investment return figures, let's take a moment to consider who stands to gain from you—the collective you, the investing masses—being invested in the market and why.

I THINK THE STOCK MARKET IS THE MOST SURE WAY FOR OUR MONEY TO ACTUALLY GROW.

When you pull your money out of the market or an individual stock, your actions, in a very small way, put downward pressure on the price per share of that stock and on the valuation of the market as a whole. The more people who pull their money out of the market and move to other investments, the more downward pressure there will be.

The opposite is also true: as you invest more and more of your money into stocks and the market in general (think: automated contributions to your retirement accounts[20]) this pushes stock prices higher.

Consider the many powerful corporations who derive their value from their respective stock's price. Think of the benefit to these companies as the masses mindlessly push their stock higher by buying their shares without any thoughtful evaluation. Many executives at these corporations have incentivized compensation directly linked to their stocks' price.

Consider the many influential people with hundreds of millions to tens of billions of their own dollars tied up in the stock market or with an individual company (think: Jeff Bezos with Amazon[21] or Elon Musk with Tesla[22]—the two wealthiest people in the world both derive more than 90% of their net worth from their company's stock—the list goes on).

---

20  As is encouraged by many advisors and pundits. The investing strategy of **dollar cost averaging**, for example, encourages people to ignore the valuation of the market and just contribute month in and month out, no matter what.

21  More than $170B of his $180B net worth at the time of this writing.

22  More than $150B of his $160B net worth at the time of this writing.

If investors en masse decide that the stock market is not, in fact, where they would like to just mindlessly store their accumulating wealth … some extremely rich and very influential people and corporations stand to lose a lot of money.

Beyond all that, think about the massive financial industrial complex …

Consider the billions of dollars raked in each year from investment firms' and their advisors' management fees.[23]

Consider the billions of dollars earned by fund companies—where millions of individuals have trillions of dollars invested (Vanguard and Blackrock, for example, both generate hundreds of billions of dollars each year from their funds).

And that's not even all …

Consider the more recent political ownership of the stock market's performance—how the market is used as a barometer of how well people think the economy or a president is performing.

**There are countless influential individuals and institutions who benefit from you (or at least, the collective you) investing in and *staying in* the stock market.**

When you understand that, it's not hard to believe that these same people and companies might want to massage the data in order to influence (read: manipulate) the way you think about investing … as uncomfortable as this reality is to fully take in.

## The Reality

The reality is it's not as easy as just calculating a simple average. This is one of the big problems with throwing out loose expectations and glossing over the details. What else can you (as the potential investor) do with them? Are you expected to take them with a grain of salt? To do your own research to understand the real nuanced connection between market movements and their potentially disastrous effect on your retirement?

Maybe you are expected to do all that … or, at least, maybe you should.

Regardless, it's safe to say that most do not. Most don't know that they should. And if they do, they don't know where to begin. Most individual investors don't know how to crack the protective and complex surface of the machine I've just described

---

23   More specific figures on this in Myth 2.

## John and Mary

You've already met John. When he and Mary were younger and newly married, they were determined to make "adult" financial decisions. Good for them!

At that point, John was making a slightly-above-average starting income of $50,000. He expected annual raises to the tune of 3%. They wanted to be able to retire at age 65 (they were 22 then) and pull out the inflation-adjusted equivalent of $50,000 every year thereafter (assuming the historically based 2.5% inflation[24]).

### Figure 2
### John and Mary's Retirement Savings Plan

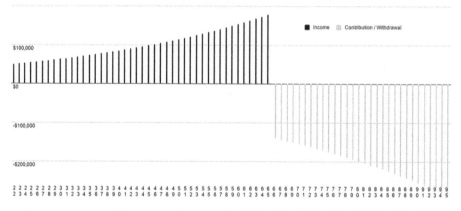

John read several popular books about planning for retirement. He listened to the podcasts of some prominent financial personalities. Several of the "experts" he was following had "proven" the stock market's historical more-than-12% return. Using that information, John put cursor to spreadsheet and built some elaborate charts. He was pleased with what he discovered: given these historically based assumptions, to be able to retire at their desired age and withdraw their

---

24  There have been periods with much higher inflation, which could greatly impact your ability to save and/or retire. More on inflation later.

desired amount, he and Mary would only need to save about 2% of John's pre-tax income each year.[25] This whole adulting thing was going to be easy.

## Figure 3
### John and Mary's Total Retirement Savings Projections

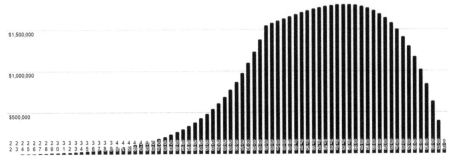

Note: John and Mary's Investment Account Balance from Age 22–95.

## Critical Consideration

Let's, together, critically consider John's conclusion here. We'll start with our primary claim-in-question of the market's average annual return.

Most advisors and pundits will use this 12% figure as an afterthought plug to help their client (or potential client) feel as though they're being conservative with their projections for the client's hard-earned dollars—a desirable trait in an advisor.

There's one financial personality, however, who defends his 12%+ claims more vehemently than any other I've seen. On his blog, in an article entitled "The 12% Reality,"[26] Dave Ramsey[27] cites similar S&P 500 historical data as

---

25  Maybe you feel as though you would be more conservative with your projections than John was here—perhaps projecting out an 8% or even 6% annualized return for your investment portfolio. I certainly hope that's the case. But even then, as you'll see as we progress through these first four myths, even relying on conservative projections like these could still leave you devastated if you don't understand the reality of the way the market works. Regardless, my point here is to demonstrate just how potentially ruinous this 12%-reality claim could be and is for some adherents.

26  https://www.daveramsey.com/blog/the-12-reality.

27  Please note: I believe that what Ramsey has done to help people get out of debt—managing to make that an entertaining conversation—is wonderful. That has been an extremely positive contribution to the financial industry. Regarding his investment advice once you're out of debt, however, I believe that to be incorrect and especially dangerous. Anyone who

evidence for his readers and concludes, "So you can see, 12% is not a magic number. *Based on the history of the market,* it's a reasonable expectation for your long-term investments."

This is the *expectation* Ramsey is setting for the millions who diligently heed his investment advice: "[12% is] a **reasonable** *expectation* for your long-term investments!" (emphasis and exclamation point added)

I should add that he is by no means the only one doing this … he just happens to be the loudest.

## Average Versus Actual

If you discovered that the *average* annualized return was different than what you would *actually* realize, about which would you care more—the average or the actual?

The actual, right? In fact, wouldn't that be the only one you care about? If the average is meaningless to where your account will *actually* be in retirement, why bother?

In the world of investments, there is a difference. And in the world of stocks, specifically, that difference can be substantial. To understand this variance, one has to look no further than the source[28] that Ramsey himself cites in his post.

Before you even get to the calculator that Dave's team used to "prove" his "12% reality" claim—right there at the top of the page—you find this warning:

> A problem with talking about average investment returns is that there is real ambiguity about what people mean by 'average.' For example, if you had an investment that went up 100% one year and then came down 50% the next, you certainly wouldn't say that you had an average return of 25% = (100% 50%)/2, because your principal is back where it started: your real annualized gain is zero.
>
> In this example, the 25% is the simple average, or 'arithmetic mean.' The zero percent that you really got is the 'geometric mean,'

---

has taken his Financial Peace University course knows that not only does he insist that your mutual funds can earn 12% per year, he often makes that sound as though it should be the expectation. With everything we're discussing in this book, you'll discover that not only is that blatantly false, it's even more dangerous than the traditional advice I otherwise reference throughout.

28  http://www.moneychimp.com/features/market_cagr.htm.

also called the 'annualized return,' or the CAGR for Compound Annual Growth Rate.

Volatile investments are frequently stated in terms of the simple average, rather than the CAGR that you actually get. (Bad news: the CAGR is smaller.)

The Compound Annual Growth Rate is *smaller.*

Unless an investment has the exact same return every single year, **your actual realized gain will *always* be smaller than the simple average.**

## Volatility

Consider the returns over 10 years of the following two investment portfolios. Which would you rather have?

### Table 2
### Portfolio Volatility Comparison

| Portfolio 1 | Portfolio 2 |
|:---:|:---:|
| 10% | 6% |
| 30% | 6% |
| 7% | 6% |
| −5% | 6% |
| 9% | 6% |
| −15% | 6% |
| 13% | 6% |
| 8% | 6% |
| −4% | 6% |
| 7% | 6% |

Portfolio 1:
- Outperforms Portfolio 2 in 7 out of 10 years
- Only has three negative years
- Its best year is up 30%
- Its worst year is down 15%

Portfolio 2:
- Only has a 6% return every single year

**A simple value calculation reveals that both portfolios have an *average annual return of 6%*. Yet, the dollar amount found in each of these portfolios at the end of this 10-year period is different.**

If you invested $100,000 in Portfolio 1, you would have made just under $170,000. The same investment in Portfolio 2 would have yielded almost $180,000. Even though these two portfolios realized the same average annual return, one yielded $10,000 less in the end—a full 10% of your starting sum.

The *actual* realized return for Portfolio 1 (the geometric mean) was 5.38%. Portfolio 2's, of course, was 6.00%. That small 0.62% difference on a $100,000 initial contribution over 10 years generated a slightly-more-than $10,000 difference between the two portfolios.

The *actual* return is smaller. This is *always* the case[29] because of how damaging negative returns are to your long-term bottom line.

## Negative Returns

When you consider the amplified impact of negative returns, it isn't hard to see why Portfolio 1 underperformed in the end. **The damage done by losing periods far outweighs comparable positive returns.**

Let's compare, for example, a 50% gain with a 50% loss. At first glance, one might think these two returns would cancel each other out. After all, the simple (arithmetic) average would be 0%.[30]

But even though it may not be intuitively obvious, in reality, that 50% loss is *much more impactful* than the equivalent gain of 50%.

Say you have $1,000. If your account goes up by 50%, you now have $1,500. If your account then goes down by 50%, your account value would drop to $750. That's 25% less than where you started even though the percentage value of the gain and loss were the exact same.

And by the way, the order doesn't matter. If your $1,000 account started with that 50% loss, it would drop to $500. Then, after the subsequent 50% gain, it would only get back up to that same $750 final sum.

Let's look at it in a slightly different way ...

---

29  Unless a return is the exact same every single year.
30  (50%–50%)/2 = 0%.

We'll take your same $1,000. As before, after your 50% gain, you have $1,500. It would only require a 33% loss to erase that $500 you just gained. A *50% gain* is counteracted by a mere *33% loss.*

If, instead, you start with that 50% loss, your $1,000 investment would decline to $500. It would now require a 100% gain to earn back that $500 you just lost. A *50% loss* requires a *100% gain* to reverse its damage.

**This reality gets worse: the impact is *exponential.*** The bigger the initial loss, the greater the gain required to make it back. For example, while a 10% loss would only require an 11% gain to offset it, a 90% loss (say, $1,000 dropping to $100) requires a *900% gain* to recoup your principal!

**Table 3**

Gain Required to Recoup Principal after Indicated Loss

| Loss Incurred | Gain Required |
|---|---|
| 10% | 11% |
| 20% | 25% |
| 30% | 43% |
| 40% | 67% |
| 50% | 100% |
| 60% | 150% |
| 70% | 233% |
| 80% | 400% |
| 90% | 900% |
| 95% | 1900% |
| 99% | 9900% |

## S&P 500

The track record of the S&P 500 provides us with 95 years worth of data points to aggregate, and there are some doozies in here that really drag on the historical geometric mean—like, 1937's −35%, 2008's −37%, and 1931's −43%.

The *geometric* average for the S&P 500 from 1926 through 2020 is 10.3%.

Although this 1.8% difference may not sound like a big deal at first, it makes a meaningful difference on a long time horizon. Assuming that 12.1% annual return, $100 invested in this S&P index in 1926 (had you been able to do so) would be worth $5MM (million) today. At the actual return of 10.3%, that same $100 investment would be worth $1MM—80% less than you would have projected!

All from a mere 1.8% difference in the annual return assumptions.

Of course, most people don't have a 95-year time horizon for which they're trying to plan. The difference is still consequential. Your actual portfolio value would be ...

- 13% less than its projected value after 10 years
- 28% less than its projected value after 20 years
- 40% less than its projected value after 30 years

As we continue to inspect these market return myths further, we'll use the following table to keep our progression organized.

### Table 4
#### Impact of Actual Versus Average on a $10,000 Investment

|  | Average 12.1% | Actual 10.3% | |
|---|---|---|---|
| Since 1926 | $529,000,000 | $107,000,000 | 80% LESS |
| 30 Years | $310,000 | $187,000 | 40% LESS |
| 20 Years | $99,000 | $71,000 | 28% LESS |
| 10 Years | $31,000 | $27,000 | 13% LESS |

That means that even if everything goes according to plan (i.e., the market actually does continue to perform as it has in the past[31]), a $10,000 investment after 30 years would only grow to $187,000 while based on the "12% reality" assumption you might have understandably projected (and planned for) $310,000.

Further, let's explore the impact this one adjustment will have on John and Mary's dream retirement. According to John's calculations, given his 12% assumption, he and Mary were expecting $1.5MM at age 65 and for that to last them until age 95. After making this "actual versus average" adjustment, however, their retirement-age reality would be 61% of that projected value, and consequently,

---

31   Spoiler alert: Myth 10 will have you questioning that!

they'd run out of money by age 73—*more than 20 years earlier than anticipated!* A far cry from anyone's retirement dream.

**Clearly, every percentage point has a meaningful impact when planning long-term.**

The takeaway: don't base any of your plans on the expectation of making a 12% annual rate of return in the stock market.

---

**MYTH:** "The Stock Market Averages 12% Per Year."

**REALITY:** The formula used to derive the 12% figure has no bearing on your *actual* return. Unless from here on out the market's returns are the same every single year, mathematically, **your actual returns *must* be smaller**.

---

I hate to break it to you, but even this 10.3% figure is still *far too high* of an expectation for your actual gain.

Now that you know how impactful every percentage point is for your long-term plans, any fee you pay better be worth it.

# MYTH 2

---

## "You Should Expect a 10% Return from Stocks"

## Advisory Fees

I still remember the day when I finally decided that I was going to buckle down and really dive deep into the investment options I was recommending to my clients. That's right, I had been recommending solutions that (if I was being honest with myself) I didn't fully understand. Yet, at the same time, I'm pretty sure I understood them better than 95% (probably more) of my colleagues—I was one of the go-tos for our region, one of the "investment guys."

After earning my CFP® (Certified Financial Planner™) designation as quickly as I possibly could so that I could finally have access to my company's investment options, I had eagerly burst onto the investment scene.[32] This was the reason I had gotten into the financial planning world: investments fascinate me.

I had mastered the language from our home office sales representative.[33] You see, our Specialty Investment Vehicles were pretty complex. There were managers on the individual fund level who were constantly researching the best positions to hold. We had experts in our home office reviewing the overlap of the underlying funds' holdings. We even boasted some additional oversight from the highest-level analysts at Morningstar. It all sounded very sophisticated.

It, if nothing else, created a compelling enough excuse for rather high fees.

---

32  Earning the MDRT—Million Dollar Round Table—acknowledgement for investment performance that year—awarded to the top 1% of the industry.

33  Don't worry if you understand nothing in this paragraph … that's kind of the point: investment management firms often use complex-sounding, obscure, over-your-head jargon to justify their elevated fees. At some point, most people just yield to their "expertise"—they stop asking questions and are left feeling inadequate and overwhelmed when it comes to their investments.

For smaller accounts, the total fees would sometimes be more than 2.5%. I had become a pro at explaining them away. You'd probably be surprised by how few people even batted an eye.

Please don't get me wrong, it wasn't that I was lying to them or trying to trick anybody. I was just doing what I was told was in their best interest. I was listening to people who had decades more experience than I did (I was in my early 20s at the time), who I felt were smarter in this area than I was, who I trusted to direct me to the best solutions for my clients.

That's what started to eat away at me though ...

Something wasn't right, and I think I had been putting off this deep dive into our solutions because I was afraid of what I might find. But I couldn't shirk my fiduciary responsibility[34] to my clients any longer, so I dug. I spent days seeking answers.

In short, I discovered that the primary solution our firm was pushing consistently underperformed the market. It had been around for more than a decade (since before 2000), and the actual annualized return for each of our models was quite a bit lower than the market as a whole—to the tune of one or two percentage points. We already discussed how much of an impact that can make.

Maybe there was an entire team of experts monitoring these models and they needed to be paid. But, if that "monitoring" is not generating a superior performance—even after more than a decade of runway—then, why?!

If our investment solutions were outperforming by more than their fees over the long run, then the value proposition might make sense. But they simply weren't. They consistently underperformed, losing my clients money, and they were expensive ... costing them even *more* money.

It wasn't long after this initial period of self-discovery that I left that firm in search of something better.

---

34  All CFPs® (among others) are held to a **fiduciary** standard. To act as a fiduciary means you must put your clients' interests ahead of your own. As in, I shouldn't continue to push my clients into an investment solution that I determine to be inferior—even if it is the only solution that would get me paid. Alternatively, some financial professionals act under a suitability standard which can lead to conflicts of interest that can end up costing the client a lot of money (more on that in Myth 12).

## An Industry of High Fees

That firm is not a small player in the investment industry. Their investment services arm is, in fact, one of the top five largest independent broker-dealers[35] by revenue[36] raking in more than $1B in commissions and fees on those complex investment strategies pushed by their massive field force.

This isn't, however, some isolated case. The list of highly regarded firms charging significant fees to manage investment dollars is upsetting.

Edward Jones, with its $1.1T (*trillion*, with a T) of assets under management, has its agents charging an ongoing 1.35% management fee[37] for a client's first quarter of a million (plus other smaller "hidden" fees and the underlying fund fees—more on those next).

- JP Morgan charges a 1.45% advisory fee
- Merrill Lynch, 2.00%
- Wells Fargo, 2.00%
- Morgan Stanley, 2.50%
- UBS, 2.50%

One of the worst culprits of this "high-fee" madness is Ameriprise Financial. With half a trillion of assets under management, Ameriprise gets away with charging a 3.00% advisory fee on smaller accounts. And that's just the advisory fee—add in the other smaller "hidden fees" and the underlying funds' fees and some clients could end up paying 3.50% or more each year in fees!

## And the Fiduciaries?

All the firms I've listed thus far are broker-dealers. But what about the fees charged by registered investment advisors (RIAs)?[38] They're actually held to a

---

35  When you're working with someone to help you invest your money, they are most likely either associated with a broker-dealer or a registered investment advisor (RIA). A **broker-dealer** is a person or firm in the business of buying and selling securities (stocks, bonds, etc.) for its own account or on behalf of its customers. One of the biggest differences for you (as a potential client) is that RIAs have to work under a fiduciary standard whereas broker-dealers do not.

36  https://www.investmentnews.com/2019-top-independent-broker-dealers-ranked-by-revenue-78864.

37  All fees cited are according to each respective firms' Form ADV filings.

38  More on this distinction and significance in Myth 12.

fiduciary standard. Meaning, they legally are supposed to be acting in your best interest. So, in theory, you'd think their fees might be more agreeable. Right?

As it turns out, they're not much better in the fee department. Work your way through Barron's 2019 list of top RIAs[39] and you'll discover more high fees eating away at investors' returns.

By far the largest RIA in the world with its more than 1.2MM clients is Edelman Financial Engines. They charge their smallest accounts a 1.75% annual fee.

The Tony Robbins–promoted[40] Creative Planning takes the second spot on that list with its 1.2% fee,[41] followed by Private Advisor Group's 2.00% annual fee on accounts under $500,000.[42] Next, you'll find Mariner Wealth Advisors with its 2.50% annual fee for "smaller" accounts.[43]

You get the idea: there are a lot of people out there paying a lot of money in fees year after year. The big question, then, is: are they worth it?

To best answer that question, you'll need to understand what the "cost" really is. Because it's not just 1.5% or 2.5% or any percentage—that's meaningless when it comes to your financial aspirations. Percentages are too disconnected from what your goal actually is when enlisting the help of a "professional." We need to evaluate this cost in terms of dollars.

Later in this text, we'll evaluate the effectiveness and value of the various strategies these firms employ.[44] This section, however, is the perfect place to evaluate and develop your understanding of that "true cost."

### The Impact

The average annual advisory fee from 2017–2019 for an investment account with $1MM was 1.02%[45] (larger accounts averaged less, smaller accounts averaged more). For this "true cost" exercise and to understand the impact these

39   https://www.barrons.com/report/top-financial-advisors/ria/2019.
40   Tony Robbins's *New York Times* Bestselling book "Unshakeable: Your Guide to Financial Freedom" was written "with Peter Mallouk," President of Creative Planning. For the most part, the book was an apparently highly effective endorsement for Creative Planning and propagates many of the myths we're dispelling here.
41   https://smartasset.com/financial-advisor/creative-planning-review.
42   https://smartasset.com/financial-advisor/Private-advisor-group-review.
43   https://smartasset.com/financial-advisor/mariner-wealth-advisors-review.
44   Myths 8, 11, 14, 15, & 16.
45   https://www.advisoryhq.com/articles/financial-advisor-fees-wealth-managers-planners-and-fee-only-advisors/#Percentage-AUM.

fees have on what your reasonable expectation for average annual growth in the market should be, let's round down to an even 1.00%.

After accounting for this average advisory fee while you have your money invested in the market, the actual realized return drops from 10.3% down to 9.2% (remember: this fee is usually *much* higher for "smaller" account sizes—i.e., sub-$1MM—which would cause that percentage to drop *even lower*).

Remember that $100 invested in 1926—that would have been projected to grow to $5MM with that initial 12.1% assumption but then, in reality, only turned out to be worth $1MM?

Well, when you add in this 1% advisory fee, it's more like $410,000. From $5MM to $410,000—that's *92% less* than what the "12% reality" would have led you to believe!

The practical implication for you? Here's how much less your actual portfolio value would be.

### Table 5
#### Additional Impact of Advisory Fees on a $10,000 Investment

| | Average 12.1% | Actual 10.3% | After Advisory Fees 9.2% | |
|---|---|---|---|---|
| Since 1926 | $529,000,000 | $107,000,000 | $41,000,000 | 92% LESS |
| 30 Years | $310,000 | $187,000 | $139,000 | 55% LESS |
| 20 Years | $99,000 | $71,000 | $58,000 | 41% LESS |
| 10 Years | $31,000 | $27,000 | $24,000 | 23% LESS |

So now, even if everything goes according to plan, your $10,000 investment after 30 years has only grown to $139,000 when you were projecting (and planning for) $310,000.

### Edelman's Reality

In his 1996 *New York Times* bestseller, *The Truth About Money*, Ric Edelman uses multiple convincing hypotheticals to encourage readers to invest in the stock market:

Although the average stock fund earned 14.5% over the past 10 years, we'll say that yours performed below average, earning only 12% a year. At that rate, [after 25 years,] your $5,000 will grow to $99,000![46]

Let's give John and Mary a break on this one and check in with my (made-up) 42-year-old friend, Brody. Reading this advice in 1996, he was convinced by Mr. Edelman's case for stock market investing and excited by his "conservative" 12% expectation. He eagerly handed his $80,000 nest egg over to Edelman's firm expecting (read: needing) that sum to grow to $1MM by the end of 2019, when Brody would be 65 and ready to retire. In theory, the math adds up: an $80,000 investment at 12% per year for 23 years (1997–2019) would grow to $1,084,000.

The reality for my poor friend, however, was far from that "conservative" $1MM projection. From the beginning of 1997 through the end of 2019, the market realized a simple average of 10.3%. A far cry from that 14.5% seed that Edelman planted in Brody's and millions of others' minds.

His *real* return was only 8.6%—leaving him with less than half of his original projection! That's right, that real 8.6% would have left him with $538,000 instead of the "conservatively" projected 12.0%'s $1MM+.

Add in Edelman's advisory fee of 1.75% for an account of that size,[47] and the effective annualized return drops to 6.7%, resulting in an account balance of $359,000—*67% less* than what Brody was expecting (*needing*).

## The Worst Offender

Edelman Financial Engines is not even the worst offender here (at least from the fee perspective it's not, but from the "12% claim" perspective, Ric Edelman is definitely on the list). The title of "Most Outrageous Fees" should probably go to the aforementioned Ameriprise Financial with its roughly $500B of assets under management[48] and 3% advisory fees.[49]

That 3% fee takes your "since-1926" number down to a mere $60,000—just 1% of your original expectation!

---

46  Actually, a $5,000 investment growing at 12% per year for 25 years would be worth $85,000. It would require a consistent 12.7% each year to achieve $99,000 … but, my objective here is not to argue Mr. Edelman's math.
47  That's his current rate; it used to be higher.
48  https://www.investopedia.com/investing/broker-dealer-firms/.
49  According to the firm's Form ADV.

## Table 6
### Impact of a 3% Advisory Fee on a $10,000 Investment

|          | Average 12.1% | Actual 10.3% | After a 3% Advisory Fee 7.0% | |
|----------|---------------|--------------|------------------------------|---|
| 30 Years | $310,000 | $187,000 | $80,000 | 74% LESS |
| 20 Years | $99,000 | $71,000 | $40,000 | 60% LESS |
| 10 Years | $31,000 | $27,000 | $20,000 | 35% LESS |

That $10,000 is only $80,000 now after 30 years ... instead of the $310,000 you were expecting.

They'd have to be providing some major value over there for this to be worth it. And I don't think fancy computer printouts and friendly customer service would do the trick—I'm thinking more like maid service, child care, a private car when you need it ... you know, the works!

## Is It Ever Worth It?

Thus far, in our analysis in this book, we don't have enough data to determine if these fees are actually worth their impact or not ... yet. It is hard to imagine that being the case for some of them, but in our honest pursuit of truth, we'd have to consider both sides of the equation—including what you actually get for all this expense. In this section, we're just looking at the bottom-line impact all the fees and adjustments have on your long-term plans. Later (Myth 12), we'll explore the other side of this—what firms are actually offering and if some are worth their elevated fees or if they've just realized that **it's remarkably easy for people to brush over these *"relatively small looking"* percentages.**

Regardless, this exploration of the impact any fee has on our real returns demonstrates that we need to manage our expectations even more.

Now, once you've come to terms with all that … let's knock those expectations down just a little bit further.

## Fund Fees

Think about where these broker-dealers and RIAs are ultimately investing. Most will invest in mutual funds and exchange-traded funds (ETFs)—both of which bring with them yet another layer of fees (the former much more significant than the latter).[50]

### Mutual Funds

Mutual funds are investment programs where investors are essentially pooling their money in order to allow a money manager to diversify their holdings.

Vanguard, BlackRock, Fidelity, and American Funds are by far the largest mutual fund families in the world[51]—each boasting more than $1.5T in assets. While BlackRock is contending with Vanguard on the "low fees" front (don't worry, they'll come up again later), Fidelity and American Funds continue to rock some pretty hefty charges on that collective more-than-$3T they manage.

Many of the mainstream financial institutions mentioned earlier rely on these old-guard behemoths to make the final underlying investment decisions. The higher fees charged by Fidelity and American Funds allows them to offer a larger cut to middlemen—e.g., the broker-dealers and their individual agents (read: sales reps). However, with Vanguard, for example, and its lower fees, there isn't as much to share.

---

50  Even when your firm invests some of your money in individual stocks (thus, not incurring a fund's fees), they tend to find a way to hurt your bottom line regardless—Edward Jones, for example, can charge you up to a 2.5% commission on money invested in that way (https://www.edwardjones.com/images/stock.pdf); Northwestern Mutual just has a flat (and relatively high) trading commission that is automatically pulled from your account every time your rep puts you in or out of an individual stock position; the list goes on—all of this is even more destructive on smaller accounts.

51  https://www.morningstar.com/lp/fund-family-150—These four have a pretty commanding lead. The next closest fund families have ~$1T less in assets under management.

## Ongoing Fees

Most of these mutual fund companies' fund fees are less than an annualized 2%.[52] American Funds's largest fund, for example, is the Growth Fund of America®[53] with $115B in assets. Its net annual expense ratio[54] is 1.4%.[55]

Obviously, another 1.4% hit to our sum would be significantly impactful. There are some advisors (even some I know personally) who will simply plug you into a portfolio of American Funds or Fidelity funds *and* charge you their own significant advisory fee on top (a 1.X% advisory fee + a 1.4% fund fee = *crazy destructive* to your bottom line).

But, to be fair, that is an extreme. Most of the advisors with those larger firms utilize a mix of mutual and exchange-traded funds.

## Exchange-Traded Funds (ETFs)

An ETF is a security[56] that is usually derived from a collection of stocks that often track an underlying index (e.g., S&P 500, Dow Jones Industrial Average). Because the funds' underlying holdings are based on whatever its respective index is doing rather than rigorous research from a team of expensive professionals, the expense ratios are considerably less—in some cases as low as just a couple of hundredths of 1%.[57]

---

52 Advisor-sold mutual funds often have different options for how you'd like to structure their fees. These different options are called **share classes**. For more information, check out the free companion resources at SpicerCapital.com/Go. Most importantly, you should know that **A Shares** charge a fee up front and then a lower ongoing fee while **C Shares** charge no upfront fee and a higher ongoing fee.

53 The ticker symbol (the abbreviation used to identify a particular publicly traded stock or fund) for the Growth Fund of America® is GFACX for its C Shares and AGTHX for its A Shares.

54 If doing this digging yourself, use caution to look for the total net **annual expense ratios** and not just the **management fees**. The total expense ratio is always larger than the management fee alone (even if that difference is, for some funds, negligible).

55 Its C Share class: https://americanfundsretirement.retire.americanfunds.com/about/funds/details.htm?ticker=GFACX.

56 A **security** in the world of finance is "paper" traded for value where profit is anticipated—it's a tradeable asset that holds monetary value. Securities include stocks, bonds, mutual funds, exchange-traded funds, variable annuities, options, and so on.

57 https://etfdb.com/compare/lowest-expense-ratio/.

With that mix of mutual and exchange-traded funds, the average additional fee incurred by those larger advisory firms (the RIAs and broker-dealers cited earlier) is around 0.4%.[58] Let's factor that into our calculations.[59]

Following the same format we've been using, here is how it will impact your return projections. Our "since-1926" number would only grow to $280,000— *95% less* than that expectation derived from Dave Ramsey's, Ric Edelman's, and a number of others' teachings.

**Table 7**

## Additional Impact of Fund Fees on a $10,000 Investment

| | Average 12.1% | Actual 10.3% | Advisory 9.2% | After Fund Fees 8.7% | |
|---|---|---|---|---|---|
| 30 Years | $310,000 | $187,000 | $139,000 | $120,000 | 61% LESS |
| 20 Years | $99,000 | $71,000 | $58,000 | $50,000 | 49% LESS |
| 10 Years | $31,000 | $27,000 | $24,000 | $20,000 | 35% LESS |

Remember: the advisory and fund fee assumptions that we're using here are *average*. That means that there are tens of millions of investors out there who, even if everything goes as planned (read: the market actually does what it did in the past), they'll be facing an even harsher reality than those we just considered.

Know where you fit in and adjust your expectations accordingly.

## Upfront Fees

Most mutual funds will provide you with a way to reduce those ongoing fees. That is, as long as you're willing to pay their hefty upfront sales charge. The

---

58  https://www.personalcapital.com/assets/public/src/Personal-Capital-Advisor-Fee-Report.pdf.

59  Even though there are several examples of large players in this space who incur higher fund fees on their millions of clients' collective hundreds of billions of dollars that they have under management, for the sake of this **conservative** example, we'll stick with that 0.4% average. We'll also drop our assumed advisory fee assumption back down to that flat 1% (as opposed to Ameriprise Financial's 3%).

Growth Fund of America®, for example, will charge you a 5.75% initial fee[60] in order to reduce your ongoing annual fee to 0.64%.[61]

That means you would immediately be down almost 6% on Day 1 of your contribution into this fund! A case could easily be made, however, to mathematically show you how much better off you'd be[62] over the long run for making this initial sacrifice.

Here is a breakdown of how a $10,000 investment would look after 10, 20, and 30 years given the actual historical return of the market. I've accounted for no advisory fees here—just how the annual 1.4% fee (labeled: ongoing) compares to the reduced 0.64% fee after accounting for that upfront 5.75% sales charge (labeled: upfront).

### Table 8
Impact of Sales Charges on a $10,000 Investment

|  | 10 Years | 20 Years | 30 Years |
|---|---|---|---|
| Ongoing | $23,030 | $53,038 | $122,148 |
| Upfront | $23,357 | $57,885 | $143,451 |

With historical market returns, it would take just under nine years for the growth of that $10,000 invested with that upfront sales charge to pass its respective value with the higher ongoing fees. You can see how easy it would be to convince a young person trying to "do the right thing" and save for the long haul to splurge on that upfront fee.

---

60    This is the Growth Fund of America® A Share class (AGTHX) referenced in an earlier footnote. https://americanfundsretirement.retire.americanfunds.com/about/funds/details.htm?ticker=AGTHX.

61    These figures vary by fund and can change over time. By regulation, the maximum allowed upfront charge is 8.5% but most fall within a 3–6% range.

62    Than with its C Share counterpart, with its 1.4% ongoing fee as explored previously.

Really, it depends on you and what your plans are. Sure, you're committed to investing for retirement, which may be a decade (or two or three) from now, but are you *that* committed to *this* particular fund?[63]

## All Together Now

Think back on Dave Ramsey's reassurances about your ability to realize 12% in the market. In that same "12% Reality" article, he encourages you to invest in mutual funds—ideally, *front-loaded* (read: with an initial sales charge) with an expense ratio under 1%, he says[64]—and to use one of his "experts" (more on them in Myth 8).

When you factor in all of this—actual (not average) returns, advisory fees, fund expense ratios—**you will be hard-pressed to realize even a 9% annualized return under the historical assumptions** these market peddlers love to cite.[65]

The two personalities mentioned thus far in this text are major influencers of everyday Americans just trying to save for their retirement goals: Dave Ramsey with his more than 14MM weekly listeners and more than 11MM books sold[66]; and Ric Edelman with his firm's more than 1.2MM clients[67].

Let's look at what those everyday Americans saving for retirement would have *actually* realized over the last 10, 20, or 30 years compared to the expectations laid out by these men (and *so* many others).

For Dave, we're assuming here a conservative advisory fee of 1% and a more-than-acceptable (by his standards) annual fund fee of 0.64% with a 5.75% sales charge.[68]

For Ric, we're assuming that 1.75% advisory fee and the low end of his firm's average underlying fund expenses, 0.3%.[69]

Assuming actual (geometric) average historical market returns and a $5,000 annual contribution, here is how far off your reality would be from the expectations they're setting.

---

63 By the end of this book, my hope is that you'll have discovered far better ways to invest your money for the long haul and thus that the answer to this question will be a resounding "NO."

64 https://www.daveramsey.com/blog/how-to-choose-the-right-mutual-funds.

65 Myth 4 explores why this practice, although seemingly simple and logical enough, is actually potentially ruinous.

66 https://www.daveramsey.com/pr/fact-sheet.

67 https://www.edelmanfinancialengines.com/about-us/edelman-financial-engines.

68 The aforementioned AGTHX's actual fees.

69 https://www.thinkadvisor.com/2018/12/06/edelman-financial-engines-cuts-fees/.

## Table 9
### Experts' Assumptions Versus the 12% Expectation

|  | 10 Years | 20 Years | 30 Years |
|---|---|---|---|
| **12% Expectation** | $103,273 | $408,494 | $1,356,463 |
| **Ramsey Assumptions** | $80,057 | $248,562 | $625,415 |
| **Edelman Assumptions** | $82,966 | $250,368 | $609,806 |

*Note:* In terms of what your investments would actually be worth after 30 years, both realize less than half of the expectation set.

A far cry from Dave's "real 12%" (despite all his comforting words of reassurance[70] along the way) and Edelman's "conservative" 12% (with that 14.5% expectation seeded in the back of many readers', listeners', and clients' minds).

But, since it can take decades for this harsh reality to come to fruition for those hard-working individuals who find themselves trusting this advice, the talking heads can continue preaching this same message, touting this same easily manipulated data, and raking in millions upon millions for their insights.

### Low-Fee Alternatives?

It may sound, at this point, as though I am simply advocating a more automated (read: anti-fee) approach. After all, for most of these advisors (really, sadly, *so* many of them), you're paying all these fees for them to just plug you into the same old stock-and-bond-only, buy-and-hold approach that you could find somewhere else for **way** less! Sure, some of them might have their own little twist[71] or claims of added value, but if you buy into that stock-and-bond strategy, why wouldn't you just go with one of the far-less-expensive alternatives who'll plug you right in at a fraction of the ongoing fees?

You have your broker-dealer options, like Vanguard and Charles Schwab with their negligible advisory fees (0.30% and 0.28%, respectively). Or there are the so-called robo-advisors, Betterment and Wealthfront (both at 0.25%).[72]

---

70   … and angry rants.
71   Most don't.
72   At the time of this writing.

We'll explore all of this in greater detail later—most importantly, the value of the advisor expertise for which you're paying;[73] and the validity of the buy-and-hold, stock-and-bond-only strategy[74]—but with all this talk of fees, these low-cost players deserved a mention here (even though you still can't count on a 12% return). Besides, I'm sure many readers were screaming about them already. I just wanted to assure you: I'm not ignoring them.

## More Complicated Still

Okay, fine, so we just use this adjusted historical return figure to manage our expectations then. Right? We came down from the simple average of 12.1% to the real average of 10.3%. And then, after accounting for average fees—both advisory and fund—the real historical return of the market dropped to 8.7%. That's it—that's the figure we should use now, right? Easy enough … so, we just need to save more or prepare for less.

YEAH, DAD...
IT LOOKS LIKE THOSE FEES YOU'RE PAYING ARE REALLY KNOCKING YOU QUITE A BIT BELOW THAT 10% MARK...

---

**MYTH:** "You Should Expect a 10% Return from Stocks."

**REALITY:** No matter how you're invested in the stock market, you're paying fees in some way. Thus, you can't expect your returns to be the same as the market itself.

---

73  Myths 8, 12, 13, 14, 15 & 16.
74  Exposed in Myths 5, 6, 7, 9, & 10.

Unfortunately, it's still not that easy. The reality is significantly worse.

# MYTH 3

---

## "You Can Count On a Return of at Least 8% from Your Stock Investments"

## Wrong Place, Wrong Time

When we were younger, my sisters and I received some money from our grandfather. Our plan was simple: we wouldn't touch it until the time came that we wanted to buy our first house. That meant that the money would be growing for years in the background[75] while we finished up our schooling.

All three of us were interested in business and financial markets (likely influenced by that same grandfather's entrepreneurial success and legacy). From asking my mother for a *Wall Street Journal* subscription for my 12th birthday to starting and running my first storefront business at 17, I was obsessed.

My sister closest to my age got married and purchased a house near the tail end of the 2001–2007 stock market bull run.

I had studied the stock market. I knew the "buy-and-hold" mantra. I was disciplined. As the market started to turn over near the end of 2007 and all through 2008, I was like a stone, immovable, without emotion. While the world around me was freaking out, this was my chance to prove my ability to disconnect from the chaos.

I succeeded beyond all expectations. I proved I had what it takes. I could "suck it up" and "stay the course" with the best of them even in the face of a roughly 50% crash. The market started its rapid recovery in March 2009. I had remained "rational" the entire time. I had not panicked in the slightest. Needless to say, in that moment, I was proud. I felt like this was my first real test, and I passed!

In the summer of that same year, I got married to my high school sweetheart. We lived in my tiny, 300-square-foot studio apartment for our first year of marriage, relishing all the money we were saving with our crazy-cheap, $250-per-month rent.

In June 2010, it was time to upgrade. I was starting to make decent money as a financial advisor, so we felt comfortable dipping into that investment account to help with our down payment. It was then (and after a conversation with that sister) that I realized just how much less I was dealing with than she had. Remember: we had invested in the exact same amount, in the exact same way, with the exact same advisor since receiving that money almost a decade prior. Yet when she had purchased her home in 2007, her investment account was more than 65% larger than mine was when I needed it in 2010.

---

75  Managed by an Edward Jones representative, in fact.

I didn't complain, nor was I at all upset (that's not the point here). I was and am to this day very appreciative for my grandfather's gift and hard work. Actually, this was the beginning of my quest to find better ways to invest—to challenge the traditional financial paradigms. It was the seed of my desire to critically consider any financial advice I heard (even if it was the common practice advised and accepted by academics and "experts" alike).

But, for my case in point here, it woke me up to the reality that the timing of *when* you need your money can significantly impact your bottom line.

## The Baader-Meinhof Phenomenon

In truth, this reality was not a huge deal for me. It didn't set me back in any way. This was gifted money, after all—money I wouldn't have otherwise had. So, in my mind at least, whatever the balance, I was ahead.

For those preparing for retirement after decades of hard work and dedicated savings, however, that difference could be devastating. Before this personal experience, I never really noticed this happening to others. But after that, for the next several years, I saw it everywhere. It was like the Baader–Meinhof Phenomenon, (the so-called frequency illusion) where upon discovering some obscure bit of information, you start to see it everywhere.

I had client after client needing to delay their retirement plans because of the 2008 market decline. Some even had to come out of retirement or pick up part-time work as a Walmart greeter. I'd see similar stories on the news and in the paper—it's difficult to fathom the tens of millions that were affected in this same way.

The frequency of these occurrences declined over the following years until in 2013 it wasn't really mentioned anymore. People who had been planning to retire in 2014-16, were relatively unaffected by that massive crash—or, at least, they had plenty of time to adjust and prepare for a different reality. They weren't slapped in the face by the same flip-of-a-coin, "sucks to be you" reality as those with the *exact same goals and circumstances* from just a few years earlier. The downfall of that earlier group was simply the fact that they were just a few years older—just a few years ahead …

Wrong place. Wrong time.

## Timing Matters

Your planning and expectations for market performance should not just be a flat X%—12, 10, 8, or even 6. It's not that simple. The amount of time you have before wanting or needing the money to achieve your goal will have a huge impact on what you should (historically) expect.

### 30-Year Horizon

It seems like most advisors and pundits, and consequently, people in general just take the 30-year average and run with it. It definitely does make this all look way more compelling on the surface. Even using real returns, a 1% management fee, and a 0.4% fund fee, the S&P 500 has averaged 9.6% per year across all 30-year periods since 1926.

**Figure 4**
S&P 500 30-Year Annualized Returns

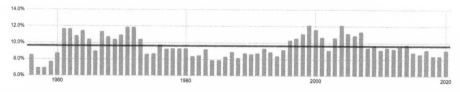

That's fantastic! Right? It is.

Of course, we're talking about an average here, so ... flip a coin: you might end up above that number, you might end up below. But even then, the historical range from best 30-year period (12.2% per year) to worst 30-year period (7.0% per year) is not very wide.

Conclusion: if you have a 30-year time horizon[76] *and* you entirely disregard our debunking of the myth that "the market will for sure always continue to go up,"[77] then sure, assuming a conservative 9% average annualized return and preparing for the "worst-case" possibility of 7% would be perfectly reasonable ... *in the beginning of your planning years.*

But, as you approach that retirement (or any other) goal of yours, wouldn't it make more sense to consider a more relevant time frame? Do the 30-year numbers really apply to you anymore? Sure, you may have been investing for 30+ years by the time you get to 65 (or whatever age you want to retire), but ... that's not really how these numbers work.

## 20-Year Horizon

When you're 20 years out from that goal, your "worst-case," historically based possibility is no longer 7%. *Far from it, in fact.*

The lowest average annual return the market has ever realized over any 20-year period since 1926 was *a bleak 1.7%.*[78] That's $10,000 growing to a mere $14,000 after 20 years instead of the $39,000 your forecasted *"worst-case"* scenario would have been (under that 7% assumption).

Over any **15-year period**, it was an average *loss of 0.8%* per year.

**10-year period**, *-2.8%* per year.

## 5-Year Horizon

But what if you're just 5 years away from your target age? This is where so many receive poor advice. Because advisors are talking to their clients about making their money work for them during retirement—about allowing it to grow in the market so that it can support them during the next 20 or 30 years while they'll be out of work—*they're still focused on that 30-year average return figure.*

---

76   So, if you're in your 30s or younger—good for you for taking this so seriously, by the way!
77   Myth 10.
78   Using all the same assumptions as previously outlined: real returns, a 1% management fee, and a 0.4% fund fee.

This is what I discovered with all those clients who had been preparing for retirement within a few years of the Great Recession:[79] they had to delay their plans due to what their previous advisors had called "unforeseeable events"—the ominous black swan.[80]

Except, it wasn't unforeseeable …

In fact, historically speaking, the 5-year (2003–08) average annual loss due to that crash (–3.8%) was a fraction of what it's been before. For instance, **the worst 5-year average annual return for the market was a *13.7% loss!***

### Feeling Lucky?

Sure, that kind of loss is not common, nor should it be expected. But it was far from "unforeseeable." In fact, 15 of the 90 5-year periods since 1926 have yielded negative average annual returns. That's 16.7% of the time. For context, you have a 16.7% chance of rolling a 1 on a 6-sided die.

But this isn't a die you'd be rolling only once every 5 years. You'd be rolling it every single year.

Think about it for a moment. If that's how it was, would you treat your investments differently? If the roll of a single die at the end of every year is what determined whether your average annual return over the previous 5 years was negative (anywhere between –13.7% to –0.9%, historically speaking, of course), would you play the same way when you're 60 as when you're 20?

I get it. It may feel as though you don't have any other option.[81] That this is the only way to really build wealth. That these are *pretty* good odds anyway. That you just have to cross your fingers and hope one of those negative spells doesn't hit right before you're about to start your retirement.[82]

### Post-Retirement Horizons

When you're in retirement, it can be even worse. If the market is down 50%, what are you supposed to do? For every one year that you maintain your current

---

79  2007–09
80  "A **black swan** is an unpredictable event that is beyond what is normally expected of a situation and has potentially severe consequences. Black swan events are characterized by their extreme rarity, their severe impact, and the widespread insistence they were obvious in hindsight." -Investopedia
81  We'll explore some other options in Myths 15 & 16.
82  All of these thoughts are rooted in financial-industry myth. By the end of this book, you will know a better way.

standard of living, you'll be shaving two years off your retirement projections (because you'll need to sell twice as many shares of stock since they're all worth half as much). Historically speaking, **there *will* be at least a couple of major crashes during your retirement.**[83]

Not only is that fixed average annual return assumption not enough to best prepare you and your assets to achieve your goals, in retirement, relying upon it could be devastating.

Understanding the time-based potential of your market investments becomes essential for creating a plan in which you can be confident. Just relying on the experts' "oh don't worry, you should expect an average 8% [or whatever] over the long haul" is not practically helpful for you in those times. It does, however, make their money management job *much* easier.

## Inflation

It's been a while since the United States suffered through a period of runaway inflation.[84] The idea of combating its ruinous potential can be a daunting task. But once again, the impact it could very easily have on the purchasing power of your invested dollars should absolutely be considered and accounted for in your long-term expectations.

The historical average annual inflation (since we officially began tracking it back in 1913) is more than 3%. That means that, on average, what it costs for you to maintain your standard of living today—that same milk, bread, and peanut butter—will go up by 3% next year ... and every year after that. Inflation is your dollar's purchasing power being reduced each year.

Thus, if your market portfolio goes up by 9% in a given year, you'll still probably lose some of that perceived gain to inflation.[85] In this case, your real rate of return after adjusting for the effects of inflation would drop to about 6%. In a year where the market dropped by 30%, well ... it'd ultimately feel more like –33%.

Take, for example, the 9-year period between the beginning of 1973 and the end of 1981. The market went up on average 7.3% per year. The actual return

---

83  We'll dive into more details about these withdrawal periods in Myth 4.

84  At least, according to the way the U.S. Bureau of Labor Statistics measures inflation. Changing the way the Consumer Price Index is calculated—which has been done several times—is yet another example of how one could potentially manipulate data.

85  ... and taxes.

was 5.1%. After adjusting for inflation, however, the return was … (are you ready for this?)

An average annual *loss of 3.8%!*

Imagine that. You retired in 1973 with a nest egg large enough to fund your lifestyle for the next 30 or so years. But, during the first 9 years of your retirement, everything became so much more expensive—inflation was significantly higher than you had anticipated based on your historical expectations.

Assuming that 8.7% return from earlier, you would have needed roughly $500,000 in 1973 in order to retire on $50,000 per year. If you maintained your exact same standard of living, given the actual inflation and market returns, you would have been out of money in fewer than 9 years.

Your stock-and-bond, buy-and-hold portfolio is not going to help you overcome this.

Ignoring that reality and just plugging in some fixed return assumption throughout your financial-planning life (as most advisors are wont to do) is a risky and lazy strategy.[86]

---

**MYTH:** "You Can Count On a Return of at Least 8% from Your Stock Investments."

**REALITY:** This can be a safe assumption when you have 30+ years before you need the funds. But as your time horizon shortens the range of possible returns is much wider, often **negative**.

---

---

# MYTH 4

---

## "A Single Return Assumption Is Sufficient When Planning for Retirement"

## The Last "But Wait There's More!"

I'm sorry to say, it gets even more complicated. When you're not putting money into or pulling money out of your investment accounts, the order of returns doesn't matter. If I reverse the order of every annual return since 1926 and apply it to our same $100 assumption from earlier, we'll still end up with the same $5MM 95 years later—even though the crash of 1929 would have just happened! We would have the same simple average return of 12.1% and actual return of 10.3%.

But how often is it the case that we're not contributing to or pulling from our investment accounts?

### Sequence Risk

Before retirement, we are (presumably, or at least would like to be) contributing to our accounts every year. During retirement, we are likely pulling from our accounts each year. During these stretches of regular contributions or withdrawals, the order of those returns actually makes an enormous difference. This is called Sequence of Returns Risk or just sequence risk.

When adding this reality into your planning considerations, you discover that historically based, period-specific highs could be even higher, and the lows … could be much lower. Meaning that –13.7% annualized return for our historical worst-ever 5-year period, could actually be even worse for an individual investor depending on the specific sequence of returns and whether they just so happened to be contributing or withdrawing.

Before we explore the now-even-more depressing historical worst-case scenario, let's evaluate a perfectly average 10-year period: 1974–1983 (ignoring inflation this time). The real average annual return over this period was 9.1% (compared to the average for all 10-year periods of 8.9%[87]).

### Table 10
### S&P 500 Returns from 1974–1983

| 1974 | 1975 | 1976 | 1977 | 1978 | 1979 | 1980 | 1981 | 1982 | 1983 |
|------|------|------|------|------|------|------|------|------|------|
| -26.47% | 37.20% | 23.84% | -7.18% | 6.56% | 18.44% | 32.42% | -4.91% | 21.55% | 22.56% |

---

87 Assuming the same 1% advisory fee and 0.4% fund fee from earlier.

## Contributions

The simple average return of these 10 years is 12.4%. If you made a $5,000 contribution at the beginning of each year (for those 10 years) into an account that's tracking the S&P 500, it would have grown to $110,000 (excluding fees) by the end of 1983.

What if we mixed up the order of those returns? What if all the worst years were first and the best years last?

### Table 11
### S&P 500 Returns from 1974–1983 Reorganized: Worst First

| Year 1 | Year 2 | Year 3 | Year 4 | Year 5 | Year 6 | Year 7 | Year 8 | Year 9 | Year 10 |
|--------|--------|--------|--------|--------|--------|--------|--------|--------|---------|
| -26.5% | -7.2% | -4.9% | 6.6% | 18.4% | 21.6% | 22.6% | 23.8% | 32.4% | 37.2% |

With all the other assumptions the exact same as last time,[88] your account would now grow to $151,000. That's $41,000—*37%*—*more* over that same 10-year period with those same returns … just in a different order.[89] That's an *effective 23.09%* return. Nice! That's *even better than the **best*** 10-year period in the entire S&P 500's recorded history (which was 18.4%).

How is that possible? How'd it go from an "average" return to better-than-the-best?

It's because we put all our bad years first and good returns at the end. But, more importantly, the reason that even made a difference—let alone a massive one—is because you were making contributions.

What happens if we put all the good years first and the bad ones last? I'm so glad you asked!

### Table 12
### S&P 500 Returns from 1974–1983 Reorganized: Best First

| Year 1 | Year 2 | Year 3 | Year 4 | Year 5 | Year 6 | Year 7 | Year 8 | Year 9 | Year 10 |
|--------|--------|--------|--------|--------|--------|--------|--------|--------|---------|
| 37.2% | 32.4% | 23.8% | 22.6% | 21.6% | 18.4% | 6.6% | -4.9% | -7.2% | -26.5% |

---

88  A $5,000 contribution at the beginning of each year for 10 years into an account that's tracking the S&P 500.

89  As in, the simple average of those 10 years was still 12.4% despite the significant difference in concluding sums.

Now, at the end of that *same* 10-year period, your account balance would be $60,000. That's $50,000—*45%*—*less* than you would have gotten with those *same* returns in their historical order. That would have dropped your actual return from 16.6%[90] all the way down to 4.1%.

**That means that, just because we were making contributions, the sequence of returns went from having absolutely no impact to having a massive one.** Depending on the order, our actual average return (*excluding any fees*) after 10 years could have been anywhere from 4% all the way to 23%! That's the difference of ending up with $60,000 or $151,000. And remember, these were the figures from a historically average decade.

Takeaway: as long as you're not contributing … you don't have to worry about this phenomenon. But aren't you contributing (or, at least, shouldn't you be) to your investment accounts during more of your pre-retirement adulthood than you aren't—especially, as you get closer and closer to retirement?

If that's the case, your historically based expectations need to swing *much* wider than discussed to this point, most importantly factoring for an even worse "worst case."[91]

## New "Worst Case"

As you're approaching retirement, aren't you—shouldn't you be—more concerned about the possibility of your returns being worse than average?

**The worst 10-year period in the market was from 1999 through 2008. The simple average return was only 0.7% per year.** After fees and factoring for actual returns, you're already looking at a figure that's more than **3% worse** than that.

When you factor in our same **$5,000 contribution** scenario from earlier, **the geometric return would have been an annualized *loss of 6.4%*. Sustaining an average annual 6.4% loss throughout the decade right before you plan to retire is devastating.**

If this were to happen to John and Mary during their home stretch (the last 10 years before their planned retirement), do you think they should take comfort in

---

90  The arithmetic average over this time was 12.4%. The geometric average (with no contributions and no fees) would have been 10.6%. Equal annual contributions (over this 10-year period), however, results in a geometric average greater than the simple average (due to sequence risk)—in this case, 16.6%.

91  Side note: it looks as though—counterintuitively—you don't actually want your good return years first while you're accumulating.

Dave Ramsey's reminder that the *previous* decade yielded a return of roughly 17% per year? That 20-year period as a whole yielded 6.8% after all—not too shabby ...[92]

Would that comfort *you* if you find yourself in this position? You were 100% on track a decade ago. You were doing so well. You were just unlucky to hit that horrific 10-year stretch where you averaged *less than* -6% per year on your stocks. Now what? Retire on less? Retire later?

Bottom line: when John and Mary are in their 50s, trying to intelligently get themselves into a position where they can retire—no matter what happens—this "hope-we-get-one-of-those-better-than-average-decades" strategy would be imprudent and irresponsible.

And, in that same vein, this "you should expect to average X% per year in the market" becomes meaningless noise.

Yet, this is the advice advisors continue to give. They, too, hope that the coming years bring solid returns. Because if they don't—as they inevitably sometimes won't—advisors lose clients. After facing such a devastating reality, investors fire their current advisor and move on to the next one. Sadly, odds are, that new advisor was offering the exact same advice a decade prior and continues to offer the same advice today ... because that's just how it's done in the industry—by professionals, pundits, and academics alike.

Oxford defines gambling as "taking risky action in the hope of a desired result."

Is this different?

You've been sold the "desired result"—not the potential reality.

---

92  Remember: this was the comforting logic used in Ramsey's "12% Reality" post: https://www.daveramsey.com/blog/the-12-reality.

## Withdrawals

One final consideration in this same vein: what about periods of withdrawals?

This reality is even more grim, if only because this represents a period where you're counting on this money to support your lifestyle—when you cannot afford for the numbers to be too far off.

Wade Pfau,[93] the Professor of Retirement Income at the American College of Financial Services, actively studies sequence risk. He observed that returns realized in a portfolio during those years immediately after one retires disproportionately impact its long-term viability.[94]

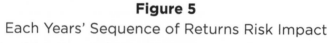

### Figure 5
### Each Years' Sequence of Returns Risk Impact

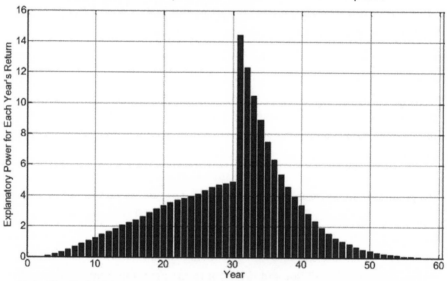

*Note*: The first thirty years represent a period when an individual is making regular contributions. Years 31–60 represent the distribution or withdrawal phase. The rate of return an individual realizes that first year of withdrawals has a significantly greater impact on their probability of a successful retirement than any other year by far. In fact, each of the first seven withdrawal years were found to have a greater impact on the viability of your retirement savings than any return during any of your contribution years.

---

93  Wade Pfau, PhD., CFA, RICP is also the founder of Retirement Researcher, https:// retirementresearcher.com/.

94  Pfau, W. D. "The Lifetime Sequence of Returns: A Retirement Planning Conundrum." September 1, 2013. Available at SSRN: https://ssrn.com/abstract=2544637.

Let's explore what that could mean for you. Once again, the biggest concern here should be sincerely accounting for one of those "worst-case scenarios" that your advisor is warning about.[95] If the better-than-average or even the best historical scenarios play out, great! Congratulations, the die roll was in your favor this time. But some people—real people—tens of millions of them, in fact—get stuck with these "historically based worst-case scenarios" during their retirement years.

Consider all those aforementioned clients from earlier in my career. They had some tough choices to make: postpone retirement, live on less, go back to work. All these were decisions they didn't want to have to be making. They weren't part of the plan. And they were in this position because their advisors and the mainstream pundits didn't help them plan for—or even consider—this all-too-real-for-them worst-case scenario.

During periods when you're withdrawing money, it's better to have your good returns early on. Let's use those same historical returns from 1974–83. We'll assume an account with $1,000,000 and a $90,000 per year withdrawal. With the best years first, your $1,000,000 account grows to $1.66MM by the end of that decade even with your annual spending. This results in an effective annualized return of 12.7% (instead of the 12.4% simple average).

**Figure 6**

## Sequence Risk During Withdrawals—S&P 500 Returns from 1974–1983: Best First

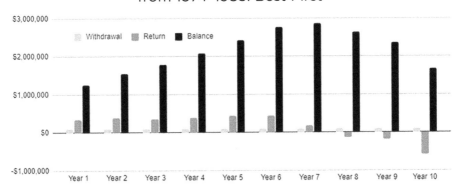

---

95   Ideally, you'll even be prepared if anything worse should happen. The significance of that should become apparent after you're through Myth 10.

With the worst years first, however, you would have realized an effective *loss of 1.4%* per year—leaving you with just $22,000 at the end of that tenth year. That means, with these assumptions from this historically average decade, your real average return could be anywhere between 12.7% and –1.4%.

**Figure 7**

Sequence Risk During Withdrawals—S&P 500 Returns from 1974–1983: Worst First

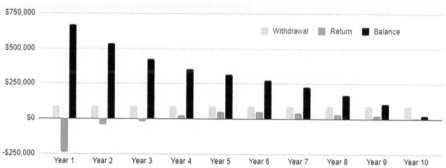

But, during withdrawal periods, it's the impact this sequence of returns has on your remaining nest egg that should concern you the most. Here, it would mean you could end up with anywhere between a healthy $1.66MM or a meager $22,000 at the end of a single decade. *And that's all without accounting for any fees!*

**Figure 8**

Sequence Risk During Withdrawals— Worst Versus Best Years First

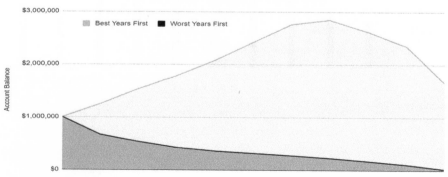

*Note:* Everything else is equal between these two hypothetical portfolios. Even the returns are the same—the *only* difference is the order in which they are experienced.

This divergence is the difference between the ecstatic "we have so much flexibility and don't have to stress about money" and the depressed "looks like we have to downsize *and* go back to work in order to survive."

### Alternate Realities

You get a taste of those two extremes when we consider the curious case of Michael and Michelle. These are two different people ... with identical lives. They retire at the exact same time—at age 60—with the exact same amount of money. They take the exact same annual income distributions from their market-based retirement accounts every single year. Their financial advisors told them that based on conservative estimates derived from the market's average historical return, they should be fine ...

And they *should* be.

... based on "the market's average historical return."

Let's start with Michael. He retires January 1, 2000 with $2MM and takes $120,000 annual income distributions.

### Table 13
#### Michael's Retirement Details

| Year | Beginning of Year Account Value | Annual Earnings Rate | Annual Income Distribution | End of Year Account Value |
|---|---|---|---|---|
| 2000 | $2,000,000 | -9.1% | $120,000 | $1,708,920 |
| 2001 | $1,708,920 | -11.7% | $120,000 | $1,403,016 |
| 2002 | $1,403,016 | -24.0% | $120,000 | $975,092 |
| 2003 | $975,092 | 28.8% | $120,000 | $1,101,359 |
| 2004 | $1,101,359 | 11.7% | $120,000 | $1,096,178 |
| 2005 | $1,096,178 | 5.2% | $120,000 | $1,026,939 |
| 2006 | $1,026,939 | 15.6% | $120,000 | $1,048,422 |
| 2007 | $1,048,422 | 4.9% | $120,000 | $973,915 |
| 2008 | $973,915 | -39.1% | $120,000 | $520,034 |
| 2009 | $520,034 | 26.5% | $120,000 | $506,043 |
| 2010 | $506,043 | 15.1% | $120,000 | $444,335 |
| 2011 | $444,335 | 2.0% | $120,000 | $330,822 |
| 2012 | $330,822 | 17.1% | $120,000 | $246,873 |
| 2013 | $246,873 | 35.3% | $120,000 | $171,659 |
| 2014 | $171,659 | 19.1% | $120,000 | $61,526 |
| 2015 | $61,526 | 15.8% | $120,000 | (67,713) |
| 2016 | -$67,713 | 19.2% | $120,000 | (223,754) |
| 2017 | -$223,754 | 31.4% | $120,000 | (451,693) |
| 2018 | -$451,693 | -10.2% | $120,000 | (513,380) |
| AVERAGE | | 8.1% | | |

His average annual return from 2000 through 2018 is 8.1%. The far-right column reflects Michael's new account balance at the end of each year—after accounting for his withdrawal and that year's percentage return. By the end of 2015, in his 16th year of retirement, Michael's ending account balance drops below $0. He is officially broke at the ripe old age of 76.

Now, let's look at Michelle. Like Michael, she retires on January 1, 2000 with $2MM and takes $120,000 out of her accounts each year. Note that Michelle averages that exact same 8.1% per year.

## Table 14
### Michelle's Retirement Details

| Year | Beginning of Year Account Value | Annual Earnings Rate | Annual Income Distribution | End of Year Account Value |
|---|---|---|---|---|
| 2000 | $2,000,000 | -10.2% | $120,000 | $1,688,240 |
| 2001 | $1,688,240 | 31.4% | $120,000 | $2,060,667 |
| 2002 | $2,060,667 | 19.2% | $120,000 | $2,313,275 |
| 2003 | $2,313,275 | 15.8% | $120,000 | $2,539,813 |
| 2004 | $2,539,813 | 19.1% | $120,000 | $2,881,997 |
| 2005 | $2,881,997 | 35.3% | $120,000 | $3,736,982 |
| 2006 | $3,736,982 | 17.1% | $120,000 | $4,235,486 |
| 2007 | $4,235,486 | 2.0% | $120,000 | $4,197,796 |
| 2008 | $4,197,796 | 15.1% | $120,000 | $4,693,543 |
| 2009 | $4,693,543 | 26.5% | $120,000 | $5,785,532 |
| 2010 | $5,785,532 | -39.1% | $120,000 | $3,450,309 |
| 2011 | $3,450,309 | 4.9% | $120,000 | $3,493,494 |
| 2012 | $3,493,494 | 15.6% | $120,000 | $3,899,759 |
| 2013 | $3,899,759 | 5.2% | $120,000 | $3,976,307 |
| 2014 | $3,976,307 | 11.7% | $120,000 | $4,307,495 |
| 2015 | $4,307,495 | 28.8% | $120,000 | $5,393,493 |
| 2016 | $5,393,493 | -24.0% | $120,000 | $4,007,855 |
| 2017 | $4,007,855 | -11.7% | $120,000 | $3,432,976 |
| 2018 | $3,432,976 | -9.1% | $120,000 | $3,011,495 |
| | AVERAGE | 8.1% | | |

Yet, when you look at her end of year account values, you notice a stark contrast to Michael's.

What gives? They both had the same amount of money to start with. They both withdrew the same amounts each year. And they both realized the exact same average annual return of more than 8%.

The *only* difference here is the sequence of returns. Look closely. They're the exact same, just in the opposite order. Michael realized –9.1% during his first year in retirement while that's what Michelle realized in her last year. Michael's last year on this chart saw a –10.2% return; whereas, that was Michelle's first year return. You'll find this is the case all the way throughout these sequences— they're the exact same returns, just in the exact opposite order.

So, who would you rather be?

Obviously, we all want to be in Michelle's position here. Sixteen years in, at age 76, Michael's broke and Michelle's swimming in more than $5MM.

So, what then, did Michelle do differently? How can we emulate her success in our own financial planning?

**We can't!** The truth is, Michelle just got lucky. She didn't outperform due to a superior strategy. They were both invested according to mainstream investment advice—that passive, stock-heavy, buy-and-hold approach. Neither one of them had more control over their outcome than the other—despite the massive disparity between their final results.

The timing and sequence of Michelle's returns just happened to work out in her favor. And that's how millions of people go into retirement—just hoping (even if they don't realize that's what they're doing) that the timing and sequence of their returns work out in their favor.

And it's not their fault—it's not your fault. It's the advisors' fault. It's the fault of that mainstream investment paradigm. You're taught to expect—you're told you conservatively *should* expect—an 8% or so average rate of return in retirement from your stock investments.

Well … that is, in fact, what Michael got.[96] Didn't work out so well for him, did it?

**That average annual return figure becomes meaningless** if you're really serious about creating a comprehensive financial plan—one that *will* get you through retirement, no matter what.

## The Magic Number

One million dollars. That's the magic number for a lot of people. That's what they're working for their entire lives. That's what they think they need to

---

96   By the way, Michael's returns were what the market actually realized over that time period. Michelle's were reversed.

retire. Maybe that's because they've heard about the so-called safe withdrawal rate of 4%,[97] and they think, "worst-case scenario, I can pull out $40,000 per year (adjusting for inflation) and get by."[98]

Let's test this with a historical "worst case." The worst 15-year period for the S&P 500[99] produced a simple average return of 4.7%. This period included some massive up years, by the way—years anyone would be ecstatic about realizing during retirement—including a 34% gain, a 48% gain, and even the market's best year ever, a 54% gain.

Performing a quick calculation (not yet accounting for withdrawals and naively not adjusting for any of the factors we've covered thus far) would generate an expectation for $1.58MM at the end of this "worst 15-year period ever."

If, however, you're not even considering any sort of worst-case scenario, and you're just running with the cliché 8% (as most advisors do), then you'd be expecting $3.2MM[100] at the end of that same period. After accounting for those "safe" withdrawals starting at $40,000 and increasing by just 2.5% per year to allow for inflation, you'd expect to be left with $1.9MM at the end of 15 years. Not bad. You'd probably feel okay as you entered retirement with those expectations.

But before you get too excited, let's apply a more critical lens to this analysis. The *actual* return after those historical-worst 15 years, would have dropped from 4.7% to 0.6%, leaving you with $1.1MM instead. That's $475,000, or 30% less than your *worst-case projections*.

After accounting for a modest 1% advisory fee and 0.4% fund fee, the effective return would have been –0.8%. With this, at the end of those 15 years you would find yourself with less than $900,000, or in other words, $685,000 (44%) less than your expected worst case.

Now, if you also withdraw that "safe 4%," you should be okay, right? Your funds should still last? After all, this is supposed to be the worst-case, *historically based*, bare-minimum figure, right?

There is absolutely data to support as much ... but here is the reality of how those numbers would play out for you: by Year 13, you are out of money.

---

97 Bengen's Rule is discussed in more detail in Myth 9.
98 As the "safe withdrawal rate" would suggest.
99 The beginning of 1929 through the end of 1943.
100 At 10% it'd be $4.2MM, and 12% would be $5.5MM.

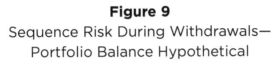

**Figure 9**
Sequence Risk During Withdrawals—
Portfolio Balance Hypothetical

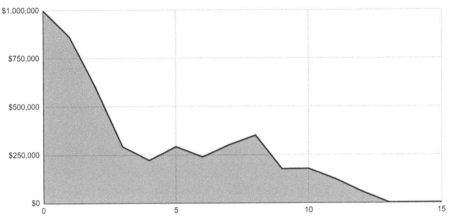

Pretty depressing if, in Year 15, you were expecting $1.9MM with your advisor's simple, rule-of-thumb calculations for your uber-conservative withdrawal projections. So, what will it be? Go back to work? Or severely cut back your bare-minimum standard of living when you see things going south just a few years into your retirement?

Are you willing to take that risk?[101]

Sadly, although you may not be comfortable with it—as you shouldn't be—it would seem most advisors and pundits are comfortable with **you** taking that risk. Because even though it's not openly discussed in the mainstream narrative, this is clearly a risk you are taking when you follow traditional investing advice.

## Modern Portfolio Theory

The industry's answer (especially for this last concern) is an ivory-tower philosophy known as Modern Portfolio Theory (MPT, for short). It's from where the buy-and-hold, stock-and-bond-only investment strategy for the average investor stems.

---

101 Especially when you don't have to, when there's a better way. Explored in Myths 13, 14, 15, & 16.

Much of this book is dedicated to uncovering and exploring the logical falla-cies and historical failings of this foundational myth. So, I'll save a more detailed explanation of how it works and where it comes from for then.[102]

At its very basic level, however, the recommendation would be to throw some bonds into the mix. A big part of the idea behind this is that bonds are considered to be less risky. At some point or another during this chapter, I'm sure more than one reader angrily shouted at their book "this is why you need to add bonds!" Sure, historically speaking (eh, there it is again) this *should* reduce those downward (and upward) surprises. Again, we'll dive into the validity of all this—and MPT, in general—very soon.

But, as for getting you closer to that expected 8%, 10%, or 12% return ... it won't.

Depending on the types of bonds we're talking about here, the historical average annual return[103] would put your expectations somewhere between 3 to 7%[104] (compared to the stock market's 10.3%). So, for now, suffice it to say that, on the whole, this addition should reduce your performance expectations by even more.

All things considered, that "conservative" 8%, at best, would be irresponsi-ble to count on—at worst, it seems like something out of a fairy tale.

## Reframing Expectations

Although there are ways of looking at the available data to validate those 8%, 10%, and even 12% per year claims, making those assertions is not particularly helpful during the planning process. In fact, it can be dangerous for the average investor, unfamiliar with just how variable actual results can be.

Think about it: even if history does just repeat itself (as the "experts" suggest), if you just so happen to get caught on the wrong side of a normal (historically based) cycle, it could mean the difference between your expected comfortable retirement and utter ruin.

This idea of "an average return over a long enough period of time" is used by the financial industry during all phases of people's lives. That is irresponsible. It's a platitude that makes it easy for the financial industry to continue to thrive. It's

---

102 Primarily explored in Myths 9 & 10. But, Myths 1–8 are all also related to various underlying aspects of MPT.
103 Geometric mean.
104 http://pages.stern.nyu.edu/~adamodar/New_Home_Page/datafile/histretSP.html.

backed by convincing-enough data that other financial "experts" repeat it without much additional consideration, **yet it's hazardous for the end-user—the investor—you.**

Unless you're a gambler, don't base the whole of your decision as to where to put your investment dollars on the misleading fact that "the market has averaged X% over X-number-of years" or the even-more-dangerous misrepresentation that "you, then, should expect to average X%."

### New Perspective

Perhaps, a more useful observation and consideration would be understanding the historic-worst-case scenario over various time periods. Additionally, one should understand the frequency of various levels of subpar performance. And all of this while factoring for periods of regular contributions or withdrawals. For example, investors preparing for retirement would benefit from understanding key data points from a chart like this:

### Table 15
### Reframe Your Expectations: Contributions

| | During Periods of Contributions | | | |
| | Worst | < 10% | < 5% | < 2% | Negative |
|---|---|---|---|---|---|
| **5 Years** | -24% | 49% | 30% | 22% | 17% |
| **10 Years** | -3% | 54% | 20% | 9% | 5% |
| **15 Years** | 0% | 60% | 20% | 3% | 0% |
| **20 Years** | 4% | 49% | 4% | 0% | 0% |
| **30 Years** | 8% | 58% | 0% | 0% | 0% |

The first column lists the worst historically recorded average annual return for each given period of time (5 years through 30 years). The remaining four columns show the frequency that returns of the indicated level (less than 10%, 5%, 2%, and negative) have occurred in the past.

**So, when you're 5 years from your retirement goal**, instead of projecting out an 8% (or even conservative-6%) annualized return, **you should be preparing—mentally, at the very least—for that historically based potential of a _24% annualized loss_** within your stock portfolio. Not that this is what you're expecting to happen, but rather, that it is something that could happen (that has happened in the past). And, if you want to make sure you can hit your goal and not just cross your fingers and rely on hope and luck ... you'll need to be prepared.

Note: all of this, of course, is relying on the limited historical data that we have—that is to say, it does not account for anything worse potentially happening in the future ... an obvious[105] yet often ignored possibility.[106]

Here's that same chart except for those who are entering retirement, preparing for withdrawals:

### Table 16
### Reframe Your Expectations: Withdrawals

|          | During Periods of Withdrawals | | | | |
|----------|-------|--------|-------|-------|----------|
|          | Worst | < 10%  | < 5%  | < 2%  | Negative |
| 5 Years  | -13%  | 49%    | 32%   | 24%   | 18%      |
| 10 Years | -4%   | 56%    | 26%   | 14%   | 8%       |
| 15 Years | -3%   | 61%    | 23%   | 5%    | 4%       |
| 20 Years | -1%   | 60%    | 11%   | 4%    | 3%       |
| 30 Years | 2%    | 71%    | 6%    | 2%    | 0%       |

Consider the following observations from this chart:

- Over any 5-year period during retirement, it'd be perfectly reasonable to expect a negative annualized return—that's happened in 18% (almost 1-in-5) of our 90 recorded 5-year periods.
- One in four 5-year periods have resulted in returns of less than 2%.
- Almost a quarter of our 80 recorded 15-year periods have brought with them average returns of less than 5%.
- There have actually been some 20-year periods where the average annual return was negative.

---

105 I hope.
106 More on that in Myth 10.

- The worst annualized return over our 65 recorded 30-year periods was a depressing 2% (compared to the 7% we examined earlier when not factoring for withdrawals—see how much of a difference that can make!).

The data on these two charts is far more practical—and **far** less misleading—than the blanket "average" return claim.

After all, as advisors (and financial professionals, in general) are telling you that you'll need to keep your emotions in check during the inevitable market fluctuations, **this information is *much more practically useful* in helping you understand how real those risks are and how painful they can actually be.**

---

**MYTH:** "A Single Return Assumption Is Sufficient When Planning for Retirement."

**REALITY:** Just accounting for a single return assumption could easily leave you surprised and financially devastated. **A sound financial plan should be preparing for a much wider range of return possibilities.**

---

As to whether or not you will, in fact, be able to just "suck it up" and control your animal instinct, keeping your emotions at bay during these inevitable chaotic swings, well … that's the subject of our next few myths.

# MYTH 5

---

## "You Can Just Ignore Your Emotions and Not Get Caught Up in the Excitement around Bubbles"

I CAN HANDLE IT. I'M PREPARED. I'M TOUGH!

## Peter Lynch

Peter Lynch is widely regarded as the most legendary mutual fund manager of all time. Perhaps what he did better than anyone else was to go out on top. Instead of milking his legend status and raking in millions in fees for years, in 1990, he retired. This ended his 13-year stint as the manager of Fidelity's Magellan Fund.

And, wow, what a run he had. When he took over in 1977, the fund had just $18MM in assets under management (AUM). By the time his tenure was over, it had swelled to $14B—boasting the title of "largest mutual fund in the world."

By stepping down when he did, Lynch sealed his track record in the annals of history. He had averaged a 29.2% annualized return for the fund over those 13 years—making Magellan the "best performing mutual fund in the world."[107]

That means that $1,000 invested in Magellan in 1977 would have been worth $28,000 when Lynch stepped down in 1990.

As Lynch reflected on his accomplishments, he wanted to know how well the average investor in his fund performed under his watch. He was shocked to discover that their annualized returns were less than a quarter than that of the fund itself. According to his calculations, investors in the Magellan Fund averaged just 7% per annum over that same 13-year period.[108]

So, instead of being worth $28,000 when Lynch was through, that original $1,000 an investor may have contributed to his fund—after all their moving in and out—would have only grown to a paltry (by comparison) $2,400, only 8.6% of what could have been had the investor just stayed in the fund.

As the fund was doing well, investors' money would flow in. All the way up until it would hit the occasional rough patch. When it hit those periods of underperformance, money would start to flow out. It would seem that investors were

107 https://web.archive.org/web/20141226131715/http://www.ajcunet.edu/story?TN=PROJECT-20121206050322.

108 Jakab, S. 2016. Heads I Win, Tails I Win. New York: Portfolio/Penguin.

consistently throwing the largest sums into the fund right at every peak, and then pulling more out at the troughs than at any other time.

This recipe of missing most of the good days and hitting the bad would explain investors' gross underperformance.

Surprisingly, Fidelity's conclusion was somehow far more grim than Lynch's. When the fund company set out with the same objective—to know how the individual investor fared—their calculations indicated an average annual loss![109]

Now, that $1,000 investment would have been worth, well … less than $1,000. Somehow, the average investor in the fund managed to realize more than $27,000 less in gains than his underlying investment (the fund itself). And that's the average—some investors realized even less!

Whether the average investor in the Magellan Fund from 1977 through 1990 underperformed the fund itself by an annualized 22% or by more than 29% is unimportant to our point here. Whatever the specifics, one thing is clear, despite having invested in what turned out to be the best mutual fund in the entire world over that period, the average investor somehow managed to still grossly underperform the market (which averaged around 15% over those 13 years).

## How Could This Happen?

When I promised the last "but wait there's more" earlier … well, I meant that was the last one for *that* section. Because these next several myths—dealing with human psychology—contribute even more to the downside of this what-to-historically-expect-from-your-market-investments calculation.

Try as we might to avoid it, we (as investors) tend to, on average, underperform the underlying funds in which we're invested, and we underperform the market in general. If these facts are just as historically documented as the

---

109 Fidelity Investments.

market's returns are, should they be ignored? Of course not—not if you're serious about whatever goal it is for which you're saving.

So, let's get to the bottom of this, shall we?

### The Behavior Gap

New York Times columnist, best-selling author, and world-famous sharpie-on-a-napkin doodler,[110] Carl Richards, has built his career on the foundation of studying and explaining this phenomenon. He calls the difference between investor and investment returns, the behavior gap.

**Figure 10**

The Behavior Gap as Illustrated by Carl Richards

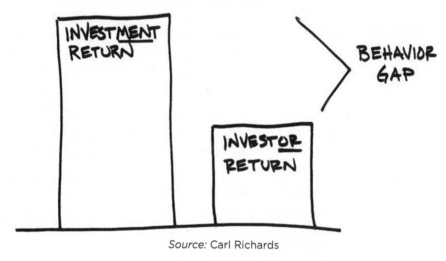

*Source:* Carl Richards

As he posits in his book, and as is generally accepted today, it is our human nature—our instinct, our behavior—that causes us to underperform no matter how well we're prepared.

Many emotional factors fuel this behavior. Two of the largest are: **herd mentality** and **loss aversion**.

---

110 At least he's investment-world-famous for it: https://www.nytimes.com/by/carl-richards.

## Herd Mentality

Herd mentality is rooted in a fear of missing out—of missing an opportunity. That fear consumes the masses—the general public—you and me. People see others making (what looks like) easy money in the market. They may not understand all the details, but at some point, that doesn't matter. The fear of missing out (FOMO) becomes overwhelming. So, they take a leap, assuming (more like, hoping) everyone else involved with this investment actually knows what they're doing.

At times, even the greatest minds fall victim to this: Sir Isaac Newton lost almost his entire life savings as a result of succumbing to the madness of the herd.[111] It would seem almost nobody—no matter how brilliant—is immune.

Even (or perhaps I should say: especially) professional money managers fall victim to herd mentality. None of them want to be the last kid to the party—assuming another professional investor has received some insight to which they are not yet privy, they make their investment decisions out of fear—the fear of missing information, the fear of missing an incredible opportunity, the fear of consequently losing their high-paying job.

They are, perhaps, comforted by the fact that if they're wrong, at least they are all wrong together. And you can't fire them all ...

So, when one big-money investor, for whatever reason, pushes a price up, for fear of being outdone, his or her closest competitors are not far behind ... whether they understand the initial mover's motivations or not. As more and more big money moves in, fearing they're simply missing out on some key information—"Clearly somebody knows something!"—they push prices higher still.

This euphoria bleeds into the mainstream—circulating through our financial news sources from the professional talking head on CNBC to the 20-year-old "stock market guru" with a YouTube channel. And once it's infected all the way down to the mom-and-pop investors, we reach a fever pitch, with almost everyone having bought in at a price far above any reasonable and fair value.

## In History

It's easy to feel superior, as though you know better ... you wouldn't so easily be bamboozled! Yet, history is rife with example after example of the masses

---

111  More on that story in a few pages.

(including some very smart people) getting fooled. Let's take a brief field trip through time to explore some of the more extreme and most interesting examples.

## Tulipomania

Our trip begins with the apocryphal tulip mania popularized by Charles Mackay's *Extraordinary Popular Delusions and the Madness of Crowds*.[112] In the 17th century, in what is now the Netherlands, tulip bulbs were all the rage. They became a status symbol. And, when a new type of tulip entered the market in the 1630s, the country wasn't prepared for the madness that was about to ensue.

Called a bizarre tulip, these bulbs had (what we now know to be) a rare virus that changed their genetic makeup—it caused the petals to be multicolored. Streaks of red and violet and other vibrant colors shot through the petals like flames. This variety was extremely rare and very difficult to reproduce. Seeds take 7–10 years to turn into a new flower (if they survive). Even then, the virus didn't carry over.

This combination of the novel, standout splendor of an existing status symbol coupled with the rarity of these bulbs, made the elites want them even more—price was no object.

As prices soared, some lucky middlemen made fortunes. Seeing how easy it was, more and more people left their jobs to enter the tulip bulb trade. As long as you could find a bulb to purchase, you'd always be able to find someone else—a Greater Fool[113]—to buy it from you for even more.

It was said that at the height of the craze one tulip sold for 10 times the annual earnings of a skilled craftsman. Another sold for 12 acres of land. In yet another account, a merchant took pity on a starving sailor. He invited him into his home, sat him at his table, and prepared him a meal. During his meal, the sailor consumed what he thought was an onion. It turned out to be a tulip bulb

---

112 As this event took place in the 1630s, our data is limited—much of the information we have comes from religious propaganda circulated during the centuries that followed. Their modus operandi: to discourage speculation. So, perhaps, some of the anecdotes we have from that time are a bit exaggerated.

113 The **Greater Fool Theory** suggests that you can profitably purchase an investment (stocks, real estate, tulip bulbs ... etc.) without consideration for the assets' actual underlying value. This strategy works, as long as there is someone else in the market also willing to buy them from you (again, regardless of true value) at a higher price in the future (i.e., an even bigger or greater fool).

that was said to be worth enough to feed the entire crew of his ship for a full year. For his mistake, the poor sailor was consequently jailed for years.[114]

As legend has it, one day a seller showed up to the public market where speculators would normally buy and sell contracts for these tulips, and for the first time ever, there were no buyers to be found. It could have been because of the bubonic plague that was wreaking havoc throughout Europe. Or perhaps, there really were no more Greater Fools. Whatever the reason, upon seeing and hearing about this, sellers finally (and very suddenly) realized: "I could actually end up stuck with all these tulip bulb contracts ..."

So ... they wanted out. They panicked. And, with no buyers on the other side of the trade, prices plummeted.

## South Sea Company

Fast forward less than a century and the rapacious masses were at it again. In 1711, the South Sea Company was formed. The company assumed Great Britain's war debts in exchange for a monopoly on overseas trading charters. They had a compelling story. With this monopoly on the riches of the New World, the sky was the limit for what this company would be able to accomplish.

This is the point on our journey where we cross paths with Sir Isaac Newton. Being an elite member of society, he was given the opportunity to invest early. With all its pomp and circumstance, how could he say no? He purchased a stake in this hot new stock for £200 per share. Within a couple of months, the price had doubled. He sold his shares, happy with his investment.

The stock price continued to climb, however. Newton didn't understand it—it seemed crazy to him. He watched as his (presumably less intelligent) friends, who were getting in at much higher prices than he initially had, made more and more money as their stock continued to soar.

Can't you just imagine his snobby friends at dinner parties poking fun at him about how his ability to understand and articulate universal gravitation was perhaps limiting his success with stocks?

Envy and greed must have worked on him enough until finally he bought back in around £700 a share. To make up for lost time, he invested way more than ever before—some of it borrowed.

---

114 This story is especially likely to be apocryphal as tulips are toxic unless meticulously prepared. Rule of thumb: in a famine, eat weeds before tulip bulbs.

Shortly thereafter, reality set in. The market peaked—turns out, in this instance, he was one of the Greatest Fools and was left holding the bag as the price of shares in the South Sea Company crashed.

**Figure 11**

## South Sea Stock: December 1718–December 1721

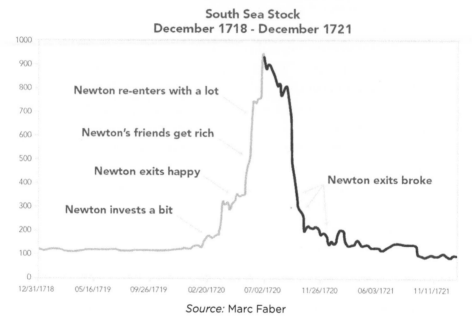

South Sea Stock
December 1718 - December 1721

*Source:* Marc Faber

He was said to have lost his entire life savings in that debacle, some £20,000 (more than 4.5MM[115] in today's pounds). Newton reflected, "I can calculate the motion of heavenly bodies, but not the madness of people."

## Mississippi Company

At the exact same time, over in France, a very similar scheme was brewing. After Louis XIV passed away, Philippe II, Duke of Orléans, was temporarily placed in charge as Louis XV was only five years old. Louis XIV's long reign and wars had left France swimming in debt. Philippe set out to rectify that.

---

115 According to data from the Office for National Statistics. The data only go back to 1750 and the South Sea Bubble popped in 1720.

He was a big fan of the Scottish economist John Law. Eager to see Law's innovative solutions play out, Philippe allowed him to form what essentially became a central bank for France. He also, over the course of several years, awarded Law and his Mississippi Company a near-monopoly on France's trade by sea (sound familiar?). Later, he even went so far as to appoint John Law as France's Comptroller General of Finances.

In 1719, Law took the Mississippi Company public. It turns out that, not only was the man a financial wizard, he was also a marketing genius. He spread rumors that the New World was filled with golden cities and ignorant natives willing to trade valuables for a fork. He had hundreds of "volunteers" parade through the streets on their way to settle and explore the New World. In reality, he had just convinced Philippe to release prisoners on the condition that they marry prostitutes and head to Mississippi! Law's machinations didn't stop there ...

The initial public offering (IPO) was for 50,000 shares at 500 livres each. Law devised a new way to allow more of the public to take part in this amazing offer. With the creativity of a late-night infomercial, people could own a share of the Mississippi Company for just 75 livres down followed by 19 easy installments of just 25 livres a month!

Like any stock with ".com" in its name in the late 1990s (we'll get there ...), the share price of Mississippi Company stock shot up almost overnight from 500 to 1,000 livres. If you were one of the few lucky enough to have scooped up one of those initial shares, your investment didn't just double in value, it went up by 667%![116] That's the power of being able to buy investments with leverage[117]— and *everyone* involved with this was doing it.

Following that initial blowout success, Law had yet another brilliant idea. The Mississippi Company would assume all the national debt (Philippe was thrilled; problem solved!), and at the same time, issue another 300,000 shares to the market at 500 livres, again following a similar scheme. Why not?! It worked splendidly last time!

---

116 Day 1: you invest 75 livres, owe another 425, and your share is worth 500. Day 2: your share is now worth 1,000 livres, 500 more than the combined value of what you invested and owe. If you sold at 1,000 and paid back the 425 you owe, you'd be left with 575 livres. After accounting for your initial 75 livre investment, your profit would have been 500. Resulting in an effective gain from the entire transaction of 666.67% (500/75)—not bad for a single day!

117 **Leverage** is a risky investment strategy where the investor uses borrowed money or special financial instruments (as in this case) to increase an investment's potential return.

Well, it worked again and by mid-1719 there were more than 600,000 shares of the Mississippi Company outstanding. Even still, the euphoria never stopped—the company's promise of future riches was extremely compelling, and the shares were relatively inexpensive (given Law's creative IPO structure). By the end of 1719, the price was up to 15,000 livres per share. More and more investors were making fortunes. In fact, the word "millionaire" was apparently coined during this time to describe the fortunes made by speculators in the Mississippi Company.[118]

Would you have been able to last a year on the sidelines thinking, "everyone's gone mad"? Or might you have started to doubt yourself? Maybe it's *you* that's missing something …

By mid-1720, however, as people started to catch on to Law's games, the share price fell faster than it rose. The Mississippi Company went under and John Law was impoverished and run out of France.

## Florida Land Boom

This time we'll leap forward a couple of centuries to Florida in the early-1920s. The state was marketed as a continental tropical paradise—all the luxury and fun of an island retreat, without even having to fly!

The state government tried every way possible to incentivize people to relocate. It was during this half-decade that they introduced much of the favorable tax treatment for which the state is still known today.

Banks got onboard with the movement and introduced easy lending policies.

Real estate companies got clever. They hired "binder boys" to stand outside properties that were for sale. They would collect "binders" from interested parties—small lump sums of money locking in their *right* to purchase the rest of the property within 30 days. These binders were for real estate what options are for stocks.[119] For the speculator, this was heaven. You could pay a $2,000 binder for a $50,000 house. Now, you have 30 days to either sell that binder or to turn

---

118 Murphy, A. E. 1997. John Law: Economic Theorist and Policy-maker. Oxford: Clarendon Press, 3.

119 **Options** are another way to use leverage (like John Law's margin terms for the Mississippi Company issue). They are financial instruments that derive their value from underlying securities—a way to bet on the direction a price will move without actually owning the underlying asset—such as stocks (in this Florida Land Boom case, however, the underlying security is real estate). The purchaser of an options contract is given the opportunity to buy (known as a "call" option) or sell (a "put" option) the underlying asset. The owner of the

around and sell the entire home. And, with the rate at which real estate prices were starting to rise, it was not unreasonable to expect that within the month, that same house would be worth quite a bit more!

Say, within your 30-day window, you sell that house for $60,000. You pay the previous owner (with whom you have this binder) the remaining $48,000 you owe. You pocket the $10,000 difference—that's a 400% return in less than a month!

It was this unique environment of low taxes, easy credit, and financial wizardry that led to the state's population increasing by 30% in just 5 years.[120] **In the context of today's technology, it's not difficult at all to imagine all the YouTube channels and social influencers that would be showing the world how easy it is to strike it rich in this new paradise.**

A favorite tale from this euphoric episode in history starts in 1920 when an elderly man spent his life savings of $1,700 on a piece of property. His sons were concerned; they were worried for his mental state. So, they did what any loving children would do … they had him committed! After a few years, however, that property was worth $300,000—175 times what he had paid for it. A lawyer was able to use this to get him released. He, of course, did what any understanding father would do … he sued his sons.[121]

I'm sure Florida is a wonderful place to live, but around 1925, Murphy[122] moved in—everything that could go wrong, did (and pretty much all at once!):

1.  Forbes published a scathing article about property valuations being based solely on the idea that there will be a Greater Fool to purchase it at an even higher price later. Other publications soon followed.

2.  The main source of supplies for all the construction down there were the big three railroads. They grew frustrated with all the bottlenecks and chaos, so they formed an embargo. For the foreseeable future, they would only be sending down food and other necessities. Luckily, Florida investors still had the harbor to get materials and supplies …

---

options contract is not required to buy or sell the asset if they choose not to—they just have the option to … hence the name.

120  From 1920–1925, the population boomed from 960,000 to more than 1.25MM.

121  Knight, T. Panic, Prosperity, and Progress: Five Centuries of History and the Markets. Hoboken, NJ: Wiley, 2014.

122  Murphy's Law: "Anything that can go wrong will go wrong."

3. On January 10, 1926, the Prinz Valdemar—a 241-foot schooner—sank in Miami Harbor. It blocked the port for weeks. No more building supplies …

4. In September 1926, the first hurricane since the speculation began hit the state.

When it rains, it pours. Property values plummeted as the state continued to get hit by more and more devastation. Nineteen twenty-eight brought with it another hurricane. Nineteen twenty-nine brought Wall Street's crash. And, in '30, a new type of fruit fly began destroying their crops. It took decades and a world war to recover.

Speaking of the stock market crash of 1929 …

## Roaring '20s

For two decades, the market had been like a rollercoaster. US investors had suffered through five boom-then-bust cycles with the ride dropping them off right back where they started. In other words, if you had invested $100 into the Dow Jones Industrial Average in 1900,[123] it would have been worth a whopping $100 in 1921.

Well, now, the Great War was over and America was itching for a bounce.

Over the next several years, investors were pleased with the market's consistent 10% per year rise. It was probably justified—long overdue, in fact. Tack on a couple of annualized 20% years and investors were singing! And then, something crazy happened.

From June 1928 through August 1929, the market soared 90%. The market had never climbed so quickly in such a short period. Pundits touted this new paradigm of economic prosperity. "Finally, the market was beginning to understand the new way to value a company," they would say.

But there were a few prominent businessmen who saw the writing on the wall. Notably, the CEO of U.S. Steel spoke out against the lofty valuations being assigned to companies (even his own). Commerce Secretary Herbert Hoover famously declared this to be an "orgy of mad speculation."

---

123 Remember, this was before our S&P 500 days, which started in 1926.

Reputable publications, like the *Wall Street Journal*, however, fought back. They claimed that Wall Street tends to be the victim of schadenfreude as demagogues need an easy target.

Although Roger Babson (a famous economist from the time) had predicted a crash several times before, markets began to waver after he forecasted one in a September 1929 speech. Babson was immediately lambasted by the press as being crazy and just plain wrong. The media went so far as to call upon one of the first celebrity economists, Yale professor Irving Fisher, to refute Babson's claims. Fisher famously stated that there was no need to worry, claiming that the stock market had reached "a permanently high plateau."

The market gradually began to slip. By mid-October, it was down about 15%. *The New York Times* reported that it expected new highs and persistent growth going forward, labeling the market as a bargain.

Then, Black Monday hit on October 28. The market cratered –12.82% in a single day.[124]

The media turned to Fisher once again. On October 30, he broadcasted a message of hope. He blamed the stock market crash on a vicious bear raid.[125] He claimed that "it was *not* that the stock market was very much too high,"[126] that its price had already reached the bottom, and that people were starting to invest again. Although the market fell another 10% on November 6, by April of the following year, it was well on its way back up. Up 50% from those November lows, it appeared as though Fisher was correct.

Herbert Hoover, now president, joined the chorus—he began broadcasting that the country and the market were already well into a recovery. He was wrong. Apparently, the orgy was more pervasive than he thought. The following three

---

124 The worst trading day the market had experienced in recorded history up to that point. The third worst trading day for the DJIA (as of this writing). The worst was –22.6% on 10-19-1987 (the other Black Monday) followed by –12.9% on 03-16-2020.

125 A **bear raid** is the practice (now illegal) of investors colluding to push a stock's price lower. They will sell the stock short (a way to profit from a stock's declining share price) and spread negative rumors about the targeted company.

126 SEC Historical Archive: http://www.sechistorical.org/museum/film-radio-television/video-player.php?vid=1809148597001&title=Professor%20Irving%20Fisher,%20Yale%20University,%20on%20stock%20market%20crash; Longer version: https://www.youtube.com/watch?v=e_Im69cn1tw.

years were a roller coaster for those with money in the market as it careened downward to a record-breaking total drawdown[127] of 89.19%![128]

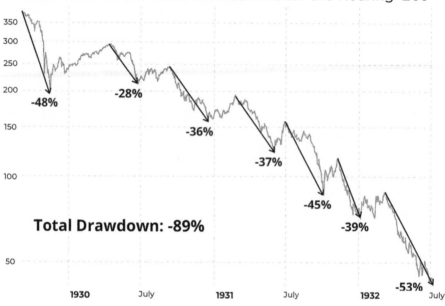

### Figure 12
### Breakdown of the Total Drawdown after the Roaring '20s

On September 3, 1929, the Dow had peaked at 381.17. It finally reached a bottom on July 8, 1932 (note: 3 years after our foremost economist of the era had predicted) at 41.22.

Our next stop? Twentieth-century Japan.

---

127 **Drawdown** is a peak-to-trough (high-point-to-low-point) drop in value during a specific period for an investment, trading account, or fund. It's usually quoted as a percentage—derived from the total drop divided by the previous peak (high point). For example, if your investment account had $100,000 in it, and the funds drop to $80,000 before moving back above $100,000, then your account realized a 20% drawdown = ((100,000-80,000)/100,000).

128 The chart is shown in a logarithmic scale to better visualize the relative percentage drops on the way down. Data from macrotrends.net.

### "Japan Can Say No"

Japan began to enter somewhat of a recession in 1986. Their central bank was eager to "save the day." Perhaps inspired by John Law's financial wizardry, they went to work authorizing whatever monetary and fiscal stimulus they could to keep the economy afloat—they slashed interest rates and began pumping money into the country's financial system.

It worked! Japan experienced an unprecedented economic boom. Urban land prices tripled from 1985 through 1989. In fact, at that time, the appraised value of the Imperial Palace in Tokyo was higher than the entire state of California!

That sounds crazy now, but back then, you better believe that people were justifying it: "Japan is finally realizing its full potential," "their central bank is on top of this situation like none other before them," and besides, "land is limited over there, obviously that's why valuations are so high." Perceived wisdom supporting astronomical market valuations is almost always presented in a believable package.

A 1989 essay entitled *The Japan That Can Say No: Why Japan Will Be First Among Equals* encapsulates the zeitgeist of the era. It argued (in a very sophisticated manner) how Japan was on a clear trajectory to becoming the next great superpower. And it was written by two very influential people—Shintaro Ishihara, the Minister of Transport who later became the governor of Tokyo (1999–2012) and Akio Morita, Sony's cofounder and chairman. These were not nobodies. They were extremely intelligent, highly regarded influencers. Like Isaac Newton of old, they'd be hard to argue or even disagree with. Thoughts contrary to their apparently well-researched and well-presented case would tend to leave *you* feeling as though *you* must be the one missing something.

The Japanese market peaked all the same. The Nikkei 225 (like the US S&P 500) reached all-time highs in December of 1989 just shy of the 40,000 mark.[129]

It's never been that high since.

Patient investors in the Nikkei experienced a prolonged, more-than-80% drawdown. While the crash of 1929 only took 3 years to hit rock bottom, this one took 20. With several significant surges and then subsequent lower lows along the way, it didn't reach its (current) low point of around 7,000 until March 2009.

---

129 In Myth 10, we'll revisit this example and look at the Nikkei 225 stock charts from that time and from today.

Here's the kicker with this one: this story still isn't over. Here we are, three decades later, and the Nikkei 225 is still right around 20,000—half its former glory. Every day, they're setting a new record for how long the market of a developed country can remain below its former high.

## Dotcom Madness

Jump ahead just one decade and we'll hit a similar euphoric blip in the US markets. This crash, however, impacted way more people than any had ever before. Back in the 1970s, trading in the market was expensive ($100+ per trade). In the 1990s, however, leveraging the advent of the internet, wirehouses[130] like Charles Schwab set out to make stock market investing much more ubiquitous with less-than-$10 trades. A news headline of the time read, "Good news: you're going to be a millionaire. Bad news: so is everyone else …"

This advent of the mom-and-pop trader facilitated the rise of mainstream market news sources. CNBC, shortly after formation, quickly shifted its focus to retail trading in order to presciently fill this void. Unfortunately, however, its very existence only fanned the flames of euphoria—everyone now felt empowered.

Warren Buffett was one of several investors of the old guard who spoke out against the crazy stock valuations of the time. In reference to the market's madness, he's famously quoted as saying: "It's only when the tide goes out that you learn who has been swimming naked." He was warning that these new market entrants were not at all prepared for what was next …

The tide, however, seemed to stay in for an extraordinary amount of time. These old school investors with their bearish[131] postures appeared to be just that: old. One of the most visible examples of this was legendary hedge fund manager, Julian Robertson. Mr. Robertson boasted an enviable two-decade,[132] 25% annualized return.[133] He, like Buffett, was a vocal bear. To him, valuations were just

---

130  The term **wirehouse** originated from the time when brokerage firms were connected to branch offices through telephone and telegraph wires. This allowed their brokers to have instant access to market data for clients. Now, it's a term used to describe a full-service broker-dealer and could range from small regional brokerages to global institutions.

131  A bear is an investor who is pessimistic about a particular investment or market and believes it's headed downward. The optimist is called a bull.

132  From the 1980 inception of his fund, Tiger Capital Management, through early 2000.

133  The S&P 500 averaged 17.5% over that same period. Tiger's outperformance is especially impressive considering the significant losses from betting against the market's madness in the fund's latter years.

so obviously insane. But, unlike Buffett who was waiting for the tide to go out, Robertson dove in headfirst to try to profit from the inevitable crash that he saw coming. He bet against many internet and technology stocks in the mid-to-late '90s (when they experienced some of their highest growth years ever). Unfortunately, the universe's timeline did not coordinate with his: the market just got even nuttier, until it peaked in the exact same month that he publicly announced the closing of his fund.[134]

Jim Cramer, of CNBC's *Mad Money* fame today, was a hedge fund manager during that time. He lectured these bears of the old regime saying:

> You have to throw out all of the matrices and formulas that existed before the web. You have to throw them away because they can't make you money anymore and that is all that matters. [In our fund,] we don't use price-to-earnings[135] multiples anymore. If we talk about price-to-book, we've already gone astray. If we use any of what Dodd and Graham[136] teach us, we wouldn't have a dime under management.

Sadly, Cramer was probably right about that last part: if he had been using Benjamin Graham and David Dodd's methodologies for assessing a stock's value, he probably wouldn't have had very much under management. People wanted tech stock exposure. They didn't want some old slow method. If Cramer (along with countless other overnight stock market savants) hadn't embraced this new paradigm, he may have never become the "authority" he is today.[137]

---

134  https://www.nytimes.com/2000/03/31/business/the-end-of-the-game-tiger-management-old-economy-advocate-is-closing.html.

135  The **price-to-earnings** (PE) and **price-to-book** (PB) ratios are valuation methodologies used to analyze the value of a particular company's stock. The former compares the stock's current price to the underlying company's earnings while the latter compares that price to the company's book value or net worth. These calculations will then give you ratios that can be used to compare to other companies within the same industry, the industry as a whole, other points in time, etc.

136  Benjamin Graham was Warren Buffett's mentor. Author of The Intelligent Investor, he is widely regarded as the father of value investing. He, with David Dodd, wrote Security Analysis, a textbook on value investing, originally published in 1934.

137  More on Jim Cramer in Myth 11.

The irony of that quote is that it's from February 29, 2000. The NASDAQ 100[138] peaked in March 2000. As Cramer was encouraging people to throw out their old valuation methodologies, the entire market for the very stocks he was promoting as the alternative was about to plummet.

Alan Greenspan is another example of an "expert" supporting the market. Chairman of the Federal Reserve at the time and one of the most highly regarded economists of our day, he initially seemed to see the problem. In a 1996 speech, he expressed concern over the "irrational exuberance" of market participants. The market shook—obviously, investors did not want to hear one of the foremost financial authorities suggesting that perhaps a drop was in store. The market didn't take long to recover, but it seemed to be enough to quiet any future concern from Greenspan. From that point on, in fact, he seemed to almost embrace the madness of the Dotcom Boom. In 1999, for example, he joked about selling Allen.com and using the proceeds to pay off the national debt.

The bullishness was everywhere. Books from "stock market experts" touted a prolonged meteoric rise with titles like: "Dow 36,000," "Roaring 2000s" (which predicted the Dow Jones Industrial Average would reach 40,000), and "Dow 100,000: Fact or Fiction."[139]

In 1999, the NASDAQ went up by about 85%. For the first couple of months of 2000, the index was just shy of tracking an annualized 200%.

One couldn't escape the euphoria. Take E-Trade's Super Bowl ad[140] as the quintessential example. After 20 seconds of two men and a monkey clapping their hands and tapping their feet off beat in a garage, the screen goes black and says, "Well, we just wasted $2,000,000."

Famous bears just kept losing. Legendary investor and George Soros[141] protégé, Stanley Druckenmiller, found himself in a similar position as Robertson. He had identified several stocks that were losing hundreds of millions of dollars without projected gains for years. These companies seemed (to him)

---

138 The **NASDAQ 100** is the index tracking the 100 largest, most actively traded, non-finance companies in the US—mostly technology stocks.

139 For context, the Dow peaked at just over 11,000 during this cycle.

140 https://youtu.be/qbBLDBohgrY.

141 Legendary investor and founder of the Quantum Fund, one of the most successful hedge funds of all time, averaging more than 20% per year over four decades: https://dealbook. nytimes.com/2011/07/26/soros-to-close-fund-to-outsiders/.

grossly overvalued. He went short.[142] But, in 1999, those stocks soared by an even higher percentage than ever before. He, like Newton, was a genius (but this time a "market genius"), who began to question his ability—his logic, his methodologies, his understanding of how markets and stocks work. It's not hard to imagine thoughts like "maybe *I'm* wrong," "I *must* have missed *something*," or "perhaps this really is a new paradigm—one I just do not yet understand ..."

It wasn't long after he finally wore himself down and had switched from net short to net long that the market peaked and began to crash. Because he was an adept, active trader (unlike most) he was able to quickly recognize his error, shift back into his short position as the market started to fall, and recover some of what was lost. As it turns out, a majority of those positions (where, for a short time, he had been net long) dropped by 99%—many went all the way to zero.

Several events could be identified as precipitating the Dotcom Crash: a negative article from the generally bullish Barron's or the Supreme Court ruling against Microsoft[143] (the largest company by market capitalization[144] at that time) as a monopoly ... but, trying to identify the exact straw that may have broken the camel's back would be a waste of time.

Bottom line: people lost their heads in the madness, as we are evidently predisposed to do, and then they lost their shirts when valuations came back down to earth.

In one month, the NASDAQ lost one third of its value. It took roughly 15 years for it to get back up to those highs.

## Real Estate Bubble

Greenspan reacted swiftly to calm the economic storm that ensued after the Dotcom Crash. He cut interest rates repeatedly down to roughly 1%, an almost

---

142 To **"go short"** (sell short, or just short) refers to the act of selling a security or financial instrument, such as the share of a stock, that the seller does not yet own. To facilitate this transaction, the seller borrows the asset (all handled behind the scenes by the brokerage firm). The short seller believes that the borrowed security's share price will drop in value, enabling it to be bought back at a lower price at some point in the future. In short, short selling is a way to profit when you believe a stock's price will go down.

143 NASDAQ: MSFT.

144 **Market Capitalization** is the total dollar value of a company's outstanding shares of stock—effectively, it's the value market investors have assigned to a particular company as a whole. It's calculated by multiplying the total number of shares outstanding by the stock's current price.

50-year low. For investors during this time, inexpensive loans were easier to come by than ever before.[145] Like 1980s Japan, we were entering a period of extremely easy credit …

But a big part of the problem that grew into the Real Estate Bubble originated much earlier than the year 2000.[146]

In 1938, as FDR's New Deal desperately tried to bring new life into the struggling economy, Fannie Mae was formed. Officially the Federal National Mortgage Association (FNMA), their purpose was to expand the secondary mortgage market. They would buy loans directly from banks, package them as mortgage-backed securities (MBS), and then sell them back to the investing public. Because this efficiently turned banks' loans into quick cash that they could once again invest, they were able to lend significantly more allowing more people to fulfill the "American dream."

In 1970, the Federal Home Loan Mortgage Corporation (FHLMC), better known as Freddie Mac, was created with an identical modus operandi. Although set up as public companies, both Freddie and Fannie were government-sponsored enterprises (GSEs). This gave both firms an implicit guarantee—the perception that the government would step in to bail them out if they ever ran into financial trouble.

In the noble "fight against poverty" and an attempt to help more lower-income families be able to take part in the joys of home ownership, the government forced FNMA and FHLMC to dedicate a certain percent of their loans to affordable housing projects. This rate was to be set by the department of Housing and Urban Development (HUD).

It was initiated at 30% in '92. By 1995, it was at 40%; 2000, 50%; 2005, 52%. And by 2008, 58%[147] of all loans purchased by these GSEs had to be to lower-income individuals.

Under these mandates, for them to be really profitable, they needed banks to issue more less-than-ideal (subprime) loans. And Fannie Mae and Freddie Mac were in no way small players. By the end of 2017, FNMA was the largest US company when ranked by total assets (with more than $3.3T).[148]

---

145  For context, rates had peaked in 1982 at 18%.
146  Heads up: there are a lot of acronyms on the horizon.
147  https://www.law.cornell.edu/uscode/text/12/4562.
148  FHLMC was not too far behind in fourth place with $2T in assets: https://www.relbanks.com/rankings/top-us-companies.

Due to this focus on lower-income loans, the rate of so-called subprime loans jumped from just 5% of all originations in 1994 to 20% in 2006.

If banks couldn't find a way to keep up, they'd be left behind. They had to get creative to find new ways to issue these subprime loans that the GSEs needed to buy. Consequently, in some cases, standards seemed to have been completely abandoned. Ninja and NegAm loans (along with a myriad of others) were devised as a solution. The Ninjas advertised No Income, No Job, and No Assets (NINJA). While with negative amortization (NegAm) loans your payments didn't even have to cover your entire interest due. You could just add the difference to your principal balance over time.

As you might imagine, these relaxed standards made the financial institutions' job of trying to resell these particular loans increasingly difficult. The challenge was getting anyone to buy subprime debt obligations as they tended to come with a low credit rating from the rating agencies,[149] meaning there was a high probability of default—of them never being fully repaid.

These credit rating agencies are companies whose job it is to assign ratings to the various bond offerings available in the market. They're supposed to be advocates for the individual investor—to be on their side—to help them know if they can rely on a particular security for future cash flows. But they also have a massive conflict of interest[150] as their revenue is primarily generated from the institutions trying to sell their bonds (ultimately to that same investing public).

A pool of those subprime obligations on their own (upon assessment of the likelihood that the debtors would be able to sustain regular payments) would likely warrant "junk" status. But ... what if you peeled off a small percentage of those loans and packaged them with some of the best loans—those from borrowers with significant income and cash flow and a perfect track record of payments?

All these rating agencies had their arbitrary line in the sand: as long as less than X% of the total bond pool was of subprime quality, the full package would receive that AAA stamp of high-quality approval. This strategy gave crafty financiers an easy way to pawn off these risky loans.

Each of these entities was trying to make money and offload their risk ...

---

149 **Rating Agencies**: Prior to being resold to the investing public, MBSs were evaluated and rated by bond rating agencies. These are companies that supposedly assess the creditworthiness of debt securities. In the US, there are three primary bond rating agencies: Standard & Poor's, Moody's, and Fitch.

150 https://corpgov.law.harvard.edu/2018/01/05/non-rating-revenue-and-conflicts-of-interest/.

- From the banks offering *you* a loan on a house
- To Fannie Mae and Freddie Mac trying to get those loans off their books
- To clever financiers trying to sell *you* a AAA-rated, "safe" mortgage-backed security

They were shifting the risk onto the next person down the line—a line that both starts and *ends* with the everyday, mom-and-pop investor.

And, believe it or not, just mixing in the bad with the good didn't eliminate the problem. Even if only 20% of the beef that goes into a hamburger patty is spoiled, the resulting rotten burger will still have a higher-than-anyone-would-like probability of making you sick.

The implications of that "spoiled beef" would have been particularly difficult to notice in the valuations of the housing market. Housing prices had not fallen in a single year (on the whole in the United States) since the Great Depression. This was a chorus that the head of Freddie Mac and the Chairman of the Federal Reserve were particularly fond of. They'd cite this statistic as evidence that housing prices *can't* drop for an extended period of time, let alone by any meaningful degree.

But that statistic (as many turn out to be) was upsettingly misleading. From 1890 through 2004 (after adjusting for inflation), housing prices had only risen by an annualized 0.4%. Yet, from 2004 through 2007, the jump was more like 100%.

Worse still, the Fed (now headed by Ben Bernanke) started ratcheting interest rates back up. After 17 rate increases, the federal funds rate[151] was back up over 5%.[152] Countless adjustable-rate mortgages (ARMs)[153] had been issued from 2005–2007 as a tactic for banks to sell more home loans. But now, due to these

---

151 **Federal Funds Rate:** The fed funds rate is the target interest rate at which large banks borrow and lend their excess reserves to each other overnight. It sets the tone for interest rates in general, most notably the rate at which you might be able to get a mortgage on your home. When this rate is at its lowest, credit is much easier for the general public to come by.

152 https://fred.stlouisfed.org/series/FEDFUNDS.

153 **Adjustable-Rate Mortgage:** An ARM is a type of mortgage where the interest rate varies throughout the life of the loan. During this period ('05–'07), banks often used super-low teaser rates to sell loans. These teaser rates would last for a fixed period of time and then adjust to a rate that was often ultimately derived from the fed funds rate. A fed funds rate that had increased by more than 5% would mean a jump of that or more for borrowers' mortgage interest rates when it came time for their ARMs to adjust, sometimes resulting in hundreds of dollars more being due each month.

rate increases, these new homeowners' monthly payments were becoming more than they had anticipated.

As more and more borrowers were unable to pay, waves of auxiliary impacts were felt throughout the financial world.

Never fear. On October 31, 2007, Jim Cramer came to the side of the "common man" and once again shared some timeless investor wisdom, "you should be buying things and accept that they are overvalued. But accept that they're going to keep going higher. I know that sounds irresponsible but that's how you make money. Right now it's 'up is down, left is right, peace is war.'"

Little did he know (yet again) that the top of the market had already been reached … on October 9.

Still, on December 7, 2007, another CNBC talking head and later Director of the United States National Economic Council for President Donald Trump, Larry Kudlow, comforted mainstream investors by saying, "There's no recession coming. The pessimistas were wrong. It's not going to happen… The Bush boom is alive and well. It's finishing up its sixth consecutive year with more to come."

Despite their calls for calm, herd euphoria gave way to loss-aversion-induced panic;[154] the S&P 500 logged its second worst year *ever* with a massive 37% loss.[155]

## Lessons from History

It's easy, when learning about these events, to (in a way) judge the people involved in the mania. The further back we go, the more "out there" the scenarios seem. It's probably easy for you to picture yourself not getting caught up in the whole tulip bulb madness, right? In hindsight, the mass-scale con game John Law was perpetrating seems pretty obvious. Doesn't it? Or, to think that the imperial palace could carry the same value as the entire state of California, you'd have to be bonkers.

Wouldn't you?

With the clear and more-complete picture that hindsight brings, it's not hard to think you're above it all. But herd mentality can be deceptively powerful and somehow—despite how glaringly obvious these examples all seem—almost impossible to detect in the moment.

---

154  Coming up in Myth 6.

155  The housing market (as valued by the US median home sale price) dropped 29% from its peak over the following couple of years.

Consider three characteristics common to manias. They're all:
- Packaged as a new paradigm,
- Shoved down your throat in a speculative frenzy, and ultimately,
- Endorsed by more and more experts.

## New Paradigm

Each boom is supported by at least one compelling reason that "this time it's different."

- During Tulip Mania, it was the new flower variant. Never before was there a commodity so valuable. That's the reason the world had yet to experience price jumps so extreme.
- The South Sea and Mississippi Companies sold the same vision. Never before had such deals been struck. This was the mystical New World that they were given rights to after all. Of course, these companies should be expected to reach never-before-heard-of valuations.
- Those lucky Floridians had discovered a one-of-a-kind continental tropical paradise! With no other land quite like it, it was a relatively rare commodity.
- The United States much-improved postwar world standing could easily explain the soaring market valuations of the 1920s. Things would never be the same.
- Japan was no longer suppressed—for the first time, its true value was being allowed to show through for the entire world to see.
- The internet was changing the world in ways we never before imagined. For that reason, you'd be silly to try to explain the valuations of this new revolutionary technology in the same terms as any company before.
- In the 2000s, we saw some crazy innovative financial and economic wizardry that made home ownership accessible to a degree never before seen. It was a new paradigm of progress and prosperity.

Although the events and the players are usually different, the narrative is the same: "The reason you don't understand these valuations (that may seem crazy to you) is because this is new—it just wouldn't make sense to value it in the same way. This thing (this time) is different!"

They're usually right with that latter sentiment: it is different. In these cases, true "fair" valuations are difficult—sometimes impossible—to determine. And then, the ensuing speculative frenzy serves to reinforce all of this.

## Speculative Frenzy

Perhaps, the more disciplined you are, the better you're able to ignore the noise, but it's often impossible to completely eliminate it. As more and more of those around you are making relative fortunes, this "new reality" is regularly shoved in your face. And the longer a bubble persists, the more it can make even the most savvy investor question her standards.

Imagine watching from the sidelines as …

- Tulip bulbs started being exchanged for 12 acres of land or 10 times *your* yearly wage.
- Shares in the Mississippi Company doubled in their first day of trading and then soared 3,000% in less than a year.
- Your elderly neighbor sells his Florida investment property for 175 times the price at which he purchased it just three years prior.
- The Dow just keeps going up in the late 1920s by more and more, year after year, ultimately climbing an unprecedented 90% in a year's time.
- One dotcom stock after another climbs by multiples of their initial public offering[156] price. In 1999 alone, you see the value of Qualcomm shares go up by 2,619% along with 12 other of the largest tech stocks going up by more than 1,000%.
- In the 2000s, the term "flipping" (with regards to investment real estate) enters the popular vernacular as countless millionaires are being made.

Careful forecasting and analysis are forgotten as everyone assumes they just don't yet understand the new paradigm, and if they wait until they do, it might be too late; they might be left behind and filled with regret! So, they throw caution to the wind and pile in …

With that kind of "success" all around you and so in your face, it'd be understandable to question your own investment standards and general understanding

---

156  An **initial public offering (IPO)** is when companies decide to offer ownership shares to the public. After a company's IPO, the shares of its stock are traded from willing sellers to willing buyers.

of valuations. Then, add to this equation experts and otherwise intelligent people reinforcing the fact that you must just be missing something.

## Expert Endorsement

When those you lean on for their expertise tell you that everything is okay—that this is just the new normal—it's hard to disagree. Who are you to suggest that this "financial expert" doesn't know what he's talking about? Or, when that person who you look up to as being one of the absolute smartest people you know, endorses the movement ... who are *you* to bet against them?

- After careful evaluation, Sir Isaac Newton threw his entire life savings back into the stock of the South Sea Company.
- The Comptroller General of all of France (surely, he must know a thing or two ...) was the Mississippi Company's biggest advocate.
- The foremost economist in the world declared that the stock market had reached a new "permanently high plateau" in September 1929.
- The cofounder of Sony and future Governor of Tokyo wrote essays about Japan's future prosperity in December 1989.
- Famous hedge fund manager, Jim Cramer, explained to everyday investors how to invest in this "new paradigm" at the height of the dotcom madness and then again at the peak of the real estate bubble.

## In the Future

As hard as we may try to avoid it, we will face markets like this again. The investment industry tends to propose solutions to the specific problems we faced in the past. In reality, however, future speculative crazes won't stem from the same sources as they did before. Whatever they are will appear as a new paradigm—something that could logically be explained away by the phrase: "This time it really is different."

A lot of money will be made. These new "investment gurus" will become YouTube or social media stars. For years, they'll rise as the experts with foresight enough to profit wildly from this new paradigm. And, while you may still be in doubt about joining in, experts and geniuses alike will push you in that direction. They might even publicly shame those who protest. **They'll make *you* feel stupid for missing out.**

It's a hand that's almost impossible to play:

- Stay on the sidelines and risk feeling like a fool as everyone else makes a fortune from this apparently obvious opportunity, or ...
- Jump in and put your life savings at risk.

Having been preceded by those several examples of historic crashes, your decision here may seem obvious. But when faced with this dilemma in real life, that decision will be far from easy. All bubbles start to climb so rapidly that anyone who wants to be involved in some way is given very little time to contemplate for fear of missing out.

And then, after months or years in this euphoric state, when at last there are no Greater Fools to continue pushing prices higher, without a solid foundation, the market edifice implodes, crushing millions.

---

**MYTH:** "You Can Just Ignore Your Emotions and Not Get Caught Up in the Excitement Around Bubbles."

**REALITY:** All evidence from **history and human psychology** would suggest otherwise. There will most likely be more than one euphoric event in your life that you do not see for what it is until it's **too late**.

# MYTH 6

---

## "It's Easy to Not Panic during Market Crashes"

## Loss Aversion

On the other side of our equation, amplifying the negative results, you find the second factor I mentioned: loss aversion.

Daniel Kahneman, a Nobel Prize–winning psychologist,[157] challenged the assumption of human rationality which prevails in Modern Portfolio Theory. In his example-rich text, *Thinking, Fast and Slow*, readers discover that as humans we are more motivated by pain than we are by pleasure.

That is to say, our fear of losing money will drive us to action even faster than our desire to gain. This concept is on display when I propose a little wager ...

I'll flip a coin. If it's tails, you lose $100. If heads, you get some money. How much would that figure need to be—that amount you could potentially win—before you're tempted to take the bet.

At $150, most people still have no interest in playing. Even though the equation is already clearly stacked in their favor. It's not worth the risk to them of losing that original $100—their baseline. At slightly over $200, however, the average person takes the bet.

Are you a gambler at heart and would take the offer at $100 even? That may sound crazy to some, but those are better odds than you'll find in any casino. Or are you extremely risk-averse and wouldn't even consider it until you have at least, say, 10 to 1 odds in your favor? Surely, there's some point when you would. Otherwise, you probably shouldn't be investing in the stock market at all ...

This proven fear of losing our money—of dropping below our baseline—leads to panic selling during those rare chaotic markets. To gain a better under-

---

157 And ... the seventh most influential economist in the world according to The Economist, 2015.

standing of how you might react and why, let's put this into a context you'll better understand.

## Snakes

What is your greatest fear?

I'm by no means deathly afraid of snakes, but I'm definitely not a fan. They probably elicit a more extreme rise out of me than uncovering a large spider (but that's a close second). When I have time to process the type of snake I'm looking at, that it's not being aggressive at all, and that most snakes where I live are not dangerous, I can collect my wits and manage to play it cool.

But, in that initial moment—that second right after I lift up the tarp, or mow down some tall grass, or move my grill and that snake slithers into sight—in that moment, I panic. There is no time for rational thought. Terrified, my heart skips a beat, I jump back, I may even emit the slightest little shriek ... In that moment, for that split second, I—a mature adult—react irrationally.

Investors do the same thing when the market starts to crash. Rational thought is fleeting, and panic consumes them, leading to this deeply ingrained, primal instinct of loss aversion. Understanding and appreciating that this is a reality for almost everybody begs the question: What is the best way to overcome—to avoid falling victim to this inability to control these emotions that plague the average investor?

Well ... if you have an advisor or have done any research on your own about managing an investment portfolio, you've likely encountered the mainstream advice: to be aware of the statistics and just control yourself the next time the market goes berserk. It's that easy. If you can do that, everything will be just fine.[158]

Let's explore just how ridiculous and impractical this advice is.

## Logic Versus Real Life

Following this line of thinking, you may consider using statistics to prove to me the impracticality of my initial panicked reaction every time I stumble upon a snake. For example, you might inform me that a person in the United States is nine times more likely to die from being struck by lightning than by snake

---

158 This is a prevailing tenet of Modern Portfolio Theory—it will not work without it. We'll debunk MPT in its entirety in Myths 9 & 10.

bite.[159] In fact, where I'm from, even a bee or wasp sting is more likely to kill you![160] And, if it's been long enough since my most recent ophidian encounter, I may convince myself that, armed with these facts, I am indeed prepared.

Consider this for yourself. Identify one of your biggest fears (heights, spiders, sharks). Explore some statistics that, on paper, should logically demonstrate the impracticality of your fear. And that's it. Congratulations! You're cured! Go enjoy your new freedom: climb to new heights, volunteer to deal with the next pesky spider you find in your home, swim carefree in the ocean!

Would that work?

No doubt, (for me at least) upon my next unexpected slithering discovery, I'll panic all the same. These types of fears—the ones that are just part of our wiring—don't work that way. They are not rational. We can't just convince ourselves to make them go away.

## Market Induced Fear Is Worse

Much like my fear of snakes, most people experience a fear of losing their hard-earned money. In fact, I believe the latter is even more difficult to overcome for a couple of reasons.

The first: **Certainty**. When it comes to snakes, there is a finite number of different types. Specifically, where I live, there are only four venomous varieties, and they all have a very distinct look. This means, after I've had a second to collect myself and then process what's going on, it's easy for me to know what to do: not worry about the harmless garden snake or ... wisely and calmly remove myself from that particular location.

The stock market is not as kind. There is no limited number of realities. No matter how much time you have to process what you're seeing, there is no Certainty. Things don't happen in the exact same way, and sometimes, they happen in a way that's worse than ever before experienced:

- The market falls faster in an hour (day, week, month, year) than ever before.
- The market falls farther from top to bottom than ever before.
- The market takes longer to hit the bottom or reach new highs than ever before.

---

159 http://ufwildlife.ifas.ufl.edu/venomous_snake_faqs.shtml.
160 https://www.uaex.edu/publications/pdf/FSA-9102.pdf.

You get the idea.

If this time—this next crash—the market is going to take longer to recover than it did in 1929 (25 years) or than it has in Japan (still not fully recovered after more than 30 years)[161] that may dramatically change *your* investment reality. Suddenly, that "safe" 6% average per year that your conservative advisor promised becomes impossible and you kind of just wish you had your principal back …

The second reason our ingrained market fear is more difficult to overcome: **Frequency**. If I'm exposed to snakes, spiders, or heights every single day, as unpleasant as that sounds, I'm more likely to come to terms with them. I probably uncover a snake up-close, once every few years. This inconsistency causes me to let down my guard. As a result, I am surprised and terrified anew every single time.

Once again, the market is even worse. Sometimes, it continues to climb higher and higher for decades, comforting the masses, helping them forget any chaos of the past. For example, in December 1999—a time when record numbers of investors and investment dollars were entering the market—a Gallup survey revealed that investors were expecting to realize an annualized 19% return over the next decade.

Their assumptions turned out to be about 20% per year too high! And that's assuming they stayed in the market. If they panicked, like most do, moving in and out with the market's violent swings, their returns were potentially even worse.

If we experienced 50% swings on a daily basis, this would be a different conversation. People entering the market would be prepared for such things—it would be expected. But, of course, we don't. Swings of this magnitude and worse are relatively rare.

But *they absolutely occur*, and unlike the rare deadly snake attack, these swings bite *every single person* with money betting on the market. Their infrequency causes us to forget—or not yet know—how painful it really is to watch our account balances rapidly evaporate. This has the potential to fill us with an unrealistic sense of being prepared.

## Emotional Exercise

Have you ever tried to imagine how you would react—the emotions you would experience—during a turbulent market? This is a prudent practice for any

---

161  More on both these examples in Myth 10.

investment you undertake. As best as you can, honestly consider the possible scenarios for your investment (I'd even recommend considering some that have never before happened) and try to understand how your emotions would impact your decision-making.

Obviously, the unpredictable nature of markets makes it impossible to do this for every possible outcome. And no imagination can fully prepare you for the emotional chaos of the real thing—but subjecting yourself to this exercise is far better than doing nothing at all.

If you've never done it, you should do it now. Go ahead. It doesn't have to be elaborate or silly; you just need to be honest with yourself. Let's give it a try real quick ...

Imagine all the money you have invested in stocks (from brokerage accounts to IRAs to 401(k)s, everything). Picture it in one big stack in front of you. The image you have in your mind right now needs to represent all of the money you have exposed to the market—whether that's $100 or $100MM. As much as you can, try to feel the same emotional attachment to this mental image as you would your actual money.

Do you have it? Are you ready?

Now, consider the next crash. Imagine the market quickly drops due to some unexpected event. That stack of cash in front of you immediately drops by 10%. If you had $1MM, your total falls to $900,000 overnight. Although painful, we could all probably shrug off a drop like that. You knew that was a possibility going into this.

At 20%, depending on how quickly it drops, you're likely a bit more concerned. But then, you remember the statistics that suggest the average investor underperforms the market, so you decide to stay the course. You're clever; you're not going to be part of those numbers[162]—you're going to be the exception that actually keeps up with the market. So, you bite your lip and stay the course. Good for you ...

But this crash—just as some others in the past—does not let up. The market continues its downslide to 30% below its former high. You call your advisor in a panic. Never fear! Trained in the ways of Modern Portfolio Theory, she regurgitates the platitudes she's rehearsed for times like these: "You just need to remain

---

162 We'll explore those statistics in detail in Myth 9.

disciplined and stay the course." "The market *always* goes back up to reach new highs." "It's the investors that panic who underperform."

Did that do it for you? It can be a compelling argument for some. Was it enough to calm your nerves or would you throw in the towel here? Your $1MM is now only $700,000, but you're staying in? You're that disciplined? Okay ...

Well, what if it keeps going? What then? It's down 40, 50, 60% ... every morning you wake up, praying it's over, and then, you look at your phone, only to realize the market is suffering a significant decline yet again. There are no signs of relief.

How do you feel? When do you just ... break?!

Maybe you didn't at 10, 20, or 30%, but when you can visually (in your mind's eye) notice that your pile of cash in front of you is half of its former glory, doesn't your stone-cold discipline begin to waver (if not just a little)? How much more of a beating can your future plans take? Were you planning on retiring in 10 years and assuming an 8% rate of return? Because ... I hate to break it to you, but at this point, that's probably not going to happen, especially if the market continues on its downward path. Now, you realize that a 0% annualized return—or worse—over that time is absolutely possible.

Your advisor is begging you to "stay the course."[163]

On the other hand, you realize that you can stop the bleeding. It is within your power. You can make the pain go away, take a moment to collect yourself, and at least be happy with the fact that you still have what you do. Sure, you want that $400,000 to grow back to $1MM. But ... you *need* $400,000 to hit your bare minimum retirement goals. So, do you risk it falling below that? Or do you just pull it out now?

Is it worth the stress of sitting idly by and potentially watching it drop another couple of hundred thousand and maybe even staying that low for decades—forcing you to work through your planned retirement?

I hope you get the idea: no matter how strong your conviction today ... at some point, all logic and reason go out the window. It doesn't matter anymore. You're not concerned with becoming a statistic. You don't care about "loss aversion." You couldn't care less what your advisor is lecturing you about. You know

---

163 Sidenote: feel free to ignore right now the fact that with most investment advisors, **if every one of their clients were to pull out of the market, they'd be out of a job**. Sounds like more than a little conflict of interest—beware the moral hazard.

it'll rebound again—probably soon—but that doesn't matter anymore: this is your life savings! It's too stressful to just sit back and observe. It is within your power to make it stop!

So, you decide to stop the pain. You indiscriminately sell. You get out. At least now you can feel a little bit more in control again.

**At some point, emotions are more impactful than any advice from an advisor.** When is that point for you? When do you "break"? If it wasn't the 60% we got down to here, is it 70%? 80%? C'mon, this is your life savings we're talking about!

And, by the way, these scenarios aren't impossible. Crashing more than 25% in just a couple of weeks has happened before.[164] A near 90% peak-to-trough drop has happened before.[165] Taking decades for the market to recover and hit new highs has happened before.[166]

Frankly, I understand. I would probably panic too if I had so much of my portfolio banking on the health of the stock market. This may sound contradictory, but I think you'd be right to panic and get out! But I'm getting ahead of myself …[167]

Statistically, more people are exiting the market at the trough (the low point) than at any other time.[168] Many are likely vowing to never subject themselves to that unpredictable ride again. It's just not worth it … that is, perhaps, until they see others profiting from a rebound, and decide to get back in, well into the recovery.

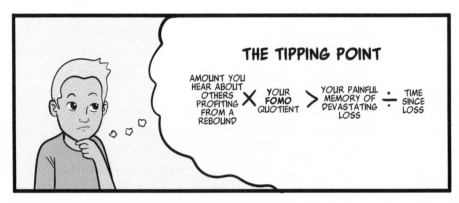

---

164  March, 2020.
165  The Wall Street Crash of 1929.
166  US, 1929; Japan 1989 (still not fully recovered).
167  Myths 9 & (especially) 10.
168  DALBAR, 2019.

That exercise can be hard—it's very difficult to be honest with ourselves or to even have an inkling as to how we would react when actual emotions are working on us in an extreme scenario like that. So, mentally prepare as you might (which I still recommend), it's a long way from a perfect or complete solution.

## One-Two Punch

It's this marriage between the herd mentality and loss aversion that leads to buying high and selling low—the exact opposite of what we all know we should do … But the cause of each of those culprits, as we've seen, is human nature. It's how we are wired. It's rooted in our survival instinct.

That means for most, it doesn't matter how prepared we are or how much we tell ourselves that we can control our emotions during a market storm. When we find ourselves in the midst of the next unprecedented chaos, we panic and act on instinct.

Carl Richards summarizes:

> It's not that we're dumb. We're wired to avoid pain and pursue pleasure and security. It feels right to sell when everyone around us is scared and buy when everyone feels great. It may feel right—but it's not rational.

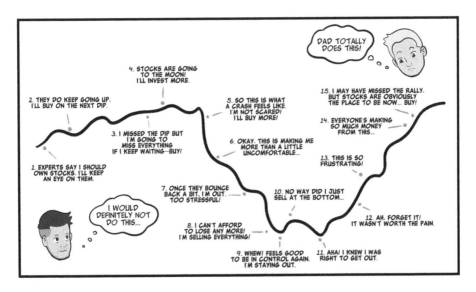

## The Gap in Real Life

So, as it turns out, humans (yes, that includes you) are emotional. Even if we have robots managing our money (robo-advisors[169]), on average as a group, we still tend to pull it out at all the wrong times. Our emotions are the culprit!

The proponents of traditional Modern Portfolio Theory will tell you that the only way MPT works long term is if people "turn off" their emotions and resist the temptation to touch their money. As much as we would like to believe we'll be able to do that—as history has repeatedly shown us—we won't. We can't. We are human, and our *survival instinct* leads to emotional decisions, which makes MPT fail.[170]

This fact is well-researched and widely accepted, yet we continue to invest in the same way, hoping we'll do better the next time the market crashes.

### Quantitative Analysis of Investor Behavior

Financial services market research firm, Dalbar, conducts a Quantitative Analysis of Investor Behavior (QAIB) every year.[171] Their research demonstrates the difference between how investments perform and the returns actually realized by individual investors. From 1986 to 2015, the S&P 500 realized 10.35% per annum, whereas the average investor with similar stocks realized only an annual 3.66% return—that's the difference between $1,000 growing to almost $20,000 versus just under $3,000!

Dalbar notes that *some* of this discrepancy is due to the fees which clients are paying their advisors and fund managers (as detailed in Myth 2). But, according to their findings, the *greatest contributor* to this difference is what they label: **Voluntary Investor Behavior**. This is where you'll discover the impact of herd

---

169 Like Betterment and Wealthfront mentioned in Myth 2.

170 Again, we'll break down the remaining tenets of MPT in Myth 9, leaving you thinking, "why would I want to try to adhere to that strategy anyway ...?" So, even if you're among the many who think you're above all this or the rare few who actually can overcome your emotions, successfully doing so could still get you into trouble ...

I sincerely do believe there are those who are actually capable of overcoming (or just suppressing) their emotions—after all, given my personal experience in 2008 (related in Myth 3), (even though I was young and the money was gifted) I confidently put myself into that category—yet at the same time, I no longer believe that's the best strategy. You'll understand why after Myths 9 & 10, and you'll understand some of those better potential solutions by the end of this book.

171 https://www.dalbar.com/.

mentality, loss aversion, and a myriad of other human nature ticks that lead to our underperformance.

The QAIB breaks out nine such behavioral biases and defines them as follows:

- **Herd Mentality**: Following what everyone else is doing. Leads to "buy high/sell low."
- **Loss Aversion**: The fear of loss leads to a withdrawal of capital at the worst possible time. Also known as "panic selling."
- **Narrow Framing**: Making decisions about one part of the portfolio without considering the effects on the total.
- **Anchoring**: The process of remaining focused on what happened previously and not adapting to a changing market.
- **Mental Accounting**: Separating performance of investments mentally to justify success and failure.
- **Lack of Diversification**: Believing a portfolio is diversified when in fact it is a highly correlated pool of assets.
- **Regret**: Not performing a necessary action due to the regret of a previous failure.
- **Media Response**: The media has a bias toward optimism in order to sell products from advertisers and attract view/readership.
- **Optimism**: Overly optimistic assumptions tend to lead to rather dramatic changes of opinion or investment approach when met with reality.

Unfortunately, even that is not an exhaustive list of all the ways our own brain is working against us. Neuroscience expert Jason Zweig[172] expounded on a few more in an article published by the European Asset Management Association in London.[173]

- **Illusion of Control**: With the proliferation of low-cost, online brokerage platforms, investors have been encouraged to believe that the mag-

---

172 Jason Zweig is the personal finance columnist for *The Wall Street Journal* since 2008 and author of *Your Money and Your Brain* (Simon & Schuster, 2007). He is also considered to be an expert on the teachings of Benjamin Graham who is considered to be the Father of Value Investing. Zweig is the editor of the revised edition of Benjamin Graham's *The Intelligent Investor* (HarperCollins, 2003), the classic text that Warren Buffett has described as "by far the best book about investing ever written."

173 http://jasonzweig.com/benjamin-graham-the-human-brain-and-the-bubble/.

nitude of their portfolio's return is directly proportional to the amount of attention they pay to it. This causes them to trade positions much more frequently than investors used to, which leads to greater transaction costs (fees charged on every trade, in and out) and an *increase in the frequency of many of the other behavioral biases.*

- **Sensation-Seeking**: Research from Wolfram Schultz at Cambridge and Read Montague while at Baylor explored the dopamine release triggered from financial gains. The less likely or predictable the gain is, the more dopamine released and the longer it lasts. All this, subtly pushing investors to participate in more (and riskier) speculation in search of their next big win (read: dopamine hit).

- **Prediction Addiction**: Scott Huettel, a neuropsychologist at Duke University, demonstrated that after something happens just twice in a row, the human brain automatically expects another repetition. Therefore, when a stock's price goes up two ticks in a row, our brains intuitively expect the next trade to be an uptick as well ... even though those past movements could have absolutely no bearing on what will happen next.

One doesn't have to fully understand the extent of all the behavioral biases at play to recognize that there is a problem—that, due to our emotional nature, the individual investor tends to underperform the market.

Dalbar has been exploring this phenomenon since 1994. Over those years and throughout the various time periods studied (each study compares time horizons from 12 months to 30 years), the underperformance due to "voluntary investor behavior" tends to range from 1–2%.[174]

## The Numbers

Let's refer, once again, to our example from Myth 1. Remember? That $100 invested in 1926—that, at our original 12.1% assumptions, would have been projected to grow to $5MM, but then, in reality (after accounting for actual returns and less-than-average advisory and fund fees) turned out to be just 5.6% of that total, a mere $280,000 (and that's not even accounting for taxes, inflation, or sequence risk) ... You remember that example, right?

---

174 DALBAR's historical QAIBs.

Well, when you honestly consider the possible impact of these "voluntary investor behaviors" on your long-term return (at least accepting the possibility that you too, being human, *might* fall victim to these very human tendencies), your actual realized return here could be less than $100,000.[175]

What would that mean for your bottom line? Even with just the low-end "voluntary investor behavior" assumption of 1%, here's how much less your actual portfolio value would be.

### Table 17
### Additional Impact of "Voluntary Investor Behavior" on a $10,000 Investment

|  | Average 12.1% | Actual 10.3% | Advisory 9.2% | Fund Fees 8.7% | After Investor Behavior 7.7% | |
|---|---|---|---|---|---|---|
| 30 Years | $310,000 | $187,000 | $139,000 | $120,000 | $90,000 | 71% LESS |
| 20 Years | $99,000 | $71,000 | $58,000 | $50,000 | $40,000 | 60% LESS |
| 10 Years | $31,000 | $27,000 | $24,000 | $20,000 | $20,000 | 35% LESS |

So now, even if the market does what it's done in the past and you behave like a normal human being … your $10,000 investment after 30 years has only grown to $90,000 when you were projecting—and planning for—more than $300,000.

---

**MYTH:** "It's Easy to Not Panic During Market Crashes."

**REALITY: Human biology and history** would suggest otherwise.

---

175 Using the low-end "voluntary investor behavior" assumption from the QAIB's findings of 1% would result in a final value of $110,000—2% of our original projection. With the high-end assumption of 2%, we're left with $42,000.

# MYTH 7

---

## "Funds Will Help You Outperform the Market"

## "Mind the Gap"

Dalbar is not the only firm curious about this differential.[176]

Morningstar, the independent investment research firm famous for its mutual fund star-rating system, has taken a different approach. Instead of comparing investor returns to the market as a whole (the S&P 500 benchmark, as Dalbar does), in their annual *Mind the Gap* report,[177] they evaluate how individual investors perform compared to the funds in which they're invested (both, mutual *and* exchange-traded[178]).

The study looks at average investor returns over five 10-year periods (the most recent report, as of this writing, examined the 10-year periods ending in 2014 through 2018). This means that the most recent 10-year period did not include all of the chaos from the market's collapse in 2008, as its range was from January 1, 2009 through December 31, 2018.[179] As might be expected, the report noted that the gap is wider during those periods that include more volatile[180] market moves. This supports the "loss aversion" premise that as markets become more chaotic, individual investors underperform by an even greater margin.

---

176 Over its more-than-25-year tenure, Dalbar's work has not been without criticism. One of the most scathingly impactful articles comes from The American College professor, Wade Pfau: https://www.advisorperspectives.com/articles/2017/03/06/a-warning-to-the-advisory-profession-dalbar-s-math-is-wrong. Pfau has to make several assumptions about the formula used to generate the conclusions in the QAIB. Given the "blackbox" nature of this formula (as of this writing), it's difficult to know for sure just how valid his criticism is. The fact that Dalbar keeps that formula under lock-and-key brings with it its own concern: either the company does indeed have something to hide, or due to the vastness of computing power today, they are legitimately worried there'd be copycats and they'd lose their value as a unique resource in the marketplace.

177 https://www.morningstar.com/lp/mind-the-gap-global.

178 ETFs were added in this most recent report. This is a welcome addition since according to Morningstar Direct there is now more money invested in Passive Equity Funds (index funds and exchange-traded funds) than their Actively Managed counterparts (both totaling more than $4T). **This addition demonstrates that, even with a "passive" investing strategy, human emotion can still haunt us.**

179 The S&P 500 lost 37% in 2008 and hit its low in March 2009.

180 **Volatile (volatility)** is defined as being liable to change rapidly and unpredictably, especially for the worse.

The study revealed that equity (stock) fund investors on average underperformed the funds in which they were invested by 0.56%. As in, if the fund realized an annualized return of 7.06%, the individual investors within the fund, on average, realized 6.50%—0.56% less than the fund itself.

For more evidence of the reality and impact of panic selling, we can study the breakdown of equity fund underperformance relative to fund volatility. Morningstar separated equity funds into quintiles based on this criterion—i.e., the top quintile contained the least volatile funds (the ones with steadier price movements over time) and the last quintile was made up of the most volatile funds (the ones with price movements that you'd expect to be more likely to induce fear).

### Figure 13
### Less Volatility Means Better Results[181]

| Standard Deviation Quintile | Investor Return | Total Return | Gap |
|---|---|---|---|
| 1 | 7.11 | 7.30 | -0.19 |
| 2 | 6.98 | 7.18 | -0.20 |
| 3 | 5.59 | 6.63 | -1.04 |
| 4 | 5.77 | 7.18 | -1.41 |
| 5 | 4.72 | 6.58 | -1.86 |

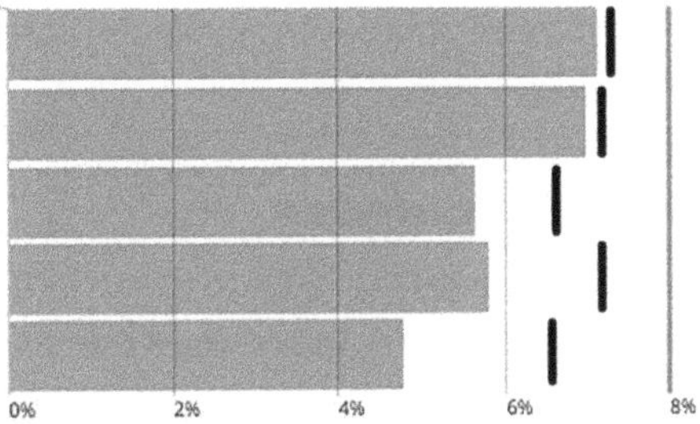

The impact of panic selling and its correlation with dramatic swings is on full display in the gap found in the lower three quintiles. The middle group had an average gap of 1.04% while the **worst managed to underperform their funds by *1.86%*.**

So, what would this mean, then, for the bottom-line figure we worked down to throughout the first several myths? That we should factor out an additional[182] 0.56% per annum? At least …

Again, I think it's important for the prudent investor to consider that this calculation is already conservative in that one of the five time periods studied

---

181 Adapted from Morningstar's Mind the Gap 2019, https://www.morningstar.com/articles/942396/mind-the-gap-2019.
182 In addition to advisory and fund fees.

does not even account for investor behavior during a market crash.[183] And that's the type of scenario for which we should be planning, right?

Historically, the market has experienced a decline of 15% or more on average about once every 4 years.[184] Don't we at least want to be prepared should a significant drop occur within 10 years of the time you'd like to be able to use your investment dollars?

Regardless, it's clear that (even when we factor in that extremely prosperous decade) there *is* additional underperformance. Now, is that underperformance due to those so-called behavioral biases? It doesn't matter. Whether we have a name for it or not—whether we understand it or not—the discrepancy is undeniably there.

I believe, however, that a more accurate (and helpful) period to learn from would be one that allows us to see the impact of having all five 10-year periods reflect the emotions present in a euphoria-panic cycle. For this, we can look at Morningstar's 2017 *Mind the Gap*.[185] In this study, the average 10-year return gap for investors in US large-cap[186] funds was an *annualized 1.41%!*

It's those emotional boom-bust times that cause humans to react in ways they weren't expecting—that ultimately lead to much greater underperformance.

## Fund Performance

But remember, *Mind the Gap* is comparing investor returns to fund returns, not our benchmark index, the S&P 500—that standard by which we formed our initial 12.1% thesis. Now, for those investors utilizing passive funds, that 0.56% gap[187] may be fair. But, for the other *half* of investors still leaning on the expertise

---

183  The S&P 500's returns (including reinvested dividends) for the 10-year period ending in 2018 were: 27%, 15%, 2%, 16%, 32%, 14%, 1%, 12%, 22%, & –4%—there was relatively-little downside volatility during this period (compared to the vast majority of decades throughout history).

184  The S&P 500 has experienced a decline of 10% or more about once every year, lasting for (from peak to trough) 114 days on average. It's experienced a decline of 15% or more about once every 4 years, averaging 270 days. And it's experienced a decline of 20% or more about once every 7 years, averaging 431 days. Source: RIMES, Standard & Poor's.

185  Morningstar, data through December 31, 2016.

186  **Large-cap** stocks tend to have a market capitalization (share price multiplied by shares outstanding) of $10B or more. Almost all the stocks in the S&P 500 meet this qualification. They represent more than 90% of the entire US equities market (as represented by the Wilshire 5000 Total Market Index). https://wilshire.com/Portals/0/analytics/indexes/characteristics/wilshire-5000-characteristics.pdf.

187  Remember, the 0.56% figure came from the study that included passive funds. The 1.41% only included actively managed funds.

of active fund managers, the gap will be even wider. So, how have these actively managed funds compared to our market benchmark in the past?

The S&P Dow Jones Indices[188] set out to solve that very mystery. Since 2001, they've published their S&P Dow Jones Indices Versus Active (SPIVA) Scorecard. And the data for 2020 aren't pretty.[189] As of December 31, 2020, more than 75% of all US large-cap funds underperformed the S&P 500 over the previous 5-year period (from January 1, 2015). But, what about throughout 2020 alone—a year with quite a bit of volatility, an environment where active fund managers claim they'll shine? Somehow, 60% of them still managed to underperform the S&P 500 itself.

Twenty twenty wasn't just a single-year anomaly either. In fact, it's on the better half of individual year performance since they started tracking in 2001.

### Figure 14

Percentage of Domestic Equity Funds *Underperforming* the S&P Composite 1500[190]

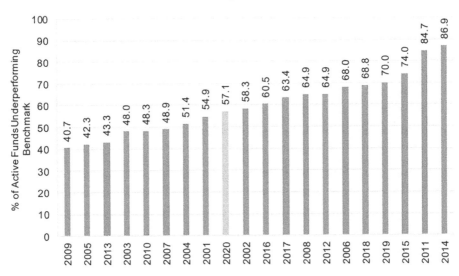

*Source:* SPIVA U.S. Scorecard 2020. S&P Dow Jones Indices LLC. Data as of Dec. 31, 2020. Past performance is no guarantee of future results. Chart is provided for illustrative purposes.

---

188 A division of the S&P Global company.
189 Find the most up-to-date information here: https://us.spindices.com/spiva/.
190 The S&P Composite 1500 represents the 1,500 largest publicly traded companies in the United States.

Don't worry, Dave Ramsey has a solution. Just find a fund that consistently beats the market. You know, one of those 25% of funds that outperformed over these last 5 years. It's that easy! Right? Ramsey Personality, Chris Hogan explains:[191]

> You want to choose funds that have a history of strong returns. Focus on long-term returns, 10 years or longer if possible. You're not looking for a specific rate of return, but you do want a fund that consistently outperforms most funds in its category.

That all sounds easy enough. But in practice, it's been proven that that's not really how fund returns work from year to year. The same funds aren't always at the top. In fact, the funds that perform the best in one period are historically *no more likely* to be on the top yet again during the following period than they are to be on the bottom …

## Luck or Skill?

The *S&P Persistence Scorecard*[192] studies this phenomenon each year. At the start of September 2015, there were 220 domestic large-cap mutual funds in the top quartile of this category. If left up to chance, 25% (or 55) of those same funds would still be in the top quartile of their class that following year. In reality, however, only 14% (31) made the cut—**far less than chance!**

By the time we get 5 years out (September 2019), even chance would leave us with one star-studded standout. Once again, however, reality was not as kind, leaving us with zero. No US large-cap funds were able to *consistently* perform in the top 25% of their category over the last 5 years.

This is not always the case in these reports—there is often a fund or two still standing. But the fact that a fund's persistence here is near or less than chance should cause you to reflect as to whether or not "still standing" is a sign of luck rather than skill.

---

191 https://www.daveramsey.com/blog/how-to-choose-the-right-mutual-funds.
192 *Does Past Performance Matter? The Persistence Scorecard*, December 2019.

Sure, maybe from year to year, consistent fund performance is no better than chance. But you care about the long term, right? What about the funds that are in the top quartile over a 5-year period? How do they fair over the next 5-year period—where there's plenty of time for those "superior" managers to outperform?

In the S&P Dow Jones Indices most recent Performance Scorecard, 30% of the funds that were in the top quartile during that first 5-year period (ending September 2014) were also in the top quartile from 2014 to 2019. Indeed, slightly better than chance (25%)!

That's not always the case, however. In 2017's Performance Scorecard, just 22% were still at the top—less than chance would have. What's even more interesting is that 28% of those top-ranked funds from the first period were in the worst-performing quartile at the end of the second 5-year period.[193] Investors basing their fund selection on past performance (as Ramsey-'n-company recommend) had **a higher chance of picking a loser than a star!**

Considering the data, it's obvious that funds underperform most of the time. But the degree to which they do so is extremely difficult to calculate.[194] One of the leading contributors to this obscurity is known as survivorship bias.

## Survivorship Bias

The fund industry has been an extremely lucrative one. The massive financial firms behind these mutual funds know how to turn a profit. They've learned over the decades what works. And what works is tantamount to throwing everything against the wall and seeing what sticks. Fund companies are constantly thinking up and churning out new mutual funds to satiate the investing public's avaricious appetite. Flip a coin, some of these hip new funds are going to perform in the top half of all funds. Surprise, surprise. If these companies can just manage to crank out a large enough number of them, even chance would allow for some to consistently outperform 5 years in a row (maybe even 10).

That's when the iron is hot for these fund companies—this is when they strike. They pour everything they've got into promoting this fund with its shiny new track record of consistent outperformance. The ROI (return on investment)

193 https://www.economist.com/finance-and-economics/2017/06/24/fund-managers-rarely-outperform-the-market-for-long.
194 This is a figure I'd like to have for our consideration here—if for no other reason than to provide us with a non-arbitrary, additional percentage by which we should adjust our calculations.

for the fund company is so high in year one[195] that it's well worth whatever it costs to get that track record plastered everywhere—the Wall Street Journal, CNBC, everywhere. The world *needs* to know how amazing this fund is!

Except, we know the truth now, don't we? **Although 5 or more years of outperformance sells, it also seems to in no way be correlated with future high returns.**[196]

So, that's what the fund company was after: it's their golden goose. They'll ride it until she stops outperforming, and then they'll move on to the next one. As long as they've continued to diligently sling enough … there will be a "next one"—the next new great track record to promote.

But, what about all those duds (the ones that consistently underperform) that they're putting out into the investing world? Well, they just sweep those under the rug. They do this either by liquidation or merger.

What would you do if the way you made your living was by hawking mutual funds and you discovered you had one of those duds on your hands? The longer the underperformance, the more difficult it'd become to drum up support and stop investor dollars from flowing out. "Darn that Morningstar 1-Star Rating!"

Well, if your fund was small enough, you could just sell off all its assets and distribute the proceeds to the fund's shareholders.[197] That would be a liquidation.

On the other hand, you could just "merge" your subpar fund with a currently better-performing one. You'd still sell off all the assets, but then you'd just immediately move them into that other fund. Voilà! Now, the poor track record from that old fund is no more! You can continue your business of promoting and selling your winners.

This process of liquidation or merger happens all the time. **Over the last 15 years, 57% of domestic (US) equity[198] funds were merged or liquidated.** For example, of the 484 domestic equity funds that were in the bottom quartile after the 5-year period

---

195 What, with investors paying those 5.75% up-front sales charges as Dave Ramsey and many financial advisors advocate …

196 I'm not suggesting it's impossible to have a fund that consistently outperforms. Perhaps, even, due to a management team that really is just that skilled. What I am saying here is that one's track record seems to be an extremely flawed, no-better-than-chance way to find that future winner. And, sadly, I'm not sure there is a better solution.

197 Some funds only last a single year, some 3 years, some 5. This complicates any sort of average-return-for-all-mutual-funds calculation.

198 Think: stock.

ending in September 2014, more than 30% (150 of them) were merged or liquidated during the following 5-year period[199]—just like that, they're gone.

Burton Malkiel, in his 2013 revision of his investment classic, *A Random Walk Down Wall Street*, anecdotally observed that when he first began work on his book in 1970, there were 358 equity mutual funds in existence. Today, there are thousands. "We can measure the long-term records of only 84 of those original funds because 274 of them no longer exist. Thus, the data in the exhibit suffer from survivorship bias. You can be sure that the surviving funds are the ones with the best records."

It would seem that for every successful fund you might be able to identify today there are dozens—maybe hundreds—who had ugly enough track records that their corporate parents cut them off entirely.

This is what financial firms do with those funds that don't "stick." And the mess it leaves behind makes it impossible to determine the average annual underperformance of mutual funds on the whole.

The evidence suggests that the probability of selecting a consistent winner (let alone a winner at all) appears to be no greater than (and in some cases worse than) chance.

Bottom line: funds clearly underperform on average and outperformance in any given year has no correlation with future outperformance.

---

**MYTH:** "Funds Will Help You Outperform the Market."

**REALITY: Funds clearly underperform** on average and outperformance in any given year has no correlation with future outperformance.

---

199 SPIVA's 2019 Performance Scorecard.

# MYTH 8

---

## "An Advisor Will Help You Overcome Your Emotional Biases"

## Advisor to the Rescue?

I GUESS THIS IS WHY THE WEALTHY HAVE INVESTMENT ADVISORS TO HELP THEM OVERCOME ALL THIS...

All of this is interesting,[200] but is it really relevant to those who employ a financial advisor? I mean, that's part of their job, right? To talk you off the ledge during times of chaos? So, does any of this—*Dalbar* and *Mind the Gap* investor underperformance data— really apply to you?

Absolutely! You see, these numbers are not just calculations for retail investors[201] who haven't sought "professional" help.[202] These numbers are derived from calculations factoring the performance of all market players. That means, the performance of all of Edelman's 1.2MM clients is being reflected in these figures—"professional hand-holding" and all.

Maybe you're thinking that most people are idiots. And that may be true. But the vast majority of the money in the market is in the control of people who are far from stupid. You may think: "I can do better than my neighbor." Again, that may be true. But ... you don't have much of a chance of being better informed or advised than Jeff Bezos or Mark Zuckerberg or probably any ultra-high-net-worth individual.

Consider those wealthiest Americans for a moment. Don't you think they'd be employing the "best" financial professionals to manage their money—to help them avoid these sad little emotional mistakes of mere mortals ... Well, they're in here too. In fact, the richest 10% of Americans own 84% of the stock market.[203]

So, not only do these Dalbar and Morningstar figures include people with advisors and professional assistance, *they're practically making up the entire figure.* It stands to reason that these numbers are fairly representative of how the average investor should expect to perform *even with professional guidance.*

---

200 To me at least ... I hope it's helpful for you as well!
201 **Retail investor** is the industry's term for the individual, non-professional investor.
202 I suspect the numbers would be even worse if we were able to only consider the unadvised, everyday investor.
203 National Bureau of Economic Research, November 2017.

## The Complete Picture

So now, with this emotional reality in front of us, let's go back to that exploration of Ric Edelman's and Dave Ramsey's advice.[204] Let's give Edelman's pricey advisors the benefit of the doubt and assume they're great at their job—able to help you limit your losses from these "behavioral biases" to the low end of Dalbar's "voluntary investor behavior" findings (1%). And Ramsey's Endorsed Local Providers[205] (ELP) are able to help you limit your emotional losses to the Morningstar's actively managed mutual fund underperformance average of 1.41% (due to the difficulty in knowing any precise value, as explored at the end of Myth 7, we'll have to ignore the obvious fact that those individual funds themselves on average underperform the market by an additional margin, thus making our final figure here a conservative projection).

### Table 18
#### Experts' Assumptions Versus The 12% Expectation

| | 10 Years | 20 Years | 30 Years |
|---|---|---|---|
| **12% Expectation** | $103,273 | $408,494 | $1,356,463 |
| **Ramsey Assumptions** | $73,705 | $207,257 | $465,778 |
| **Edelman Assumptions** | $78,247 | $220,182 | $495,212 |

Factoring for these historically average considerations, leaves you with only about 35% of your original expectation (and this is all without inflation, taxes, or sequence risk). Although imperfect, these are historically based measures of the very real consequences of behavior biases on our actual long-term returns.

---

204 From the end of Myth 2.

205 This is just Dave Ramsey's name for his lead generation system. People trust him, so they enter their name on his site. He then forwards that name to three so-called ELPs who cover the territory wherein the lead resides. Those ELPs (all three of them) are then encouraged to contact the lead as quickly as possible to secure the business. Today, his investment industry ELPs are called SmartVestor Pros.

    Even though I greatly (and publicly) disagree with Ramsey's investment philosophy, he offered me one of the eight ELP spots available for my territory. All for the low monthly payment of just $750! Securing a spot in the larger MSAs (metropolitan statistical areas—bigger cities) currently costs participating advisors more than $900/month.

They alone have shaved yet another six-figure sum[206] off the 30-year projections given these experts' assumptions.

You may be thinking, "I'm above average. I don't need to account for that extra 1% or 1.41% 'emotional' discount." And you very well may be above average. (In fact, I'm confident at least half the readers of this book *will* be …) But some readers also have to be below average. And their returns can be far worse than what we just explored here. Unfortunately, it's really impossible to know beforehand which you'll be. The potential panic-inducing events that we're discussing here are few and far between and all very different from any of the previous instances!

## Overconfidence

The funny thing about averages is that way more than half of people think they're above average at most things. Which, of course, by definition, is impossible. This is another of those "behavioral biases." With overconfidence, you naturally believe yourself to be above average. In one study, for example, 81% of new business owners thought they had a 70% or greater chance of succeeding, but that only 39% of their peers did.[207] Another study found that 82% of young drivers in the US rated themselves in the top 30% of their peers when it came to safety.

In their book, *In Search of Excellence*, Peters and Waterman present a psychological study conducted on a random sampling of adult males. After being asked to rank themselves on their ability to get along with other people, "*all* subjects, 100%, put themselves in the top half of the population. 60% rated themselves in the top 10% of the population, and a full 25% ever so humbly thought they were in the top 1% of the population."[208]

You may very well be above average (honestly, I'm sure you are, since you're reading this book), but the aforementioned gaps have left quite the chasm for you to bridge.

On top of that, this overconfidence in the world of investing can, ironically, lead to *even greater underperformance*. If you really think about it, the above-average investors who are diligently adhering to the mainstream's "stay the course" mantra might ultimately get hurt the worst. Carl Richards summarizes:

---

206 When compared to our previous (pre-behavioral biases) evaluation of this same chart at the end of Myth 2: $159,637 for Ramsey's and $114,594 for Edelman's.

207 Ervolini, M. A, 2014. Managing Equity Portfolios: A Behavioral Approach to Improving Skills and Investment Processes. Cambridge, MA: MIT Press.

208 Peters, T. J. and Waterman, Jr, R. H. 1982. In Search of Excellence. New York: Harper & Row, 56–57.

The terrible irony in all this is that the people who are trying the hardest to stick to their plans—the ones who hold out the longest before they finally capitulate—are the ones who end up getting hurt the worst because they buy nearest the peak. Once those hard-core holdouts give in, you know the top can't be far away, because there is no one left to buy.

I would posit that the opposite is also true. As markets free-fall, it's the "disciplined" investors who hold out the longest—and suffer the most—prior to their ultimate capitulation.

### For Those Truly Capable of "Staying the Course"

Even if you are 100% certain that you wouldn't "break," our next two myths will put some doubts in your head about that strategy. They should make you reconsider your stone-cold desire to hold out *no matter what.*

Remember, I was that person. I've sat on the sidelines during euphoric upswings as friends and colleagues tried to get me on board. I've remained disciplined during chaotic crashes.[209] I've proven to myself that I could stay that mainstream course, no matter what … *if* I wanted to.

You see, at this point, after all my research, I've discovered that simply "staying the course" with a stock-and-bond portfolio is not the panacea it's made out to be. I've discovered that it could even be the exact wrong course of action for you in the future.

---

**MYTH:** "An Advisor Will Help You Overcome Your Emotional Biases."

**REALITY:** The data we've reviewed thus far primarily consist of investors who have advisors trying to "help them." The evidence suggests that an advisor "talking you down" does not equal superior performance in the market.

---

209 My experience during the Financial Crisis of 2008 detailed in Myth 3, for example.

# MYTH 9

---

## "You Just Need to Buy and Hold Stocks and Bonds"

## Understanding MPT

The prevailing solution to this whole "emotion problem"—to help prevent you from getting in and out at all the wrong times—is an academic concept known as Modern Portfolio Theory or MPT, for short. It's evolved into the go-to investment strategy used by advisors and promoted by academics and pundits the world over. For the most part, it's unchallenged and widely accepted as "investment gospel."

> "I think buy-and-hold is a crock of sh*t."
> **—Mark Cuban**

The theory was pioneered by Harry Markowitz in a 1952 paper for the Journal of Finance.[210] The world of finance loved and has embraced this theory so much that they later awarded him a Nobel prize for his contribution.[211]

Modern Portfolio Theory is a "theory on how risk-averse investors can construct portfolios to optimize or maximize expected return based on a given level of market risk."[212] It's the idea that with the proper mix of stocks and bonds[213] one can diversify away any risk that might be in excess of what they can tolerate.

To that end, stocks and bonds have become the simple building blocks for the majority of individual investors' portfolios.

---

210 Markowitz, H. M. "Portfolio Selection." The Journal of Finance 7 (1). March 1952, 77–91.

211 Never mind his observation that the model was **never intended to be applied to the everyday investor**, so … just like the financial world at large, we'll conveniently overlook that point for the time being. Don't worry, we'll circle back around to it shortly.

212 Investopedia, 2020. https://www.investopedia.com/terms/m/modernportfoliotheory.asp.

213 A **bond** represents a loan made from an investor to a borrower, usually a corporation or government. It is generally considered to be a more conservative investment than a stock as it represents a specific amount due at the end of the loan term and usually includes payments from the borrower to the investor along the way. For a more detailed exploration, explore the free companion resources at SpicerCapital.com/Go.

## Self-Evaluation

Now is as good a time as any for you to consider all your investments. Go pull up your accounts. Let's see what your overarching portfolio looks like today. Go ahead. Really. I'll wait.

So, what's your stock/bond allocation? 60/40? 70/30? 80/20? Is your portfolio entirely derived from stocks and bonds? Maybe you have 5–10% peeled off for other investments, like real estate or commodities. Do you think that's enough to mitigate the risks of being exposed to only two overarching asset classes (stocks and bonds)? Others exist, you know. And after all, diversification is a key principle behind MPT, yet most practitioners still advise you to invest almost exclusively in stocks and bonds.

# Diversification

The importance of diversification and correlation are *critical* to understanding the inadequacy of MPT, so make sure you get this part. The concept of diversification is encapsulated in the cliché of not putting all your eggs in one basket. The idea is that by mixing certain asset types together in your portfolio, you realize higher returns with less risk. We don't have to get into the weeds of the math behind this for it to make sense.

### An Easy Example

In the early 20th century, there were hundreds of independent manufacturers trying to succeed in the auto industry. By the end of the 1920s, it was dominated by Ford and GM. If you had purchased Ford stock at its inception, you'd be sitting pretty today. But what if you picked wrong and put all your savings on the wrong horse—one of the many auto manufacturers who ultimately went bankrupt?

Enter the very basic need for diversification. What if, confident in the auto industry, but unsure on which individual company to bet, you simply purchased a little stock in every single one of those hundreds of manufacturers?

Sure, you would have experienced a lot of relatively tiny failures, but the few long-term successes would have netted your investment portfolio significant returns. Betting on the auto industry as a whole was safer and more profitable than attempting to divine the winning horse. Markowitz called this phenomenon "the only free lunch." Through diversification, at no additional cost, an investor can reduce his risk while also increasing his projected return. *It's something for nothing.*[214]

## Easier than Ever

Diversifying within an asset class has never been easier. Today, if you wanted to bet on the auto industry, you could find an Exchange-Traded Fund (ETF) that tracks an index that follows that particular industry. Investing your money in such a fund would be like purchasing a little stock in every single public company that operates within that respective industry or sector. In fact, investors can utilize ETFs to diversify across most types of investments.

Investing in an ETF that tracks an index instead of investing in individual stocks removes the risk of a single stock going bankrupt, and you consequently losing all your investment. It allows you to diversify across an entire investment class, like large US companies.[215]

An ETF is a cost-effective way to do this. These funds invest their underlying assets based on set rules often just systematically tracking and simulating the exact composition of their respective indices. As such, they don't require an expensive manager or much in the way of overhead.[216]

If you invested in an S&P 500 ETF, you would own a small piece of each of the 500 companies[217] that make up that index, and it would cost you very little time or money to do so. Considering the thousands of companies in the United States and tens of thousands in the world, utilizing ETFs provides a relatively inexpensive way to get a more diversified exposure, spreading your risk. This diversification smooths your returns, making them more predictable and less volatile.

We already explored the *significant* long-term benefits of reducing volatility back in Myth 1. Remember the comparison of the two portfolios, where the one that outperformed in 7 out of 10 years still underperformed on the whole?

---

214 Technically, it's not "nothing" you're giving up: you are reducing the possible returns (not to be confused with projected returns) that can accompany speculations or gambles.

215 Via an ETF that follows the S&P 500, for example.

216 Annual fees for ETFs go as low as 0.02% (ETFdb, May 2020. https://etfdb.com/compare/lowest-expense-ratio/). That's 20 cents for every $1,000 invested. Super cheap!

217 Fun fact: there are often more than 500 stocks represented in the S&P 500 as some companies have multiple share classes, like Berkshire Hathaway and Alphabet (Google). At the time of this writing, there are 505 stocks in the S&P 500.

The reason for this apparent contradiction was ultimately because losses weigh heavier on an account than do gains.[218]

And then again, in Myth 7, we saw how more volatility within a mutual fund or ETF results in even worse returns for the underlying investors.[219] In short, a reduction to volatility is a welcome addition to a viable financial plan.

One of the primary goals of diversification is to minimize losses. That's why it's so important your investments are well-diversified.[220] You can diversify within an asset class, like the ETFs we just talked about. You can also diversify across various asset classes—having some money in large company stocks, some in international stocks, some in government-issued bonds, and so on.

This is where correlation comes in: it helps you diversify in a stable fashion.

## Correlation

Understanding correlation can help you substantially reduce the volatility of your entire investment portfolio. Based on historical data, correlation measures the degree that two assets move in relation to each other. This relationship is assigned a value between 1 and –1. This number is known as the **correlation coefficient**.

A positive correlation exists when assets move in tandem. If one goes down, the other goes down. If one goes up, the other goes up. The closer the correlation coefficient is to 1, the more in sync the assets have been. For example, US and international stocks tend to maintain a correlation close to 1: when stocks in one developed country do well, stocks in other developed markets all around the world, on average, also perform well. A coefficient around 0 implies little to no relationship at all.

A negative coefficient implies the assets tend to move in opposite directions—when one is up, the other tends to be down. For example, stocks and bonds have *historically* displayed low correlation. In the past, their coefficient was mostly negative—they moved in opposite directions. Since 1990, however, bonds have tended to move in the same direction as stocks (a positive correlation), although that correlation is still relatively low (closer to 0 than to 1).

---

218  If you don't remember that, you should go back and learn it again—it's such a critical concept to understand if you want to get the most out of the rest of this text ... including, when we explore some potential solutions in Myths 15 & 16!
219  From Morningstar's 2019 Mind the Gap Report.
220  But not over-diversified, which we'll discuss in more detail in Myth 15.

Incorporating uncorrelated assets in your portfolio can make your returns more consistent from year to year. As one asset class is down, another uncorrelated or negatively correlated asset class might be up. This consistency reduces the portfolio's volatility, which as we have seen, can lead to higher long-term returns.

Today's Modern Portfolio Theory suggests that investors are served best by buying and holding a stock-and-bond portfolio using broad-based, low-cost ETFs to fund each asset category (large company stocks, small company stocks, corporate bonds, etc.). Since stocks and bonds historically have a low correlation, the idea is that this combination reduces risks and smooths returns.

---

Warren Buffett and Charlie Munger discuss Modern Portfolio Theory during the question-and-answer period of a Berkshire Hathaway annual meeting ...[221]

Munger: "Much of what is taught in modern corporate finance courses is twaddle."

Buffett: "Care to elaborate?!"

Munger: "You cannot believe this stuff: Modern Portfolio Theory ..."

Buffett: "... it has no utility ... It is elaborate. There's lots of little Greek letters and all kinds of things to make you feel that you're in the big leagues, but there is no value added."

Munger: "I have great difficulty with it because I am something of a student of dementia. But Modern Portfolio Theory involves a type of dementia I just can't even classify! Something very strange is going on."

---

221 https://buffett.cnbc.com/annual-meetings/.

## 'Worst-Case' Hypotheticals

Now that you have a solid understanding of how and why MPT is supposed to work, let's put your resolve to the test. Modern Portfolio Theory relies on historical data to support its assumptions of providing you with a risk level you can tolerate. But it's always quoted in terms of average returns and standard deviations[222] which makes it difficult to comprehend the extremes.

Let's consider a couple of those worst-case scenarios. If you have money in the market now, then make these considerations with your own money in mind. If not, take note as this should impact the strategies you ultimately implement for your long-term savings.

### History's Worsts

The worst 20-year period for the US stock market came during the crash following the Roaring 20s. The market peaked at $381 on September 3, 1929 and hit its low point at $41 on July 8, 1932. It took 25 years to hit new highs. Over the 20 years from 1929 through 1948, the market averaged just 1.7% per annum.[223]

The worst 20-year period for a developed nation's stock market was the one experienced by Japan in 1989. The market[224] peaked at $38,957 on December 29, 1989 and hit its low point at $7,054 on March 10, 2009. It still has yet to fully recover, i.e., reach new highs.[225] Over the 20 years from 1989 through 2009 (it closed out the year at $10,546.44), the market averaged –4% per annum.[226]

---

222 **Standard deviation** is a statistical measurement used in finance to account for historical volatility. Securities and markets with a wider range of past prices (higher highs and lower lows) will have a higher standard deviation. Thus, a smaller, more volatile stock would have a high standard deviation, while that of a stable large company is usually much lower. The stock market has historically had a higher standard deviation than the bond market.

223 If you were reinvesting the dividends earned from the stocks held, it would have only taken you 15 years of "staying the course" to recoup your initial investment. Note: if the goal of this text was just to prove a point, we could leave out the dividends. But that's not the goal—the goal is an honest exploration of our investment reality, so that we can best adapt and thrive long term no matter what happens. Thus, allowing for dividend reinvestment in this case is more realistic.

224 As represented by the Nikkei 225.

225 As of this writing, more than 30 years later, it still sits around half its former high.

226 Both these figures (1.7% and –4%) are assuming the below-industry-average advisor and fund fees outlined in Myth 2 (1% and 0.4%, respectively). They do not, however, account for inflation or taxes. Adjusting for average inflation over this time period makes the return an investor would have actually realized an almost 7% per year loss!

What would these scenarios have done for your portfolio?

Let's assume average historical US bond returns[227] and that you're not making contributions or withdrawals during this period—as we've seen (Myth 4), this has the potential to make these returns we're about to study *even worse* …

We'll also assume (and this is a big assumption) that you stay invested the whole time. As discussed in Myth 6, this is unlikely for most investors, especially considering the fact that we're talking about a rapid—in just 3 short years—89% drop for the first scenario and a slow, painful, 82% downward trending rollercoaster for the other.

Would you sit through drops like that? Would you want to?[228]

## The Portfolio Impact

Given those aforementioned assumptions, here's how various portfolio makeups would have performed over each **20-year** scenario.

### Table 19
### Portfolio Annualized Returns Given History's Worst-Case Scenarios

|  | 100/0 | 80/20 | 60/40 | 40/60 |
|---|---|---|---|---|
| **US Great Depression** | 1.70% | 2.37% | 2.97% | 3.50% |
| **Japan's Lost Decades** | -4.00% | -0.92% | 0.99% | 2.40% |

*Note:* The first number in the labels at the top of each column represents the percentage of your hypothetical portfolio that you allocated to stocks; the second number, the percentage to bonds. The percentages displayed in the chart show the annualized returns of each portfolio given the assumptions outlined above for each scenario.

That $100,000 you invested 20 years ago only grew to $140,000 (100/0) or $199,000 if you were somehow invested with a 40/60 stock/bond mix for *all* 20 years. Compare that to a common "conservative 7%" assumption of $387,000. Even with bonds in the mix, those negative years can really throw a wrench in your long-term plans (especially if you're solely dependent upon MPT).

---

227 The index most commonly used to represent US investment-grade bond performance is the Bloomberg Barclays US Aggregate Bond Index (it is to bonds what the S&P 500 is to stocks—representing approximately 43% of the US bond market). Over the last 15 years, the index averaged an annualized 4.44%.

228 More on why you might not even want to in our next myth.

If you accept those Japanese stock assumptions as a *possibility* in the US marketplace (of course they are, why wouldn't they be?) then, the potential "worst-case" is even more frightening. Your $100,000 after 20 years, would only be worth somewhere between $44,000 (100/0) and $160,000 (40/60).

Again, this is all assuming you're "staying the course" the entire time, despite all the chaos, and are *not subjecting yourself to sequence risk by contributing or withdrawing.* These factors (plus taxes and inflation) make the reality even more grim.

But, with these examples, you can see some of the value bonds can add to your portfolio, given periods of particularly poor stock market growth. In both of these extreme scenarios, bonds did a great job at significantly improving your overarching returns—even if those "improvements" were far below any mainstream 20-year projection.

## Bad Time for Bonds

But this has all been assuming bond returns derived from a recent historical average. Why not, at least explore a sort of worst-historical-case scenario by mixing into these abysmal stock scenarios the worst period for bondholder returns. Because, honestly, I don't think that's too unrealistic an assumption for the more immediate future of bond performance. Warren Buffett agrees: "Bonds are not the place to be these days… Fixed-income investors worldwide—whether pension funds, insurance companies, or retirees—face a bleak future."[229]

Remember: bonds have a low correlation with stocks and things that are uncorrelated tend to move independently. Meaning, both stocks and bonds could do well at the same time, stocks could do well while bonds do poorly and vice versa, and of course … *both stocks and bonds could perform miserably over the same period.*

Bonds have been a welcome addition over the last several decades, as they have been in a raging bull run (to the extent a relatively tame bond-bull can rage). This has correlated with the gradual and extended decline in interest rates since the 1980s: in other words, interest rates and bonds are negatively correlated. When interest rates go up, bonds do poorly. Interest rates go down, and bonds do well.

Today, however, interest rates are touching 0%. Last time they were this low, the following decades did not bode well for bondholder returns. Consider the

---

229 Warren Buffett's 2020 annual letter to Berkshire Hathaway's shareholders: https://www.berkshirehathaway.com/letters/2020ltr.pdf.

decades before our current bull run began. From 1953 to 1981, as interest rates rose from roughly 1% to almost 20%[230] bonds averaged an annual return of only 0.2% after inflation.

### Figure 15
### United States Interest Rates: 1953–2021

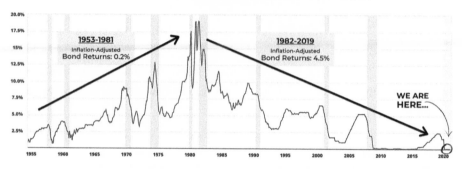

*Note:* US recessions are shaded.
*Sources:* Interest rate data (as measured by the Effective Fed Funds rate) from the Board of Governors of the U.S. Federal Reserve System, and Morningstar Direct. For Equities we use: S&P 500 TR; for Fixed Income: Barclays U.S. Agg Bond TR.

---

"The economics of investing in bonds has become stupid."

**—Ray Dalio**

---

## An Even Worse 'Worst-Case'

The worst, non-inflation-adjusted, 20-year annualized return for a diversified bond portfolio was 0.79%.[231] Consider the impact on your portfolio if this were your average return over the next couple of decades (as you prepare for retirement, or even worse psychologically, as you enter retirement).

With that one change, here is what your returns would look like.

---

230 https://fred.stlouisfed.org/series/FEDFUNDS.
231 From 1940 through 1959, a diversified bond portfolio consisting of 3-month treasury bills, U.S. treasury bonds, and investment-grade corporate bonds, given the same advisory and fund fee assumptions as we've been using throughout, would have realized a 0.79% annualized return. Bond data from: http://pages.stern.nyu.edu/~adamodar/New_Home_Page/datafile/histretSP.html.

### Table 20

## Portfolio Annualized Returns Given Even Worse Historically Based Assumptions

|  | 100/0 | 80/20 | 60/40 | 40/60 |
|---|---|---|---|---|
| **US Great Depression** | 1.70% | 1.53% | 1.35% | 1.17% |
| **Japan's Lost Decades** | -4.00% | -2.62% | -1.54% | -0.64% |

*Note:* The first number in the labels at the top of each column represents the percentage of your hypothetical portfolio that you allocated to stocks; the second number, the percentage to bonds. The percentages displayed in the chart show the annualized returns of each portfolio given the assumptions outlined above for each scenario.

The more bonds you added to the US hypothetical, the *worse* your results—cutting your $140,000 down to $126,000 (40/60). And, with the Japan hypothetical, bonds still weren't able to bring about a positive *20-year* annualized return. Even with the "super safe" 40/60 portfolio (a portfolio that might, according to modern theory and practice, be recommended for a 60-year-old to ease into), you still weren't able to break even—only having $88,000 left in your account at the end of those 20 years.[232]

How much do these returns differ from your "well-diversified" plan's assumptions for growth? If you're around 30 now, how would this affect your retirement planning—your ability to hit your goals? If you're around 60, how badly would this affect your quality of life in retirement?

Are you comfortable with this reality? That you just looked at your 80%-stock portfolio and realized that, despite the traditional diversification, there is realistic (historically based) potential to lose more than 2% on average every year for the next 20 years.

Is it impossible for any of these 20-year, **nightmare scenarios** to play out in the future? Is it crazy to **accept that potentiality?**

*Of course not.* Why would it be?

It's not a pleasant thought. It's not convenient. It makes a financial advisor's job much more difficult. But these scenarios are possible. Don't get me wrong, **I'm not suggesting they're likely.** But even if you don't perceive them as likely, **they are *very real* possibilities**. After all, they were pulled straight from history (where the academics—the originators of these theories—love to focus).

---

232 Again, factor in a retiree's withdrawals and these returns are drastically worse (due to sequence risk, explored in detail in Myth 4).

The reason I repeat several times in this section that these figures are "historically based" is two-fold:

1. Because it is particularly important to the context of this principle that you keep in mind where these data are coming from: no one just made them up; they actually happened.[233]

2. But also, history only provides us with a limited dataset. In other words, **there is absolutely *no reason* something worse—something entirely unexpected—could not happen in the future**.

Again, not a pleasant thought, but times are changing ...

> "The simple stock-bond mix needs to be fine-tuned."
> **—Burton Malkiel, author of *A Random Walk Down Wall Street***

## New Correlation Reality

Consider Markowitz, back in the early 1950s, as he devised this theory that hinges on uncorrelated assets. It's not difficult to imagine assets being less correlated back then than they are today. We live in a world of smart devices at our fingertips, allowing us almost-instant access to pretty much whatever data we desire. That information can travel from city to city and even overseas in milliseconds. We're more connected now than ever before—let alone, than was even thought possible in 1950.

The Great Recession of 2008 serves as a stark reminder of this new interconnected reality. When things go badly in one area of our global economy (the United States real estate market, in this example), it's felt everywhere. This new paradigm is obvious when you examine what happened to the growth of the entire world GDP per capita through 2008 and 2009.[234]

---

233 Even though these stock and bond worst cases happened at different times, they did both happen, and given the admitted lack of correlation between these asset classes, there is no reason they could not happen at the same time.

234 http://data.worldbank.org/indicator/NY.GDP.PCAP.KD.ZG?end=2015&start=2004.

**Figure 16**
World GDP per Capita Growth (annual %)

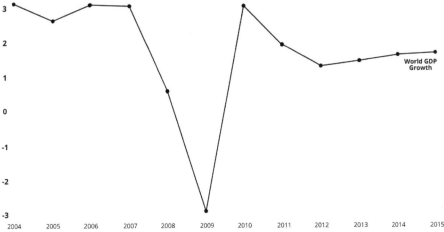

*Note:* The numbers on the x-axis represent the annual growth percentage.
Source: World Bank Accounts Data and OECD National Accounts Data Files.

Where diversification was supposed to protect us, almost every market fell together—domestic stocks, international stocks, real estate, commodities … all fell!

**Table 21**

Asset Class Performance: 2008 Financial Crisis

| Asset Class | Return between Oct '07 and Feb '09 | Months to Recover after Feb '09 |
|---|---|---|
| Investment-Grade Bonds | 1% | 0 |
| Junk Bonds | -35% | Not yet recovered |
| Commodities | -40% | 24 |
| US Large-Cap Stocks | -53% | 48 |
| US Small-Cap Stocks | -53% | 24 |
| International Stocks | -60% | 144 |
| Emerging Market Equities | -62% | 143 |
| Real Estate | -68% | 52 |

*Note:* As measured by: Vanguard Total Bond Market ETF (BND), iShares High Yield Bond ETF (HYG), TR/CC CRB Index, S&P 500 Index, Russell 2000 Index, Vanguard FTSE All-World ex-US ETF (VEU), iShares MSCI Emerging Markets ETF (EEM), and MSCI US REIT Index (RMZ).

Many asset classes—including international stocks, US high-yield bonds, real estate investment trusts, and even commodities—have become increasingly correlated to the S&P 500 since the 2008 Financial Crisis.

A more recent reminder of this global connectivity came in March 2020 due to the economic uncertainty surrounding Covid-19.

**Table 22**
Asset Class Performance: March 2020 Crash

| Asset Class | Return in March 2020 |
|---|---|
| Investment-Grade Bonds | -1% |
| Junk Bonds | -10% |
| Commodities | -13% |
| US Large-Cap Stocks | -12% |
| US Small-Cap Stocks | -22% |
| International Stocks | -13% |
| Emerging Market Equities | -15% |
| Real Estate | -22% |

These days, when investors panic and pull money out of the markets … they appear to be pulling them *indiscriminately* from everywhere—preferring the comfort of stashing their money under the proverbial mattress to chaotic uncertainty.

And it's not just the overarching asset classes that are becoming increasingly correlated. Even the individual underlying assets are moving more in sync than they used to. According to Morningstar, correlations between individual S&P 500 stocks have trended upward over the last two decades.

**Figure 17**

Average Individual S&P 500 Stock Correlation

Source: Morningstar, "The Correlation Conundrum and What to Do About It"
and SSGA, May 2, 2012.

Based on the average daily correlation over the trailing 6 months (remember: 0=uncorrelated, 1=totally in sync), correlations rose from roughly 0.1 in 1994 (read: almost no correlation) to 0.5–0.7 in 2011 (read: much more correlated).[235] **This increasing correlation has an adverse impact on the effectiveness of diversification strategies.**

Morningstar elaborates on the concerning significance of this new reality, "For simplicity, consider a portfolio of just two assets—stocks ABC and XYZ— that are held in equal proportions. Shares of ABC have a volatility of 40%, and XYZ have a volatility of 30%. If the two stocks have a correlation of 10% [0.1], the overall volatility of the portfolio would be 26%. However, if the correlation between the two stocks rises to 66% [0.66], the volatility of the portfolio increases to 32%."[236] And as we now know, all else equal, a higher volatility results in even worse actual returns for the buy-and-hold investor.[237]

---

235 At the time of this writing, this correlation of the stocks comprising the S&P 500 was between 0.5 and 0.8. You can find the most up-to-date figures here: https://www.cboe.com/ index/dashboard/kcj#kcj-overview.

236 Rawson, M. "The Correlation Conundrum and What to Do About It." Morningstar Advisor. May 2, 2012. https://www.morningstar.com/articles/549350/the-correlation-conundrum-and-what-to-do-about-it.

237 Referencing the lessons learned in Myth 1 about the negative impact of increased volatility.

## To Markowitz's Credit

To Harry Markowitz's credit, individual stocks and overarching asset classes used to be relatively uncorrelated. But things are different today. Whatever the reason, the trend has quite clearly changed.

And, when you lose the correlation constant, Modern Portfolio Theory falls apart. There is no way Harry Markowitz could have predicted the level of reliance and connection that we experience in our world today. After all, he formulated this theory more than a decade before the first prototype of the internet[238] was created! This theory was born in a world of "slow data" and that was just starting to globalize again.

## An Industry Confused

In reality, Markowitz never intended for these to be *your* issues. The industry seems to have mistakenly taken his 1952 research and applied it to the everyday investor when in fact that was never his intent.

After winning the Nobel Prize, he was asked to write an article explaining how Modern Portfolio Theory applied to household investors. Surprisingly, Markowitz responded that he had *never thought about it* before. He said that was not his specialty; his theories were designed with institutions in mind. In that 1991 article for the *Financial Services Review*, he wrote, "An evening of reflection convinced me that there were clear differences in the central features of investment for institutions and investment for individuals."

Wade Pfau elaborates,[239] "He recognized Modern Portfolio Theory was never meant to apply to households. He had developed it for large institutions like Mutual Fund companies... Households in retirement, face an asset liability matching problem—they have to fund expenses over an unknown length of time. Modern Portfolio Theory is much more simple."

> "Everything should be made as simple as possible, but not simpler."
> **—Albert Einstein**

---

238 https://en.wikipedia.org/wiki/ARPANET.
239 https://www.youtube.com/watch?v=pudX6_M_a54.

Mistaken or not, the financial industry latched on and refuses to let go—despite the loss of the correlation constant and even despite the revelation of Markowitz's original intent.

## Same Questions; Different Answers

In 1942, Albert Einstein was teaching at Oxford. He had just given a Physics final to that year's seniors. One of his students stopped him in the courtyard and asked, "Dr. Einstein, weren't those questions on that final exam the same as last years?"

Einstein chuckled and said, "Why, yes, yes they were."

"How is it that you can give the same test every year?" his student inquired.

"Well … the questions may be the same, but the answers … well, this year the answers are different."

Our financial questions today are the same as they were back in 1952. Where should we invest our hard-earned money? How can we best protect it without sacrificing gains? How can we best prepare for retirement? And so many more.

Academics, pundits, and practitioners alike continue to respond in the same way month after month, year after year, decade after decade. even though the answers are in dire need of an overhaul.

### Bengen's Rule

Consider the so-called safe withdrawal rate (SWR) referenced in Myth 4. This commonly accepted rule of thumb was first articulated by William Bengen in a 1994 *Journal of Financial Planning* article.[240]

After studying 75 years' worth of data, Bengen concluded that retirees who withdraw no more than 4% of their investment portfolio in their first year of retirement, and then adjust that figure for inflation every subsequent year, can live without fear of running out of money (a big risk/concern for retirees).

After being popularized by a Trinity University study,[241] the 4% safe withdrawal rate became a staple of the financial services industry. The message to clients was that with this combination of …

---

240 Bengen, W. P. "Determining Withdrawal Rates Using Historical Data." Journal of Financial Planning, October 1994, 14–24. http://www.retailinvestor.org/pdf/Bengen1.pdf.
241 Cooley, P. L., Hubbard, C. M., and Walz, D. T. "Retirement Savings: Choosing a Withdrawal Rate That Is Sustainable." AAII Journal 10 (3). 1998, 16–21. https://www.aaii.com/files/pdf/6794_retirement-savings-choosing-a-withdrawal-rate-that-is-sustainable.pdf.

- An MPT-inspired stock-and-bond portfolio plus
- That 4% "safe withdrawal rate" rule of thumb plus
- The constitution to "stay the course no matter what"

… they could be confident in the fact that they would not outlive their money during their retirement.

Why? Well, because *in the past*, that would have worked.

Unfortunately, throughout the first decade of the 21st century, following this advice—answering this question with the same answers as before—was ruinous for millions of retirees.

## T. Rowe Price Study

After experiencing a decade with two savage market crashes, T. Rowe Price wanted to put this 4% SWR to the test.[242] They assumed a $500,000 portfolio invested in 55% stocks and 45% bonds upon entering retirement on January 1, 2000. Let's explore their findings through the lens of our example couple just trying to prepare for this whole retirement thing …

John and Mary had done their research and were sold on the math and science backing a 4% safe withdrawal rate. They agreed to withdraw $20,000 from their account while adjusting for inflation each year (increasing their withdrawal by 3% annually). They had an advisor run a Monte Carlo simulation[243] for them just to be sure. At that time, it revealed an 89% probability of not outliving their income.

---

242  https://www4.troweprice.com/iws/wps/wcm/connect/
e3c2ec8045961707ba69bf32e4e97423/DismalDecade.pdf?MOD=AJPERES.

243  **Monte Carlo Simulations** are used to model the probability of different outcomes especially when random variables are involved. A Monte Carlo simulation applied to portfolio science, for example, will take historic annual returns of the stock market. It'll do the same for the bond component. Then, it will run hundreds or thousands of scenarios randomizing those returns into the future. The product of this exercise is a probability of "success," i.e., your likelihood of not running out of money during your retirement.

These simulations project out the impact on a portfolio of a randomized set of historically based returns—i.e., the S&P 500's worst possible year in one of these models might be 43% (because that's what actually happened in 1931).[244] But you'll never see an accounting for any potentially worse returns. They might run these projections 10,000 times to produce a range of historically based possibilities. When combined with a "safe withdrawal rate," these simulations can produce a percentage chance that you don't run out of money in retirement (historically based, of course). The inverse of this percentage being the probability that you do run out of money and have to go back to work or in some way massively alter your life plans.

An 89% chance of success doesn't sound too bad. John and Mary could retire with confidence!

The traditional advice at the time was to "stay the MPT and SWR course" no matter what—these strategies had been proven with decades of evidence. It was those who panicked in the past that lost the most.

## The Study's Findings

This clichéd wisdom about those who panic turned out to be true here as well. Those who panicked to the extreme after the Dotcom Crash and followed their knee-jerk reaction to move all their money into the "safe" asset—bonds—well, when a Monte Carlo simulation was run again in March 2009 to assess how they were doing, it was discovered that they consequently had a 0% probability of "success"—of *not* outliving their income over their remaining *21 retirement years.*

That's a 100% chance of failure (based on the historical data)!

But nobody ever thinks they'll be the one to panic, so what about those that were "disciplined" and "stayed the course" as they were told? Well, after applying the actual market returns to John and Mary's portfolio and then rerunning that same Monte Carlo simulation at the bottom of the second bear market (March 2009), the study revealed *a mere 6% chance of "success"* from that point through their remaining 21 years.

---

244 Although many won't even go back that far. They'll randomize market returns from the last 15 or 20 years to project out forever into the future …I hope you can now see the problem with that.

That's a **94% chance of failure**—a 94% chance that John and Mary will have to cut their retirement plans short, go back to work, significantly cut back their lifestyle, mooch off a loved one, or some other equally undesirable option—**all because they diligently adhered to the prevailing market wisdom of the time.**

**MYTH:** "You Just Need to Buy and Hold Stocks and Bonds."

**REALITY:** Millions of people have been financially devastated by blindly adhering to that advice. **Modern Portfolio Theory is not the best way for everyday savers to invest.**

## Lesson Learned?

The study proposed a couple of alternative strategies that would have worked better over this period, like reducing withdraws by 25% or taking no annual inflation adjustments for 3 years after each bear market bottom (good luck determining when those are in the chaos of the moment ...). But even those would have left John and Mary, now 9 years into their retirement, with a mere 43% or 26% "chance of success," respectively—both a far cry from the 89% comfort they had as they made the decision to retire.

These proposed alternative solutions are how the financial industry (academics and professionals alike) tends to react to everything—retroactively, with the benefit of hindsight. If an advisor had suggested these "radical" adaptations to the SWR back in 1999, practitioners might have accused him of being overly cautious and ultimately not doing what was in the best interest of his clients, after all there was empirical evidence to support the MPT+SWR theory.

Since his cautiousness would have (historically-speaking) resulted in slightly lower returns and a worse outlook for his clients' retirement prospects, he likely would have lost business as a result.

The industry is rife with pressure to stick with the traditional investment paradigm—to just "fall in line" and not challenge what everyone else is doing.

## Consequences

But just think about the millions upon millions of investors, diligently adhering to mainstream advice, who have to delay their retirement each time we have an "unexpected" and never-before-experienced sequence of events. **Are you really expected to leave your life plans subject to that kind of roll of the dice?**

Today, the industry embraces a revised version of the "safe withdrawal rate"—the so-called dynamic withdrawal rate. This newfangled solution is simply the current iteration of the financial industry's backward-looking answers designed to account for past events ...

Our lauded experts are particularly good at providing solutions that would have worked super well after the fact!

But is that it? Is that all we should take away from this? Is this "dynamic SWR" really the best solution? The be-all and end-all? This time they thought of everything? We can all rest easy now?

Right ...?

What if, instead, we learned something else from all this? Something bigger?

What if, instead, we learned a different lesson from those millions who suffered—forced out of retirement or to live off way less than planned—during the first decade of the 2000s due to this faulty, backward-looking, industry advice?

What if, instead, we learned that **for some things—like major life plans—historical data is just not good enough?**

# MYTH 10

---

## "You Can Use Past Data to Prove What the Market Will Do in the Future"

## Long-Term Capital Management

In 1994, the hedge fund world had its eyes on a promising new fund called Long-Term Capital Management (LTCM). Their star-studded roster was packed with financial industry heavy hitters of the MPT and efficient market[245] inclination.

The fund was founded by Wall Street heavyweight, John Meriwether, the former vice-chairman and head of bond trading at Salomon Brothers. With his influence, he was able to attract the best traders in the industry and beyond. His pull stretched into academia where he even attracted the likes of two Nobel laureates.

### The Laureates

Anyone who has ever traded or studied stock options[246] is familiar with the Black-Scholes model for pricing these popular derivatives. Investopedia defines this model as follows:

---

245 The **efficient market hypothesis** (EMH) states that share prices reflect all information. This belief is a cornerstone of Modern Portfolio Theory.

246 A **stock option** gives one the right, but not the obligation, to buy or sell a stock at a specific price before a certain date. There are two types of options: **put options** bet that a stock will fall while **call options** bet that a stock will rise.

The Black-Scholes model, also known as the Black-Scholes-Merton (BSM) model, is a mathematical model for pricing an options contract. In particular, the model estimates the variation over time of financial instruments. It **assumes** these instruments (such as stocks or futures) will have **a lognormal distribution of prices**. Using this assumption and factoring in other important variables, the equation derives the price of a call option.[247]

Myron Scholes and Robert C. Merton, two of the academics behind this esteemed model, signed on with Meriwether. The models they built for LTCM were rooted in the idea of efficient markets and "a lognormal distribution of prices." In other words, they were **using *past data* to make "*sure bets*" about what would happen in the *future*.**

Sound familiar?

Put simply, their models—"definitively proven" by historical data and backward-looking analyses—would identify arbitrage[248] opportunities in the market. Then, LTCM's traders would go to work, leveraging their immense portfolio to the extreme in order to squeeze every last dollar out of each and every opportunity.

Alright, the stage is set. It's time to put these historically based academic theories to the test—that is, these theories that are reliant upon the same dataset and logic, as is Modern Portfolio Theory, to "definitively" draw their conclusions!

## Initial Success

To the LTCM partners—and to the many high-profile banks and investors who fell all over each other to get a piece of the pie—their strategy was foolproof. With the salesmanship of Merton, Meriwether, and Scholes, by the time they launched in February 1994, the fund had amassed more than $1B in start-up capital—an unprecedented feat for a brand-new hedge fund.

---

247 Emphasis added.
248 **Arbitrage** exploits the price differences (market inefficiencies) of related financial instruments in different markets or in different forms. It generally involves buying and selling assets at the same time in order to profit from those discrepancies.

The firm was wildly successful at first, generating returns of 28% in 1994, 59% in '95, and 57% in '96. In 1997, LTCM still managed to realize another 25%[249] despite controlling more than $100B in assets.[250]

In his book, *When Genius Fails*, Roger Lowenstein observed:

> Merton's theories were seductive not because they were mostly wrong but because they were so nearly, or so nearly often, right. As the English essayist G. K. Chesterton wrote, **life is 'a trap for logicians'** because it is almost reasonable but not quite; it is usually sensible but occasionally otherwise. 'It looks just a little more mathematical and regular than it is; its exactitude is obvious, but its inexactitude is hidden; its wildness lies in wait.'[251]

To most, it seemed as though they had cracked the code. There were a few reputable names in finance, however, who expressed concern with LTCM's overconfident reliance on past data. Most notably, Paul Samuelson, the first economist to win a Nobel Prize and Merton's MIT mentor, had his doubts from Day 1. "The essence of the Black-Scholes formula," Samuelson observed, "is that you know, *with certainty*, not what the deal of the cards will be but what kind of universe is being sampled." Lowenstein elaborates:

> The beauty of cards is that the universe is known; there are 52 cards in a deck, and only 52. Life insurance is a bit different: since new people are always being added to the universe, actuaries rely on samplings. They aren't perfect, but they work, because the sample of people is very large and mortality rates change only very slowly. But in markets, we are never sure that the sample is complete. The universe of all trades looked one way throughout the 1920s and another way after the Great Depression. The pattern changed again during the inflationary 1970s, yet again in the effervescent 1990s.

---

249 After LTCM's hefty fees the investor returns were still impressive: 20%, 43%, 41%, and 17%.
250 The larger a fund is the more difficult it is to find and take advantage of opportunities. LTCM controlled this much in assets through the use of leverage—a risky practice that left the fund more exposed. But, since the fund was making what they deemed to be mathematically safe bets, they were not concerned.
251 Emphasis added.

After which of these periods was the picture 'normal,' and **how do we know that the next new period won't change the story again?**[252]

We will never have a complete dataset when it comes to stocks and markets and economies. One thing we can be sure of, however, is that the story for each new period will—in some likely unanticipated way—be different.

## Ultimate Demise

At the end of 1997, the story did indeed change. Long-Term Capital Management was highly exposed to a "one-of-a-kind" financial crisis in Asia. This was an event for which Merton's and Scholes's historically based models had not prepared. But the fund survived ...

That is until the following year when *yet another* "one-of-a-kind" financial crisis wreaked havoc in Russia. The Russian government defaulted on its domestic local currency bonds—a decision very few thought possible ... especially those at LTCM with their backward-looking data.

By the end of August 1998, the fund had lost more than $1.85B worth of capital. Lowenstein offers this perspective:

> Theoretically, the odds against a loss such as August's had been prohibitive; such a debacle was, according to the mathematicians, **an event so freakish as to be unlikely to occur even once over the entire life of the Universe and even over numerous repetitions of the Universe. But it had happened to Long-Term** not quite four years after Meriwether had written to the firm's investors, confidently endorsing Merton and Scholes's so finely tuned assumptions ...[253]

According to their mathematical models, the financial fluctuations that resulted from these rare events were for all intents and purposes ... impossible. Yet, the "historically based impossible" seemed to keep happening to them. In the first three weeks of September, Long-Term's equity crashed from $2.3B to $400MM.

---

252  Emphasis added.
253  Emphasis added.

Long-Term Capital Management put **MPT's backward-looking logic** to the test. And their **remarkable failure** took place on the world stage. Yet here we are—advisors, pundits, and academics still trying to use historical data to predict *forever into the future.*

What became of LTCM? The fund effectively lost 92% in 1998 before, under pressure from the Federal Reserve, a consortium of Wall Street banks reluctantly bailed them out.

## Fundamentally Flawed Assumptions

The previous myths, along with Merton's and Scholes's assumptions, are predicated on the idea that the market will continue to do what it has done over the last 100 to 200 years—i.e., go up. As we explored ad nauseum in Myth 1, the United States' market has, thus far, always gone up. It's gone up since the beginning of our S&P data officially starting back in 1926. It's gone up since the New York Stock Exchange (NYSE) was founded more than 200 years ago. No matter what happened—world wars, scandals, terrorism, depressions—we overcame, and the market continued on its destined path ... onward and upward!

It's a seemingly easy point to prove. Advisors will point to that trusty statistic (myself included back in my early, unquestioning days) that shows that given a long enough time period (15 years now), the market has always recovered. That logic seems sound enough.

But then again, this would be true with anything that's on an upward trajectory. As long as you pick a point before that thing is coming back down ... the trend of all past data *will imply* upward movement ad astra.

### Balloon Charts

Study the chart pattern created from tracking a millisecond-by-millisecond analysis of the height of a helium balloon released outdoors at a child's birthday party. For the most part, the balloon is moving farther and farther from the ground. There is, however, an occasional gust of wind that, depending upon its strength, will push the balloon downward to varying degrees. Plotting the balloon's height against time in this way might reveal a chart like this:

## Figure 18
### Balloon Charts to the Moon

The clever child scientists might deduce that the balloon will obviously continue this trajectory forever. After all, all the data suggest as much.

Of course, we know this won't happen (although, perhaps, we spare the child—allowing their imagination to run wild). We know that, at some point, our inspirational balloon will hit an all-time high, never again to return. For the balloon, Archimedes's Principle[254] stands in the way of our dreams of seeing it drift off into space. At some point, new outside forces (a different makeup of the surrounding air) will act on the balloon, dramatically impacting its ability to continue its ascent.

If you were just looking at that chart and knew nothing of science, you might be surprised to learn of this drastic change.

---

254 Archimedes's Principle says that balloons will stop rising once their density matches the surrounding air. Fun facts: the average toy balloon bursts at around 6 miles. Weather balloon, 19 miles. The record is held by Dr. Takamasa Yamagami and colleagues from the Institute of Space and Astronautical Science. Their balloon made it 33 miles (about halfway to the official edge of space) before breaking the trend for good!

## Historical Charts

History is full of trend-changing "surprises" like this that have altered the course of our world.

The early Egyptian Empire controlled the most valuable land in the known world. They had secure borders and strong diplomatic ties. They were experiencing unprecedented prosperity. I don't know why they would have exactly ... but if the occasion arose, it's not hard to imagine an advisor to the pharaoh pointing to their more-than-3,000-year uptrend in prosperity and boasting something like: "Since the dawn of time, Egypt has been a dominant nation. Sure, there have been bumps along the way, but we always rise up stronger than before. There is no reason to expect that we will not forever be the world's most dominant superpower!"

Mentally picture yourself in Rome at the height of their power, roughly AD 117. How easy do you think it'd be to imagine a world where the Roman Empire did not reign supreme? They had one of the most formidable militaries the world had ever seen. Their population grew to more than 20% of the world's inhabitants. Can't you picture the advisors to the newly approved Emperor Hadrian inspiring him with facts like, "For more than half a millennium our nation has grown ever-dominant. Our military is unstoppable, and our people love us. At this pace, we will rule the world in no time at all!"

Imagine witnessing the conquests of Genghis Khan across early 13th century Asia. Through military, political, and economic genius, the Mongol Empire grew from nomadic tribes to the largest contiguous land empire ever in the history of the world. Experts of the day could have easily claimed, "United for only a few short generations, and already the Mongol Empire spans more connected land than any empire ever! After winning hundreds of battles, the data are clear: nothing can stop them!"

The British Empire in 1920 held sway over 23% of the world population and claimed 24% of the Earth's total land area. Their growth to this point was supported by roughly four centuries of data points—the uptrend was dramatic and undeniable. Experts might have easily pontificated, "For centuries, we have expanded our world dominance, despite major setbacks along the way—*cough*cough* American  Independence … This last century, we have been a global hegemon with our unrivaled naval prowess. Clearly, nothing can stop our superiority!"

For most of these examples, far more data than we have for the US stock market today could have supported these claims—hundreds and thousands of years' worth of uptrending statistics to prove them! Yet …

- The Egyptian Empire lost its "superpower" status far quicker than it was attained and has yet to get it back.
- The Romans' fate was only downhill from there with their capital ultimately torn to pieces by barbarians.
- Unforeseeable forces led to the passing of Genghis Khan and the abrupt rupture of the Mongol Empire.
- And that point in 1920, marked the "all-time high" of the British Empire's reach.

These worldwide, future-impacting changes all came about by events that were unexpected—things that had never before happened. Clearly, historical data does not guarantee future results, no matter how much data you have!

Decades, centuries, or even millennia of convincing data can be wrong.

## Solon's Warning

In the sixth century BC, Croesus the King of Lydia was thought to be the richest man in the world. According to Greek legend, a renowned wise man by the name of Solon visited the Lydian King. Croesus sought acknowledgement of his own grandeur by asking Solon to identify the happiest man he had ever met.

Solon told Croesus of a peasant he had met in Athens who worked hard, raised his family, was content with all he had, and died happy.

This was not the answer for which Croesus was fishing; he continued to press. After enough unsatisfactory responses, he finally just asked Solon directly if he were not the happiest person he had ever met. In Nassim Nicholas Taleb's retelling of the legend,[255] Solon responds:

> The observation of the numerous misfortunes that attend all conditions forbids us to grow insolent upon our present enjoyments, or to admire a man's happiness that may yet, in course of time, suffer change. For the uncertain future has yet to come, with all variety of future; and him only to whom the divinity has [guaranteed] continued happiness until the end we may call happy.

After which, Taleb simplifies Solon's message:

> The modern equivalent has been no less eloquently voiced by the baseball coach Yogi Berra, who seems to have translated Solon's outburst from the pure Attic Greek into no less pure Brooklyn English with 'it ain't over until it's over,' or, in a less dignified manner, with 'it ain't over until the fat lady sings.'

Up until that point in time, Croesus's life, if plotted on the statistician's trusty XY-graph (wealth/good fortune/happiness on the y-axis over time on the x-axis) would have revealed that familiar-by-now upward trend. Solon, in his wisdom, knew those past data points did not guarantee Croesus's future.

Sure enough, shortly after this encounter, the King's luck began to change—his son was killed in a hunting accident and his empire was conquered by Cyrus the Great of Persia.[256]

## Buffett's Warning

Through his management and growth of Berkshire Hathaway, Warren Buffett has become the epitome of a savvy investor. Ten thousand dollars invested

---

255 As related in Chapter 1 of Fooled by Randomness by Nassim Nicholas Taleb.
256 According to Croesus and Fate, Leo Tolstoy's short story retelling of the Greek legend.

with the Oracle of Omaha in 1965 would have grown to more than $274MM by the end of 2019. Compare that to the $1.9MM you would have realized from the same investment in the S&P 500 over that same period.

In his 2018 letter to shareholders, Buffett offered a Solon's Warning of sorts for investors in Berkshire's insurance subsidiaries:

> A major catastrophe that will dwarf hurricanes Katrina and Michael will occur—perhaps tomorrow, perhaps many decades from now. 'The Big One' may come from a traditional source, such as a hurricane or earthquake, or it may be a **total surprise** involving, say, a cyber attack having disastrous consequences **beyond anything insurers now contemplate**. When such a *mega-catastrophe* strikes, we will get our share of the losses and they will be big—very big.[257]

Buffett is acknowledging the reality that some catastrophe that has never before been experienced—whether it's tomorrow or decades from now—**will** happen. To that end, Buffett is cautious, holding a large cash reserve and always attempting to not be overexposed to any one surprise event.

> We use debt sparingly. Many managers, it should be noted, will disagree with this policy, arguing that significant debt juices the returns for equity owners. And these more venturesome CEOs will be right *most* of the time. At rare and unpredictable intervals, however, credit vanishes and debt becomes financially fatal. A Russian Roulette equation—usually win, occasionally die—may make financial sense for someone who gets a piece of a company's upside but does not share in its downside. But that strategy would be madness for Berkshire. **Rational people don't risk what they have and need for what they don't have and don't need.**[258]

## The Russian Roulette Equation

For those of you not familiar with Russian Roulette, it's the game where you have a six-shooter pistol but only one bullet in the chamber. You spin the cylin-

---

257 Emphasis added.
258 Emphasis added.

der, hold it to your head, and pull the trigger. There are five chances that nothing will happen. And one that you end up dead.

In his illuminating book, *Fooled by Randomness,* Nassim Taleb references a similar sentiment as Buffett does here. Taleb adds money to the equation. If a deep-pocketed—and perverse—thrill-seeker offered you $1MM if you survived after playing one round, should you do it?

A strict analysis of the potential possibilities reveals that (from a financial perspective, at least) playing is clearly in your favor. There's an 83% chance that you walk away with $1MM free and clear! Of course, however, in that 1-out-of-6 chance that you do happen to find the bullet in the barrel, well … you're dead.

As Buffett said, "a Russian Roulette equation—usually win, occasionally die … would be madness … Rational people don't risk what they have and need for what they don't have and don't need."

With Russian Roulette, you're aware of the odds: they're 5 to 1. Taleb points out, however, that in the world of investments, the odds aren't known. Yet, most professionals and academics proceed as if we do know them. As consumers, we buy into their narrative perhaps because we want it to be easy; we want it to all make sense. But in reality, if we're talking about that *mega-catastrophe* the likes of which has never been seen—"The Big One" that Buffett called it—the odds of that happening, versus a normal day in the market where the action is within a range that you'd expect, are 1-to-1,000s or tens of thousands. So, as those catastrophic events don't happen—because they don't very often—people start to think that they won't—that they can't …

### "Don't Worry, Honey!"

During chaotic markets, advisors flood social media with general statistics, charts, and graphs of market recoveries from the past. They say, "You don't need to worry. The one thing all these crashes have in common is that the market has *always* recovered!"

Every time I see or hear this, I can't help but imagine that advisor sitting out on his front porch, relaxing with his wife, watching his kids run around in their front yard.[259]

All of a sudden, two of their children run across the busy street in front of their house without paying much attention. His wife yells, standing from her

---

259 Weird, I know, but you'll see …

chair, ready to nip this dangerous behavior in the bud, when … the advisor calmly grabs her arm. He says, "Don't worry, honey. They'll be just fine. I've seen them run across that busy street dozens of times and nothing bad has ever happened!"

## An Appeal to Ignorance

This line of reasoning that convinces so many otherwise intelligent people, relies on a logical fallacy known as an *Appeal to Ignorance* (argumentum ad ignorantiam or arguing from ignorance). This logical fallacy abounds in everyday conversation, politics, and marketing. The Oxford University Press explains, "in this fallacy, someone argues that a proposition is true simply on the grounds that it has not been proven false (or that a proposition must be false because it has not been proven true)."[260]

You see, you can prove that it's possible for something to happen, just by one occurrence. But unfortunately, you can't do the opposite—you can't prove that something will **never** happen solely because it has never happened in the past … no matter how much time passes without occurrence.

Here, we can use history—this time I'll even stick with *financial* history—to prove the point.

### Case Study: 1987 Dow

Before October 1987, the Dow had never experienced a daily loss greater than 13%. Can't you imagine advisors and pundits saying that a drop of much more than that would be impossible? "There is no way that your investments will lose 15% or more in a single day!" After all, it had never happened before—there was roughly 90 years' worth of evidence that it wouldn't. So, surely it couldn't … right?!

Wrong.

260 https://global.oup.com/us/companion.websites/9780199331864/stu/supplement/.

Way wrong! On Black Monday, October 19, 1987[261], the Dow Jones Industrial Average fell a devastating 22.6% in a single day.

Pundits were blindsided. Advisors panicked. The sky was falling—no one knew what to do. Everyday investors lost **big time** in the chaos! They didn't realize an event like this was possible, so they didn't prepare—their portfolios or themselves (mentally).

Roger Lowenstein explains how unlikely—impossible even—this event truly was when basing one's analyses off historical models:

> Economists later figured that on the basis of the market's historic volatility, had the market been open every day since the creation of the universe the odds would still have been against it falling that much on any single day. In fact, had the life of the universe been repeated *one billion times*, such a crash would have been theoretically 'unlikely.' But it happened anyway. **Obviously, past volatilities do *not* prepare investors for shocks that lie in wait**—nor do they signal in advance just when such shocks might choose to occur.[262]

Just because something has never happened in the market before, that does not mean it can't or won't.

## Where Buffett Is Wrong

Somehow, despite this logic, Buffett's solution to that "expect the unexpected" mantra is surprisingly lacking. He—like so many others—just blindly looks to the stock market for safety:

> If my $114.75 had been invested in a no-fee S&P 500 index fund [in 1942], and all dividends had been reinvested, my stake would have grown to be worth (pre-taxes) $606,811 on January 31, 2019 (the latest data available before the printing of this letter). That is a gain of 5,288 for 1. Those who regularly preach doom because of government budget deficits (as I regularly did myself for many years) might note that our country's national debt has increased roughly

---

261  Black Tuesday for you Australian readers.
262  Emphasis added.

400-fold during the last ... 77 year[s]. That's 40,000%! Suppose you had foreseen this increase and panicked at the prospect of runaway deficits and a worthless currency. To 'protect' yourself, you might have eschewed stocks ...

He uses these data to suggest that you should obviously be invested in the stock market, even if you are concerned about things being different today than they were before. In spite of any unprecedented economic realities causing you to want to find a better way, Buffett points to the past to "prove" how the future will play out.

The facts he presents here are great lessons *for a student of history*. Yes, the national debt has been able to balloon to previously unthinkable levels without causing the stock market to come crashing down[263]. But this information—these data from the past—cannot (should not) be used to prove what will happen in the future. Life just doesn't work that way. Facts, reality, proof ... just don't work that way.

Sidenote: I do still appreciate the perspective that Buffett brings to this reality. He's right: if you told me today that the US national debt would increase by 40,000% over the next 77 years (to roughly $10 quadrillion ... that's $10,000,000,000,000,000), well, I'd say "NO WAY! Impossible. Something will break first." I think most people would say that. And he's probably right: if presented with that same statistic 77 years ago, I might have thought it outlandishly impossible. Yet, here we are ...

Although I find that fascinating, it is in no way proof that "American mettle" (as he puts it) can continue at this pace if we finally suffer through the consequences of that out-of-control national debt. All his observation about the past does is prove that it is **possible** for the market to continue upward in spite of it all.[264] It does not, however, prove any likelihood of that scenario playing out going forward.

Possible? Fine. I'll give you that.

---

263 ... yet. More on this idea later in this myth.
264 Or at least, that it was possible, given the state of everything 77 years ago. In actuality, it doesn't really prove much of anything for our future given how many variables are involved and how different they all are today. But I understand his point.

Highly improbable? What do you think? A national debt of $10Qa[265] without any long-lasting negative consequences to the growth of the US economy or value of the stock market?[266]

*Don't fall for this Appeal to Ignorance*—even when it comes from a highly regarded industry authority.[267]

## "Lower Levels of Probabilities"

Following the 2020 coronavirus lockdowns, Buffett quickly sold all of Berkshire's massive airline holdings for a loss of billions of dollars. By way of explanation, he said that events like that calamity are "on the lower levels of probabilities that happen."[268]

Whether it's the national debt or otherwise, a "mega-catastrophe" of which *he* warns could absolutely impact the stock market in ways *never before thought possible* by the majority of the investing public. And you can be sure that "The Big One" will be one of those rare events that falls even further down on Buffett's "levels of probabilities."[269]

## It'll Be Too Late

It isn't hard to imagine how pundits and academics would react if the stock market were to drop by 50%. "Stay the course," they would say. "History proves it's the right thing to do in a precarious situation like this." Your trusted financial advisors, too, coached in "how to *handle* emotional clients" and pumped full of the same Kool-Aid, would provide words of comforting wisdom during these troubling times, just as I used to. They'd point to past performance to prove that the market always recovers—a forward-looking conclusion drawn from limited backward-looking data …

What would you do? Let's take this seemingly bizarro scenario one step further. Imagine the market never recovers during your lifetime. What if the market stayed below that 50% cut for decades to follow?

---

265 I admit: I had to look up the abbreviation for quadrillion.
266 That seems highly unlikely to me. I think something will have to give …
267 Which coincidentally happens to be another logical fallacy called an Appeal to Authority. More in Myth 11.
268 https://www.cnbc.com/2020/05/02/warren-buffett-says-berkshire-sold-its-entire-position-in-airlines-because-of-the-coronavirus.html.
269 Although, I can't imagine that offering much comfort if your savings were just wiped out …

You were 30, 45, or 60 years old (whatever, all devastating) when it began its descent. You waited for it to come back. You were "strong" and "responsible." You "stayed the course." You believed your financial advisor's rules-of-thumb, waited for the "8% average annual market return," and relied on their "4% safe retirement withdrawal rate."

But this time they were wrong ...

Here you sit, 30 years later, surrendered to a new paradigm: "On occasion, albeit rare, the market might not go back up in a lifetime ..."

Improbable? Perhaps.

Impossible? Absolutely not.

How can we be so confident in Modern Portfolio Theory? Are we so secure and comfortable as to not, at least, prepare? Is this idea such a stretch in your mind that it should warrant disregard?

## Case Study: 1989 Japan

Forget the depressing hypothetical then ... Let's briefly recall our journey through history from Myth 5. The story of Japan provides a reality similar to the scenario posited above. From 1949 through 1989, the Nikkei 225[270] soared from around $40 to just about $40,000. Overall, it was a fairly consistent climb. Every time there was a dip, it predictably came right back and continued on up. Once again, you could have found yourself with decades of compelling data. "This is what the Japanese market does—it just continues to go up. It always bounces back and reaches new highs." So, if there ever was a dip or crash or recession, obviously you should just "stay the course and wait for the inevitable rebound" because over the long run the market *always* goes up ...

Sound familiar?

---

270  Like our S&P 500.

**Figure 19**

Japan's Nikkei 225 ($USD): 1949-1989

*Source*: MacroTrends.net.

Well, as you know by now, that was the absolute wrong advice for someone investing in Japan in the late 1980s. The market fell more than 80% over the next couple of decades and today still hovers around half that former high—even though that had *never* happened before ... in *any* developed nation!

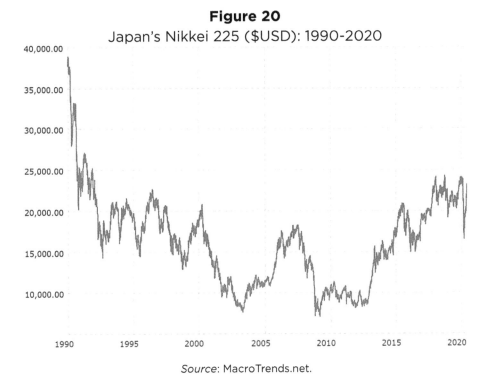

**Figure 20**

Japan's Nikkei 225 ($USD): 1990-2020

*Source*: MacroTrends.net.

For that proverbial retiree, this **clichéd wisdom** would have proven her **financial downfall**.

## The Professional's Dilemma

Warren Buffett and other industry authorities are backed by a hoard of financial advisors touting that stock-market-returns-are-always-positive-over-any-15-year-period statistic. I'm afraid I, too, helped perpetuate this false sense of long-term security in those I was attempting to serve. So far, mindlessly staying in the market would have proven lucrative throughout the history of our nation—through numerous corrections, recessions, and depressions. Unfortunately, that fact will attract many "experts" unable to see it any other way.

That is, until it is far, far too late.

And, if they did accept it as reality, what could they do about it? There are no mainstream strategies to counteract these problems. The generally accepted strategies *are* the problem.

Investors, too, will struggle to accept this reality. Psychologically, we want things to be easy. We don't want to feel hopeless. And, believe me, I've felt hopeless at times on my journey to finding a better way. This road has been arduous and was incomplete for an uncomfortably long time. There wasn't a clear path—it's taken me half-a-decade of dedicated research to fully comprehend some of these problems, let alone the potential solutions!

## Consequences of Accepting the Reality

Thus, not only would acceptance of this reality by a financial professional result in her not knowing what solutions to recommend, but it would also make it much more difficult to attract new clients. Before she'd even have the chance to try to explain these non-traditional solutions, she'd have the grueling task of trying to help them comprehend this harsh investment reality that goes against an entire industry backed by a body of apparently Nobel-worthy academic work.[271]

That's a tall order! It's much easier to just go with the flow—to not challenge the traditional investment paradigm. As Upton Sinclair said, "It is difficult to get a man to understand something, when his salary depends on his not understanding it."

If a practicing professional accepts the potentially ruinous nature of Modern Portfolio Theory, she must either ...

- Struggle to find and understand better solutions and commit herself to a life of uphill battles convincing clients of not-yet-experienced dangers or ...
- Feel guilty as she continues to push clients into that traditional, stock-and-bond-only, buy-and-hold, plug-and-play system.

This is one of the main purposes of this book: a greater understanding of this reality; that everyday investors will demand and actively seeking out better solutions; that knowledgeable advisors will be able to spend their time helping those open-minded investors; that researchers will begin to explore even better strategies ...

But, just like the 12 Steps of Alcoholics Anonymous, it all starts with *acceptance* **that there** *is* **a problem!**

---

271 More on this "Nobel-worthy academic work" in Myth 11.

## The Science of Investing

The fact of the matter is, there's just not enough data to know definitively what the future of the stock market holds. In the world of a scientist, how many data points does he need before he can confidently draw a conclusion?

To get an article published and to even be taken seriously in the scientific community, you better have sufficient data to support your claims. Published journal articles will have hundreds, thousands, sometimes millions of data points.

The average pharmaceutical company clinical trial, for example, generates up to 3MM data points[272] before decisions are made about a drug's efficacy.

So, how many crashes and bear markets do we have as data points to study? Upon how much data are the prevailing MPT conclusions—notably, that the stock market will always go up—being drawn?

### Relevant Data Points

The Dow Jones Industrial Average was first published on May 26, 1896. The history of the US stock market does, however, go back much further than that to the formation of the New York Stock Exchange in 1817, or the Buttonwood Agreement of 1792, or even the Philadelphia Stock Exchange formation in 1790, but data from that first century is sketchy at best.

Using the S&P 500 (as we have been and as most MPT proponents do) gives us more than 90 years' worth of data. Is that enough? It is, after all, more than 1,000 months—more than 20,000 trading days. Not bad. But isn't what we're really attempting to understand here how the market will perform after a catastrophic event. That's the claim, right? "After the market falls, it always comes back, because it always has."

In that case, for our scientific analysis here, we should be examining those crises we've overcome—the ones that are always used as "proof" and inspiration that you should "stay the course." "You see, the market bounced back from XYZ Crash, there's no reason to believe it won't recover from this one as well ..."

---

272 Institute of Medicine (US) Roundtable on Research and Development of Drugs, Biologics, and Medical Devices; Davis JR, Nolan VP, Woodcock J, et al., editors. Assuring Data Quality and Validity in Clinical Trials for Regulatory Decision Making: Workshop Report. Washington (DC): National Academies Press (US); 1999. Final Comments. https://www. ncbi.nlm.nih.gov/books/NBK224576/.

## How Many Bears Are There Anyway?

In financial parlance, a crash is a sudden, sharp drop in stock prices over a relatively short period of time, ranging from a single day to a couple of weeks.

Bear markets, on the other hand, are sustained declines. Once the market has fallen by more than 20%[273] from its most recent high, it's technically considered to be a bear market.

Officially, since 1900, we've experienced 33 bear markets[274]—that's 33 prolonged drops of 20% or more from recent highs. And yes, it is true: the market has recovered from each and every one of them ... yet I doubt even an aspiring scientist would be convinced of any conclusion drawn from only 33 data points.

## Bowling Alley Theory

A professional bowler makes an appearance at your local alley one night. At first, you and your friends were all just casually watching as he expertly posted strike after strike. But now, without realizing it, your game is on pause and you're all staring. This guy's on fire. He hasn't missed. You look up at his scoreboard. He just bowled his 12th strike in a row—a perfect game. He doesn't stop. You and your friends are enthralled, whispering his running total to each other as he continues in the zone.

He's on his 3rd game now. You hear the satisfying crash of the pins signifying his 30th strike. And there's 31. 32!

You watch him calmly bowl his 33rd strike after just as many attempts. Your friend yells in your ear over the roar of the crowd, snapping you out of your daze. "Let's make this interesting ..."

If you knew this man planned to bowl 5 games that night (an opportunity for 60 straight strikes[275]), which of the following two bets would you feel more comfortable making?

1.  100% of your life savings that he will set a new world record and bowl five straight perfect games—60 strikes in a row. If so, you'll double your

---

273 Entirely arbitrary but industry standard.
274 The exact number may be give or take one or two depending on who you ask and precisely how they're calculating a bear market.
275 The world record is 47 set by Tommy Gollick in May 2019. Fun fact: It's not that he fell short when attempting to extend his streak to 48. Gollick just stopped after 47. The game was over; he was done.

life savings. But, if he ends those games with 59 or fewer, you'll lose everything.[276] Or …

2.  A quarter of your life savings that he will bowl strikes on **most** of his remaining attempts—at least 14 of his remaining 27. If that proves to be the case, you'll double up that portion. Otherwise, you'll lose it.

How does the historical data you have in front of you now (the 33 strikes on 33 bowls) influence your decision? How does it influence your confidence level?

Even though there's less money to be made and despite the perfect record thus far, almost everyone chooses Option 2. Because … obviously, a perfect past record does not guarantee a perfect future performance, and we're talking about your life savings here!

When theorizing about the stock market, then, wouldn't we be more correct to say that the historical data we have suggests that the market **almost always** trends upward after major crashes? And thus, feel confident that it will continue to do so ***most* of the time** … rather than obstinately concluding that the market ***will* always** trend upward *no matter what*?

It's a subtle difference, but it's a meaningful one. A subtle difference in understanding that could save you from a potentially devastating reality.

## Scientific Control

But this bowling analogy is not even a fair comparison though, is it? The bowler had the luxury of predictable surroundings. He was able to use the same ball and wear the same shoes. The temperature and ambience were relatively consistent throughout the games. He was in a controlled environment.

When you start to manipulate these surrounding variables, the future results become much more unpredictable. The 33 data points become even less reliable. Unfortunately, the environment in which our "investing experiment" is taking place is anything but controlled.

You see, each one of these bear markets—and the even fewer crashes—involved very different conditions:

---

276 I know what you're thinking … your friend obviously has a gambling problem …

- The circumstances leading up to the Wall Street Crash of 1929[277] were very different from the Cuban Missile Crisis and Cold War backdrop during the Kennedy Slide of 1962.
- The internet euphoria surrounding the late-90s Dotcom Bubble[278] was entirely different from the crash following the Standard & Poor's downgrading of the United States government in 2011.
- The easy credit environment during the early 2000s that led to the Global Financial Crisis of 2007–08[279] in no way resembled the environment that led up to 1987's chaotic Black Monday fueled by the unforeseen consequences of portfolio insurance.[280]
- The railroad magnate power struggle that led to the Panic of 1901 ruining thousands of small investors was made up of entirely different variables than the Coronavirus Crash almost 120 years later causing global stock markets to plummet more than 30% faster than ever before.[281]

A major reason we can't use past performance to *prove* how markets will behave in the future is the same reason that it's difficult to actually prepare ourselves for market panics:[282] they're almost always different. The political, social, and economic climates leading up to crashes or bear markets are different. The number and competence of players involved in the market (affecting the often-frenetic pace at which it moves) is different. In fact, we're always experiencing a unique combination of factors many of which have never before been experienced in quite the same way.

This means that after each crash, people—experts included—can honestly say, "Whoa! I never could have seen *that specific* event coming. That's never happened before ..." Many of these experts will use statements like that to excuse

---

277 Explored in Myth 5.
278 Explored in Myth 5.
279 Explored in Myth 5.
280 Portfolio insurance is a hedging technique popular in the 1980s designed to limit investors' losses by buying and selling stocks in reaction to changes in price rather than changes in fundamentals. Specifically, they sell when the market is falling, without regard for any fundamental information. As demonstrated in October 1987, when enough people have this "protection," there is potential to create a market-destabilizing feedback loop.
281 In most G20 nations.
282 Explored in Myth 5.

their lack of preparedness. Perhaps, many will take comfort from the fact that "at least we were all wrong together."

I'm assuming, however, that since you're still reading this, that's not good enough for you …

## Cookie Dough Economics

Each time I bake cookies with my boys, our delicious baked treats come out remarkably similar. This is because I have a go-to recipe that I use. I use the same amounts of the same ingredients every time.

The ingredients that went into building up and causing each and every one of those aforementioned instances of stock market chaos are very, very different from one bear market to the next.

If I allowed my 3-year-old to exercise his own culinary creativity with each batch from here on out, I would obviously not be as sure about what to expect each time. Imagine him using twice as much sugar for one batch of cookies, 50 times the salt in another, and subbing out the chocolate chips for anchovies in a third batch. Using widely varying amounts of ever-changing ingredients will produce a broad range of results. After 15 or 30 or 100 iterations, even if the results have—up until that point—always been edible, that should in no way serve as a guarantee for you that the next batch won't cause you to vomit!

To make this matter worse, when we're talking about the economy and the stock market, the number of ingredients at work is **_unquantifiably_ greater** than my cookie recipe. It's preposterous to assume that we can project how things will play out after future crashes without knowing their unique circumstances. Here's Nassim Nicholas Taleb's conclusion on the matter:

> We know from chaos theory that even if you had a perfect model of the world, you'd need infinite precision in order to predict future events. With sociopolitical or economic phenomena, **we don't have anything like that**.

## Massive Macroeconomic Variables

Let's explore a couple of these market ingredients that will obviously change in the future and contemplate their vomit-inducing potential for our mainstream investment recipe. Consider briefly, the following major economic phenomenon and how much of a variable it represents for our projected return calculations …

## Country Life Cycles

First, think about the life cycle of successful businesses. After going through a rapid and exciting growth phase companies reach maturity—where things start to slow down quite a bit and ultimately decline.

Ray Dalio posits a similar theory regarding the life cycle of a company. Dalio is arguably the world's greatest macroeconomic visionary alive today. Over the last few decades, his insights have allowed his investment fund, Bridgewater Associates, to profit from unexpected economic shifts both good and bad all around the world. His success, derived from his dedicated research, has allowed Bridgewater to grow into the world's largest hedge fund.

It's from this unique experience, that Dalio has parsed together his research-backed theory.[283] He breaks a country's life cycle into five stages.[284]

In the first stage, "countries are poor and think that they are poor." This stage makes up the early part of any established civilization. During this period "they have very low incomes and most people have subsistence lifestyles, they don't waste money because they value it a lot, and they don't have any debt to speak of because savings are short and nobody wants to lend to them. They are undeveloped."

In the second stage, "countries are getting rich quickly but still think they are poor." This stage is similar to the growth stage in a successful company's life cycle. Despite the growth, however, the people tend to "behave pretty much the same as they did when they were in the prior stage but, because they have more money and still want to save, the amount of this saving and investment rises rapidly. Because they are typically the same people who experienced the more deprived conditions in the first stage, and because people who grew up with financial insecurity typically don't lose their financial cautiousness, they still work hard, save a lot, and invest efficiently in their means of production, in real assets ..."

In the third stage "countries are rich and think of themselves as rich." In the business world, this stage is known as maturity. When this happens to a country, "the prevailing psychology changes from a) putting the emphasis on working and saving to protect oneself from the bad times to b) easing up in order to savor the fruits of life. This change in the prevailing psychology occurs primarily because

---

283  In fact, his new book is entirely dedicated to a thorough dive into this research. https://www.principles.com/the-changing-world-order/.

284  These five stages were originally published on Bridgewater's site: http://bwater.com/.

a new generation of people who did not experience the bad times replaces those who lived through them. Signs of this change in mindset are reflected in statistics that show reduced work hours (e.g., typically there is a reduction in the average workweek from six days to five) and big increases in expenditures on leisure and luxury goods relative to necessities."

In the fourth stage, "countries become poorer and still think of themselves as rich. This is the leveraging up phase: i.e., debts rise relative to incomes until they can't anymore. The psychological shift behind this leveraging up occurs because the people who lived through the first two stages have died off or become irrelevant and those whose behavior matters most are used to living well and not worrying about the pain of not having enough money. Because the people in these countries earn and spend a lot, they become expensive, and because they are expensive, they experience slower real income growth rates. Since they are reluctant to constrain their spending in line with their reduced income growth rate, they lower their savings rates, increase their debts and cut corners. Because their spending continues to be strong, they continue to appear rich, even though their balance sheets deteriorate. ... They increasingly rely on their reputations rather than on their competitiveness to fund their deficits. They typically spend a lot of money on the military at this stage, sometimes very large amounts because of wars, in order to protect their global interests ..."

In the fifth stage, countries "typically go through deleveraging and relative decline, which they are slow to accept. After bubbles burst and when deleveragings occur, private debt growth, private sector spending, asset values and net worths decline in a self-reinforcing negative cycle. To compensate, government debt growth, government deficits and central bank 'printing' of money typically increase. In this way, their central banks and central governments cut real interest rates and increase nominal GDP growth so that it is comfortably above nominal interest rates in order to ease debt burdens. As a result of these low real interest rates, weak currencies, and poor economic conditions, their debt and equity assets are poor performing and increasingly these countries have to compete with less expensive countries that are in the earlier stages of development. Their currencies depreciate and they like it. As an extension of these economic and financial trends, countries in this stage see their power in the world decline."

Although the lengths of time associated with each of these stages differ for countries throughout history, the pattern has been the same. This reality explains why our understandably optimistic experts from our historical scenarios at the beginning of this section were ultimately proven dead wrong. The ancient Egyptian, Roman, Mongol, and British empires all experienced those periods—during stages three and four—when it would have been near-impossible for anyone alive in that moment to sincerely imagine a time without their supremacy and without perpetual growth.

But they all eventually, as civilizations always do, slipped into that fifth stage and began to decline. [285]

Into which stage do you think the United States and many other developed nations fall?

**In which stage has the US been during the majority of those 100 or so years of stock market data we've been relying upon—that *everyone* relies upon ...?**

Do you think a country's stock market returns should be expected to be similar during the various stages of their life cycle? Obviously, any market returns during the struggle of the first stage would be very different than those experienced during the

prosperity of the third. But, what about from the tail end of the fourth stage and beyond, when a country's growth slows? **Is it still reasonable to expect the same market trajectory as was realized during prior stages?**

Remember Lowenstein's question? "How do we know that the next new period won't change the story again?"

It almost certainly will ...

## Reserve Currency Status

What kind of impact do you suppose having the U.S. Dollar as the world reserve currency has had on the performance of the stock market over the last 90+ years?

---

285 In Dalio's more recent theorizing on this subject, he has added the (what used to be implicit) sixth step: the general chaos—civil wars and revolutions—which can ultimately lead a civilization anew to Stage 1.

**Figure 21**

Global Reserve Currencies since 1450

*Source*: DoubleLine.

History suggests the U.S. Dollar will not always maintain this position. Yet, this is the only reality we've known throughout *our entire sampling of S&P 500 historical data.* How could losing this status in the not-too-distant future impact our expected market returns going forward?

Honestly, I don't claim to know. I don't think we can know. That's precisely the point: this is not a variable for which our past data accounts.

My goal is not to pontificate on precisely what might happen as these massive variables change, rather it's to help you see that there's no reason to believe that they won't change. And when you have such large variables changing like this—as would be the case with any science experiment—it is illogical to expect similar results to what we've experienced in the past given these new and entirely different market conditions.

## Today's Tulip Revisited

Finally, let's consider in more detail one of these worrisome macroeconomic variables that we've never had to account for in quite the same way. It's in that same vein of concern Buffett presented earlier: the national debt. Our global central banking policy crisis—i.e., developed nations just printing as much money as they'd like—is out of control. More and more countries are printing more, spending more, and racking up more debt than ever before. Also, countries with negative interest rates[286] (a relatively new concept in and of itself[287]) now make up more than 20% of global GDP.[288]

I could go on listing off countless ways the market is different today than it ever has been at any point in the past, but I know you get the point: **we have *never* been here before.**

So, why do we pretend to know how everything will play out over the long run?

The circumstances in which we find ourselves today are unlike anything we've ever experienced. I don't claim to know exactly how all this will shake out, but there has to be a reckoning at some point. It's hard for me to imagine that not happening during my lifetime ... but of course, I couldn't tell you. No one can. *It's dangerous to doubt the financial wizardry and machinations of the powers that be and their ability to kick the proverbial can down the road for future generations.*

But whenever that reckoning does come, it's difficult for me to see a non-painful way out of this.[289]

---

286 Negative interest rates exist when borrowers are paid interest from—instead of paying interest to—their lenders (banks, the government).

287 First used by Switzerland's central bank in 1972 but never before to this extent on a global scale.

288 https://www.reuters.com/article/us-bis-markets/acceptance-of-negative-interest-rates-vaguely-troubling-bis-idUSKBN1W70N0.

289 I admit: something absolutely could change. Maybe some brilliant economist teams up with an altruistic politician and solves the riddle, finding a way to get us out of this mess without a massive Japan-like-or-worse slump and is somehow able to successfully pitch their plan to a rational public ... seems a little far-fetched, but I suppose it is possible.

## Apples Aren't Oranges

Trying to understand how our stock market will perform after a global-central-banking-crisis-induced crash based on how it recovered after the Panic of 1907,[290] for example, is *ludicrous*.

And, even if it's not this unique global debt crisis that sets off a bear market like we've never before seen ... there's always the possibility that something else could. Think: the out-of-nowhere nature of COVID-19, for example ... but worse. The economic chaos that ensued in March 2020 could not have been anticipated—it blindsided most investors.

Who knows what could break this couple-hundred-year trend in a long-lasting way?

Don't get me wrong: I'm not predicting a worse-than-ever-before crash here.[291]

**The point is: you can't use historical data—no matter how much you have—especially when the inputs are all so different ... to predict what will happen *forever* into the future.**

The claim that the market always trends upward after major downturns seems a bit unqualified with only 33 or so data points pulled from very different (read: non-controlled) environments!

But this is what we (as humans) tend to do. We want shortcuts. We want heuristics. We want things to be easy. So, in the absence of sufficient data ... we guess! We hypothesize. Which, in and of itself, would be fine, except ... the industry is not treating MPT as the educated guess that it is. They're treating the theory as fact—as though it's been conclusively proven. As such, it's become financial doctrine, when in reality ...

... it is just a guess.

> "The greatest enemy of knowledge is not ignorance, it is the illusion of knowledge."
> **—Daniel J. Boorstin**

---

290  When the New York Stock Exchange fell almost 50% following the downfall of New York City's third-largest trust, the Knickerbocker Trust Company.
291  Now, I won't be surprised if that does happen, but that's not the point you should take from all this.

## Understanding Reality

It is at least within the reasonable realm of possibility that for those who are relying on the past to predict forever into the future—investing according to Modern Portfolio Theory, with their buy-and-hold, stock-and-bond-only port-folios—that a time will come when they will be **financially devastated**.

That can be a difficult pill to swallow. I get it! It means you'll need to take more responsibility for the way you're investing. Which means more stress, more concern. That's a hard reality—I understand. I'm not selling sunshine and rainbows ... that'd be **much** easier.

### The Doomsayer Perspective

Although it may sound this way right now, this isn't a message of fear. That's not the point. Instead, it's a message of practicality—of being aware of what's possible—of not being blindsided—of being prepared no matter what happens.

I'm not predicting a near-term loss of global superpower status for the United States, or the downfall of the European Union after a worldwide currency crisis, or that due to our country's life cycle stage that it'd be impossible for the stock market to average anywhere near as much over the next couple of decades ...

But I know for a fact that each of those—along with countless other scary scenarios—is a real possibility.

When some people hear this message, they immediately write it off inter-preting it as me suggesting a total economic meltdown—utter chaos—the actual doomsayer scenario: that the stock market is no more; that all businesses go bankrupt; that the country is literally on fire.

That is not, in fact, what I'm saying ...

### The Honest Perspective

The reason I spend so much time helping you understand and accept these possibilities is that once you do, you open yourself up to the reality of any future outcome in between. Sure, maybe a higher-than-ever-before, 30-year period of growth for the stock market is possible. It is. But, given everything we just looked at, that hardly seems as likely as the possibilities in the other direction. Not to mention the fact that that wouldn't be a scenario for which you'd really need to "be prepared." If that happens: yay. Throw a party.

But, if the range of possibilities for our market investments also includes many average returns below those explored in the first several myths, we might not want to invest quite so much of our life savings according to the mainstream strategies ...

You see, the alternative to the stock market averaging between 7% and 12%[292] over the next 30 years, is not the market totally imploding and everyone losing all their money. No! It's your stock portfolio averaging an effective:

- 0% per year over the 20 years leading up to your planned retirement.
- 2% per year for the rest of your life.
- An annualized 1% loss throughout your retirement.
- And so on.

When you realize that there is a very real possibility—even if you view it as slim—of those things happening ... you realize that all the rates of return in between are also all very real possibilities. All things considered, some of them are not even that difficult to imagine, even if they have never happened before ...

And these are possibilities for which **we can absolutely prepare**. It's even possible to do so **without sacrificing upside potential**.[293] Plus, preparing for them comes with the added benefit that if any of those extremist doomsayer scenarios actually become reality, well ... you'll just so happen to be in a position with much less downside risk—you'll be ready!

---

292 The historically based, 30-year average high and low points from Myth 3.
293 We'll explore some specific strategies in Myths 15 & 16

**MYTH:** "You Can Use Past Data to Prove What the Market Will Do in the Future."

**REALITY: It is illogical to use past data to predict forever into the future.**

### A Better Way

Honestly, if it was between the stock market or hiding all your money in a safe under your mattress, then sure, we should probably just push our luck. That's kind of how I felt during the first several years of my research—as though those were investors only two options ...

Fortunately, as rational investors preparing for the long term, those aren't our only options.[294]

Unfortunately, however, it's extremely difficult to know who you can trust in your search for those better ways ...

---

294  We'll explore the best potential solutions I've found in Myths 15 & 16.

# MYTH 11

## "You Should Just Do What the 'Experts' Say"

## All 24 Chromosomes

In 1923, American zoologist Theophilus Painter declared that humans had 24 pairs of chromosomes. This "reality" was disseminated on his expert authority from the 1920s through 1956, despite subsequent counts with the correct number of 23. There were even textbooks with photos clearly showing 23 pairs of chromosomes that incorrectly labeled it as 24 due to the authority of the consensus of the time.[295]

The 24-chromosome-reality being presented as an "established fact generated confirmation bias among future scientists. Painter was so influential by that point, that many researchers accepted his count over actual evidence. There are even records of scientists modifying or discarding their own data to agree with his count.

This erroneous claim took decades to refute until microscope technology finally made the error unmistakable.

### An Appeal to Authority

The reason it took so long to uncover the truth despite clear evidence to the contrary stems from yet another logical fallacy:[296] an Appeal to Authority. This is when the beliefs of an authority on a topic are used as evidence to prove a theory instead of any actual data, logic, or research.

In our honest pursuit of understanding our complicated world of investments, we would do well to heed the words of American astrophysicist, Carl Sagan:

> One of the great commandments of science is, 'Mistrust arguments from authority.' ... Too many such arguments have proved too

---

295 Glass, Bentley (1990), Theophilus Shickel Painter, Washington, DC: National Academy of Sciences, pp. 309–37 http://www.nasonline.org/publications/biographical-memoirs/memoir-pdfs/painter-theophilus-shickel.pdf.
296 In addition to the Appeal to Ignorance found in Myth 10.

painfully wrong. Authorities must prove their contentions like every-body else.[297]

I understand: it is extremely difficult to disagree with an authoritative fig-ure especially when regarding a question outside your field of expertise. But, just because a "recognized expert" says something, that doesn't make it a reality. Consider …

- The US Postmaster General under President Dwight D. Eisenhower, Arthur Summerfield's authoritative declaration that, "Before man reaches the moon, your mail will be delivered within hours from New York to Australia by guided missiles. We stand on the threshold of rocket mail."[298]
- Musical director for the wildly popular *Ed Sullivan Show*, Ray Bloch's forecast regarding the future of The Beatles: "The only thing different is the hair, as far as I can see. I give them a year."

These were experts in their respective fields. Yet their claims were so wildly inaccurate.

> "It ain't what you don't know that gets you into trouble.
> It's what you know for sure that just ain't so."
> **—Ironically, most often erroneously attributed to Mark Twain**

Sometimes an "expert's word" doesn't have much bearing on the way we live our lives. But, at other times, if everyone had just blindly followed authoritative assertions, our lives would be vastly different today. Consider …

- Aristotle's theory that there are only five elements that make up our known universe.

---

297 Sagan, Carl (2011), *The Demon-Haunted World: Science as a Candle in the Dark.*
298 Fun fact: the US Post Office did test so-called Missile Mail in 1959. A submarine launched a rocket off the coast of Florida to a naval base. After 22 minutes, its cargo of two mail containers was successfully delivered. Sadly, the initiative was never pursued any further …

- IBM President Thomas Watson's[299] claim about the future of computers: "I think there is a world market for maybe five computers."
- 20th Century Fox Executive Darryl Zanuck's expert prediction that "television won't be able to hold on to any market it captures after the first six months. People will soon get tired of staring at a plywood box every night."
- Ethernet co-inventor and industry leader Robert Metcalfe's[300] confident assertion in 1995 that the Internet would "soon go spectacularly supernova and in 1996 catastrophically collapse."[301]
- Microsoft CEO Steve Ballmer's expert opinion from 2007 that "there's no chance that the iPhone is going to get any significant market share. No chance."

Think about where we would be if people took those experts at their word— never questioning, never challenging, never considering alternatives. When authorities are challenged and better alternatives sought, our lives often improve.

And sometimes, blindly following "expert advice" can be devastating. Before the Titanic's maiden voyage, Philip Franklin, vice president of the company that produced the ship, famously declared, "There is no danger that Titanic will sink. The boat is unsinkable and nothing but inconvenience will be suffered by the passengers."

After the tragedy, a humbled Franklin apologized: "I thought her unsinkable, and **I based my opinion on the best expert advice.**"[302]

## Market Experts

You have the opportunity here to avoid potentially titanic losses by questioning the inadequate norms and seeking a better way.

If you have a decent amount of your life savings in stocks, you likely start to stress a bit whenever the market starts to precipitously fall. Would it calm your

---

299  Legendary president of IBM from 1914 until his death in 1956.
300  He was also a Harvard PhD, a professor at the University of Texas at Austin, and the founder of the 3Com digital electronics company.
301  Fun fact: Metcalfe promised that if proven wrong, he would "eat his words." Obviously, he was. So, during a 1997 speech, he placed the magazine article with his quote into a blender and consumed the puree in front of a live audience …
302  Emphasis added.

nerves—or at least encourage you to "stay the course"—if a world-renowned economist and ivy league professor told you not to worry? If he convincingly informed you that stocks were due to bounce up any day now and would likely never hit these lows ever again, would you feel better?

If you then turned on the news and heard the same message from your favorite expert pundits, and then again from your advisor, would that convince you that you're overreacting—that you should remain "disciplined" and just "stay the course"?

Because that is what happened in 1929 right before the worst crash to date in US history.[303] Right before all the chaos, to ease the naive public's nerves, Irving Fisher declared that "stock prices have reached what looks like a permanently high plateau." Other experts (in the public's eyes at least) found reasons to support Fisher's claim. Who were *they* to disagree with *him*?

And so, pundits and advisors the world over sang a similar song. And who are *you* to disagree with *them*?

Despite his brilliance—and despite the fact that almost every financial expert seemed to be on the same page here—he could not have been more wrong, and those who listened to him and blindly followed his advice suffered for it. As we know now, the market had already peaked earlier that month and it took another 25 years before we finally broke back through that "plateau …"

## The Laureates

It can be even more difficult when several of our authorities here have been recognized by the Nobel Committee for their contributions to our particular matter-in-question. But even a Nobel Prize does not make an expert infallible.

- Long before he took home the prize 20 years later, Paul Krugman pontificated in 1988 that the internet would have no greater impact on the economy than the fax machine …
- Eugene Fama and Robert Shiller shared the prize in 2013 "for their empirical analysis of asset prices." Yet they hold contradictory theories about key aspects of this issue (specifically, whether markets are "effi-

---

303 Detailed in Myth 5—in the part about the "Roaring '20s."

cient"[304] or not[305]). Despite each making their own authoritative claims on the matter, obviously at least one of them must be wrong.

- And then there are our friends from Myth 10, Robert Merton and Myron Scholes. They "developed a pioneering formula for the valuation of stock options. Their methodology has ... generated new types of financial instruments and facilitated more efficient risk management in society."[306]

Hooray for their "more efficient risk management in society ..." Am I right?! We already saw what happened to them and the billions of dollars they managed[307] when they had the opportunity to put their Nobel-worthy, expert ideas to the test with real money on the line.

## Influencers

Just like the scientists with their 24 chromosomes, there is no shortage of financial personalities interested in taking these industry authorities at their word—never thinking to question. They predicate their own reputation and influence upon their regurgitations of those "experts." It creates an understandably confusing mess for the layperson just trying to plan their financial future.

Most of the outspoken financial personalities out there don't understand Modern Portfolio Theory's flaws. They don't understand all your investment options—they just keep regurgitating that same easy buy-and-hold, stock-and-bond-only mantra. Many aren't experienced in the industry and they're definitely not your fiduciary. Not to mention the fact that many are incentivized by ulterior motives.[308]

And let's be honest here: whether you go seeking their advice or not, it's impossible to ignore some of these mainstream voices screaming for our attention.

---

304 Need a reminder of what is meant by "efficient" markets? Here's the footnote definition from Myth 10: The **efficient market hypothesis** (EMH) states that share prices reflect all information. This belief is a cornerstone of Modern Portfolio Theory.
305 Personally, I'm with Shiller on this one ... they're obviously not.
306 https://www.nobelprize.org/prizes/economic-sciences/1997/press-release/.
307 Explored at the beginning of Myth 10.
308 We'll explore the world of financial professionals further in our next myth.

Whether you like it or not, if you're not careful, they can and likely will influence your investment and other financial decisions.

> "Blinding ignorance does mislead us. O! Wretched mortals open your eyes!"
> **—Leonardo da Vinci**

## Those Who Are Loudest

In Homer's epic poem, *The Odyssey*, Odysseus must sail past the land of the Sirens. Warned that their song would lure him and his crew to their watery grave, he ordered his sailors to plug their ears with beeswax. But Odysseus, ever the curious traveler, longed to hear the song of the Sirens. He ordered his crew to tie him tightly to the mast and not let him free, no matter how much he begged.

Tempted by the Sirens' beautiful song, he commanded his men to untie him. Fortunately, they heeded their previous orders and bound him tighter. Despite his precognition, even the strong-willed Odysseus would have fallen victim to the Sirens' seductive calls.

In the treacherous world of investing, the Sirens' cry assumes many forms. Unlike Odysseus and his crew, however, we do not have foreknowledge of exactly how or when they will try to lure us to our demise. All we know is that it *will* happen.

It's dangerous to underestimate the Sirens' persuasiveness. Most investors won't perceive the song for what it is until it's too late. If history is any indication, the temptation will become too strong even for the most intelligent[309] and legendary[310] among us.

The risks to which Odysseus and his crew were exposed were greater than ours today—death versus *mere* financial ruin. However, I don't think the solution will be quite as straightforward for us as it was for those daring seamen. It's unrealistic to assume we won't be able to shake off whatever restrictions we attempt to place upon ourselves, and it's growing increasingly impossible to block out every last note of financial noise.

---

309  Think: Sir Isaac Newton, explored in Myth 5.
310  Think: Julian Robertson or Stanley Druckenmiller, explored in Myth 5.

## Talking Heads

Most people recognize that pundits often say what will get them the highest ratings. You know you shouldn't let it influence you, but sometimes you just can't shake what they said.

One of my favorite examples is watching pundits and experts laugh at the economist Peter Schiff as he presciently forecasted the 2008 crash.[311]

There are countless examples from every past crisis. History has shown us that a majority of pundits and experts are consistently on the wrong side of these issues. They often attempt to make those who disagree with them look crazy. And in the moment, those pundits are very good at what they do: convincing viewers. So be careful.

These prognosticators spew their convictions with such confidence it can be extremely difficult to ignore. CXO Advisory Group, a provider of market research and analysis, set out to see how right the lime-light market "experts" really are. They studied more than 6,500 individual forecasts about the performance or direction of US stocks offered publicly by 68 experts over a 7-year period.[312]

On average, the gurus were right only 47% of the time. So, when you hear one in the future making a bold call, maybe you should try to associate their voice with the sound of a coin dropping ... since the "expert" will be correct *almost* as often as a coinflip.

Talking head expert, Jim Cramer, tied with the guru-average: 47%. He speaks and millions of everyday investors listen. Here's a stock-specific gaffe you can add to your already-long list[313] of Cramer's upsetting advice ...

When a caller to his show on March 11, 2008 asked if they should be worried about Bear Stearns, Cramer emphatically insisted "NO! NO! NO! Bear Stearns is fine. Don't move your money from Bear, that's just being silly."

---

311 You can watch a compilation of several such interviews here: https://www.youtube.com/watch?v=sgRGBNekFIw.
312 https://www.cxoadvisory.com/gurus/.
313 Remember his optimistic advice for investors at the market tops both in 2000 and again in 2007 (explored in Myth 5).

In case you're not aware, that turned out to be one of the banks the government allowed to "go under." Five days after that call, Bear was purchased by JP Morgan for just $2 per share. When Cramer made that authoritative declaration on March 11, Bear was trading at around $60 per share.

I sincerely hope you cross pundits off your list as a resource for your future financial decisions. Not only are their interests in no way aligned with yours, they don't even have a track record of solid advice.

## Online Gurus

Every time we go through extended or rapid periods of stock market growth, teams of financial neophytes begin to laud their success. It's the …

- Dotcom genius with an insane 5-year track record. Most of the public didn't realize that this was due to him using extremely high leverage on very risky stocks rather than any real knack for the trade.
- Millionaire house flipper in 2007. He wasn't particularly skilled at spotting or negotiating a good deal. He simply got lucky: taking the right risk at the right time and scaling until the housing bubble popped … losing everything.
- Skilled craftsman who left his well-paying job to get into the tulip bulb trade. He likely looked the savant to all his friends … for a few months at least.

Following the advice of any of these successful individuals would obviously not have been a wise long-term strategy. There have been countless of these overnight successes (read: perceived experts by many…) during every prosperous period of any market. And, as technology progresses, their destructive influence is becoming greater.

I have no doubt that if social media existed in the late 90s, there would have been loads of famous financial influencers teaching you "all you need to know" to be able to live the high life like they were then. Just imagine if John Law[314] had been able to leverage affiliate marketing through influencers' YouTube channels. … Think how long his scheme could have dragged on and how much larger the Mississippi Company could have grown before its ultimate demise.

Today, these financial and investment "authorities" are everywhere. They have podcasts to which pretty much anyone anywhere could listen. They have massive Instagram followings. They're dancing on TikTok as they "teach" you how to become financially free. Just think of all the YouTube channels showing you how to invest … run by people who have only been in the market since 2009 or later (i.e., during a prolonged period of stock market success).

These influencers often set themselves up as guides—as experts. And millions of people, generally younger generations, listen …

Remember, when we're talking about your life savings, experience matters. I'm absolutely not saying a young person (or new person to the field) cannot have valuable insights. They can. But in the case of social media and YouTube, people often confuse an influencer's financial success (or apparent success) attributable to their social presence and activities with their actual expertise and know-how.

Just, be careful. When you find that you like someone who you've been listening to and are now tempted to take advice from, make sure they're using sound logic, data, and research. Seek counterpoints. Come to your own informed conclusions.

## Extremist Doomsayers

Finally, what about the extremist doomsayer? The one that is actually prophesying an imminent crash (not just informing you of the nonzero probability as I am)? Advising you to pull all your money out of the market and put it under your mattress or all in gold …?

---

314 John Law and the Mississippi Company explored in Myth 5.

They're out there, and some of them are extremely well-researched and convincing.

As a rather tame but relevant example, there were several highly intelligent people warning of the overvalued technology market in 1995. They may have been right, but if you had pulled all of your money out then, you would have missed out on an incredible opportunity that a tactically managed, well-diversified portfolio[315] would have captured. In fact, many brilliant hedge fund managers were ruined during this time as they defiantly shorted[316] that sector during its climb in the late '90s.[317]

The problem is, even if the doomsayer is right, there is no way to know when their prophecies will actually take place.

There are highly influential and powerful people that have a vested interest in those doomsayers not being validated on their watch. No president or member of Congress or Fed Chair wants a crash while they're in power. So, they implement a policy that works for the short term (perhaps, at least, until they're no longer in office), but consequently makes the long term even more bleak, effectively delaying that foretold imminent crash.

That's why, as I've said before, we're not talking about just shoving all your savings under your mattress. There are better ways for us to prepare ourselves and our life savings.[318]

## Building Your Own Mast

Those are just some of the many voices out there screaming for your attention. The odds appear to be stacked against you. And, when we're talking about something as important as your life savings, you can't afford to trust blindly.

---

315 More on those in Myths 16.
316 Need a reminder of what it means to "short" something? Here's the footnote definition from Myth 5: To **go short** ("sell short," or just "short") refers to the act of selling a security or financial instrument, such as the share of a stock, that the seller does not yet own. To facilitate this transaction, the seller borrows the asset (all handled behind the scenes by the brokerage firm). The short seller believes that the borrowed security's share price will drop in value, enabling it to be bought back at a lower price at some point in the future. In short, short selling is a way to profit when you believe a stock's price will go down.
317 Remember the example of Julian Robertson and Tiger Management from Myth 5.
318 Myths 15 & 16.

You can't afford to just say, "Oh, okay, you're a financial advisor, so I'm going to do whatever you say." "Okay, you're paid six figures to speak to me on television. You must know what you're talking about so I'm going to listen."

Question and challenge everything until you actually understand why you're doing what you're doing. That includes challenging me and my ideas! Only then will you have true conviction with your ultimate decision.

Anytime you hear a new idea, try to find someone who is well-versed in its opposition. Listen to both sides. Try your best to not make up your mind until you've heard them both out. Both sides will likely sound convincing. Once you've heard the differing perspectives, take a step back, and then see how you feel. And, if you're still not sure, keep researching, keep finding reliable sources.

It may not be fun to take the time to do that, but I hope by now you can see the gravity of your financial decisions and the significance of finding resources you can truly trust ...

This is important. This is your life savings. This is your legacy.[319]

In this world that is so predictably unprepared for the next unexpected panic, you'll need to construct your own mast to which you can cling. You do that by taking the time to:

- Understand these mainstream issues. *Check! You're off to a good start.*
- Sincerely vet any source of financial information. *We're working on that now.*
- Discover and actively implement solutions that you know to be better. *That's coming up!*

It won't be perfect; I'm no Odysseus. By no means will this make you impervious. But this will put you in the best possible position to financially thrive no matter what unexpected chaos lies ahead.

---

319 ... assuming you care about that sort of thing.

**MYTH:** "You Should Just Do What the 'Experts' Say."

**REALITY: The "Experts" are wrong often enough.**

# MYTH 12

---

## "Financial Advice Is All the Same"

## Finding Hope

If such highly esteemed experts can be wrong, you might feel as though there's no hope. It can be overwhelming; that's for sure. Remember, that's where I found myself for those first couple of years after leaving the established firm where I started my career. "Who am I to question?" "How am I possibly going to be able to find *better* solutions than what these guys came up with ...?"

But I had to do something. The problems were becoming increasingly obvious the more research I did. Navigating this treacherous world of investments can be confusing. There's a lot of intelligent-sounding, but bad advice out there. It's easy to get overwhelmed and lost. I was challenging everything—as I've encouraged you to do.[320]

People who honestly do that and consider all the data, research, and logic from our first ten myths often find themselves feeling a little lost. They want help, but now they're not sure where to turn ...

In a world filled with unqualified advisors, unoriginal pundits, and extremist doomsayers, who can you trust? Where can you turn for advice?

I'm going to walk you through that process and help make you aware of the traps into which *most* people fall. As we navigate this gauntlet, we'll gradually build out our list of criteria you should look for in your trusted financial authorities.

There are absolutely some amazing and reliable resources out there. But there are *so* many financial "experts" vying for your attention and business—some that will be better prepared to help you now with your new-found understanding of these investing myths than others. You just have to be careful; you need to be an informed consumer.

You're looking for someone you can trust. But not just someone you can trust to not try to sell you something all the time, but also ...

- Someone you can trust to understand these problems.

---

320 As I said at the end of Myth 11: You should challenge the people who are trying to give you advice. And that includes me. If you take that approach, you will ultimately be stronger in your convictions.

- Someone you can trust to use critical thought and logic when considering your complete financial picture.
- Someone you can trust who is familiar with all your potential investment options.

Some readers who already employ a financial professional should seriously consider how they proceed given the significant industry problems we've covered thus far. Others—those who already have a decent amount of money to invest or who just have a complex-enough financial situation that they could profit from the help—will need to proceed with caution as they search for guidance. Other readers still will just want to do everything on their own, parsing through all the information they can get their eyes on.

Regardless, you'll need to know to which of the horde of financial professionals and other influential personalities on the subject you should listen. They're all fighting for your attention. Who should you give the time of day?

I'm often alarmed by how little consideration most adults give this important decision.

## Commitment Issues

Think about how much thoughtful consideration you would (or should) give before discussing the prospect of marriage with a beloved companion. You would want to know that you could trust them with such an important commitment. Although not *quite* as important as selecting a life partner, you *should* do the same with your money: scrutinize every source before you determine that you can trust it.

In our search for those resources you can trust, you're going to get a feel for what's out there. And … most of it's not great. You've probably gathered that much already—that is, after all, a big reason this book needed to be written in the first place. There is a dearth of reliable resources available.

## The Pursuit of Trustworthiness

First off, on our journey through the world of financial professionals, you'll meet those who will go out of their way to aggressively push their services upon you. Most readers have likely already experienced the pleasure of one of these encounters:

- Your "local Ed Jones guy" just making the rounds in the neighborhood, knocking on all the doors, letting you know he's "here to help."
- The "your friend thought that you and I would enjoy meeting" Northwestern Mutual rep offering to throw together a financial plan for you for 'free!'
- The family member or friend who included your name on the list their firm had them put together as initial sales targets on which to "practice" while they're getting started.

Sadly, this is the vast majority of what you're going to find (or rather, that will find you).

## Commission-Based Salesfolk

This horde of financial representatives all jockeying for your attention work on commissions. They often work for the large insurance companies or investment brokerage houses. They're trained to paint this in a positive light: "Because I'm paid on commission, it's only when I find the right product for you that I get paid. And because I love this all so much, I'll just put together a financial plan for you for free!

"Incidentally, most of the plans I put together say that you need a lot of insurance and the particular insurance products I can recommend are all laden with commissions ..."

I'm not saying that the insurance products with commissions are inherently bad,[321] but those advisors are often extremely restricted—why would they ever offer you the options that pay little or no commissions? They're undeniably confronted with this massive conflict of interest every time they go to put together recommendations.

---

321 Insurance products are not inherently bad. In fact, some are critical for a sound, comprehensive financial plan. The point is, when you make your livelihood by identifying needs for commission-laden insurance products, you tend to label more things as "needs" and use products with higher commissions than you otherwise might.

The same is true with the investments they can recommend. When you go to a commission-based financial representative for investment advice, you should consider that the investments that their firm allows (or incentivizes) them to offer, are the ones that allow the firm to make money.

Often over the long run, with these "free" financial reps you actually end up paying more.

In 2020, the North American Securities Administration Association (NASAA) released a report[322] comparing the sales practices of Broker-Dealers[323] and Registered Investment Advisors. Representatives of the former are generally not bound by the fiduciary standard[324] whereas those of the latter always are.[325] The commission-based salesfolk in question are often associated with the broker-dealer side of the industry.

The study revealed that when complex products with hefty commissions were sold, broker-dealers were as much as nine times more likely to recommend them.[326]

Remember my example from Myth 2 about how I was able to explain away the exorbitant fees my firm was charging for me to manage my clients' money? I was able to justify it all because the solution I pitched sounded complex. These "complex products" with their elevated commissions make the reps and the companies more money. It's no wonder that when you remove that fiduciary responsibility—or when a firm has a more corporate, bottom-line-focused mind-

---

322  The NASAA study included more than 2,000 firms and 360,000 practitioners working with 68MM retail investor accounts.

323  Need a reminder of the difference between broker-dealers and registered investment advisors (RIAs)? Here's the footnote definition from Myth 2: When you're working with someone to help you invest your money, they are most likely either associated with a broker-dealer or a registered investment advisor (RIA). A **broker-dealer** is a person or firm in the business of buying and selling securities (stocks, bonds, etc.) for its own account or on behalf of its customers. One of the biggest differences for you (as a potential client) is that RIAs have to work under a fiduciary standard whereas broker-dealers do not.

324  Need a reminder of what it means to operate under a "fiduciary" standard? Here's the footnote definition from Myth 2: To act as a **fiduciary** means you must put your clients' interests ahead of your own. As in, I shouldn't continue to push my clients into an investment solution that I determine to be inferior—even if it is the only solution that would get me paid …

325  As of the time of this writing. There is a lot of pressure to change the laws regarding this issue so that all practitioners would be operating under a uniform fiduciary standard.

326  They were seven times as likely to recommend private placements, eight times as likely to recommend variable annuities, and nine times as likely to recommend non-traded REITSs.

set—that you'll see these types of risky products recommended up to nine times more often.

Through this report, states found significant differences between broker-dealers operating under a suitability standard and RIAs operating with a fiduciary responsibility. For instance, RIAs generally took more conservative investment approaches, "avoiding higher cost, riskier, and complex products. Investment advisers also reported more robust due diligence, disclosure, and conflict management practices," NASAA said.

Studies like this have shown that if you just paid a fee for your financial advice—even though it feels like more because it's all disclosed and out there in the open—in the long run, it can actually end up saving you money.

I'm not saying it would be impossible for you to find someone within these ranks that you could trust,[327] they just have a severe uphill battle as they fight against their firm's sales incentives and limited options.

I recommend you avoid this route all together.

• Not a Commission-Based Sales Rep

## Suitability Standard-Bearers

But if you insist, here are a couple things to keep in mind. First, make sure they're a fiduciary.[328] That means their recommendations are legally supposed to be in your best interest.[329]

The alternative to a fiduciary is a representative operating under a suitability standard. That means they only have to justify whatever recommendation they provide. Think about how easy that is: if it has to be in your best interest there's really only a few products that could be justified as that ideal fit. But, if they simply have to be able to demonstrate suitability,[330] that opens the door to many

---

327 I have friends who are still working with broker-dealers. I know them to be honest and trustworthy. I also know they're making great money and have families to feed. It can be hard to walk away from the golden handcuffs those companies have brilliantly devised to keep their best salespeople around ... even if they do suffer from a change of heart.

328 There are circumstances where even a broker-dealer's reps could be fiduciaries. For example, if they have their Certified Financial Planning™ designation.

329 Of course, a legal obligation is not a guarantee, but it's better than the alternative. Also, you would have legal recourse should you ever later determine that your advisor did not act in your best interest.

330 With the **suitability** standard, a representative merely needs to be able to show that their recommendation is in line with their client's objectives.

more products, including much more expensive products that will pay them much higher fees. Those products could still be suitable; they may just not be the best for you …

So, make sure they're a fiduciary.

☐ Fiduciary

## Restricted Agents

Next, you'll want to understand the limitations to the options they're allowed to recommend. By providing you with "the best they have to offer" an advisor can still satisfy their fiduciary responsibility without actually providing you the best that the *market* has to offer.

When I was working with that top-five brokerage firm early in my career, I was for the most part only allowed to sell insurance solutions from one company … theirs. There was understandably no support for anything else. The investment solutions I could offer were limited to those mutual fund companies that charged significant upfront and ongoing commissions.

This structure is common in that broker-dealer space. You want an advisor whose hands are not tied as to the solutions he can recommend. That's where I found myself before I left: knowing there were better options out there for my clients but not being able to do anything about it.

☐ Independent

Make sure your advisor is actually in a position to provide you with the best solutions.

## Misaligned Incentives

Next, be sure you understand their compensation structure. If they'll make more money selling you one product instead of another, surely you'd like to know that.

Also, try to understand their motivations. This one can be tough to discover, but when you know this can be a problem, you might understand why your rep is all the sudden so pushy. Let me explain with an example …

Suppose your financial representative's firm has a competition going where, if he hits certain sales goals, he'll qualify for a cruise for himself and his family.[331]

---

331 This is a very common practice in the insurance and broker-dealer space.

It's the last day of the competition, and he's one sale away from qualifying. You are his last appointment of the day. He just needs that one sale, and it doesn't look like he's going to get it from anywhere else ...

Do you think that might impact the way he approaches your meeting—his recommendations even—and the way he presents them?

Even if your rep is a very well-intentioned and trustworthy friend, don't you think this has the potential to influence his behavior—even if just a little bit?

☐ Aligned Incentives

These large insurance companies and broker-dealers have been around for a long time. They know how to motivate a sales force. Keep that in mind during your interactions if that is the path you choose.

But hopefully, you feel compelled as I would, to cross the "free" financial representative off your list of potential candidates to come to your aid here.

Next up: let's check out some of those advisors who see the light and do go off on their own.

## Investment Outsourcers

Over time, more and more advisors have become disenchanted with the salesy nature of the financial industrial complex that I just described. Many will leave and set off on their own. I was surprised to learn that a lot of them—only armed with the investment knowledge they received from school and perhaps their previous broker-dealer employer—will just outsource their investment advice to a robo-advisor.[332]

Many good financial advisors—the ones who aren't just trying to sell you something—train to be holistic financial planners. That's a broad topic which requires a general understanding of several different areas of focus, like retirement planning, tax planning, estate planning, insurance planning, and investment planning. You can dive deep into any one of those fields of study in the

---

332 Discussed toward the end of Myth 2.

financial planning universe, just as I've chosen to do with investment planning. But that takes a lot of dedicated study, and consequently, time.

So, most advisors are only armed with that general investment knowledge, like they are with all areas of financial planning. And for the most part, that broad understanding is enough in those other areas.[333]

With investments, however, that can be dangerous (as outlined in Myths 1–10).

But, rather than turning potential investment business away, it's difficult for many advisors to refuse such an easy upsell: "If you already trust me as your financial planner, and you don't want to go through the hassle of researching and finding someone else to manage your investment dollars … Why wouldn't you want me to manage your money?"

And if the advisor said, "No, I'm not going to manage your investment dollars for you since that's not my area of expertise…" they'd risk damaging their relationship and would be "leaving money on the table." So, how can they manage their client's money without really having to do anything? They outsource it to a robo-advisor, collecting an ongoing "management" fee as the middleman.

Most often, you could just invest directly with that underlying robo-advisory firm and incur *way* less in fees. The onus is on you to figure out who is actually investing your money for you. And, if you're okay with the answer there: Is there a way to get that exact same service for a smaller fee?[334] Don't be afraid to ask questions.

Next stop: let's consider those advisors who just want to plug into the traditional investment paradigm …

---

333 Unless you have a complex estate or offshore tax-haven assets, for example. At which point finding an advisor or team with an expertise in estate and/or tax planning would be prudent.

334 Consider, for example, Betterment: As of February, 2021, there were more than 600 advisory firms doing this via their so-called Betterment for Advisors platform: https://www.thinkadvisor.com/2021/02/11/betterment-for-advisors-now-lets-advisors-choose-the-investments. That's not to say that those firms are not offering other services that may justify their fees above what their clients could just as easily set up on their own via Betterment directly. But this is all information you should be aware of and consider should this be the reality for an advisor you're considering.

## Plug-and-Play Passive Practitioners

By this point, you understand some of the most serious problems with mainstream investment advice. Obviously, that stock-and-bond-only, buy-and-hold, set-it-and-forget-it strategy isn't good enough for you anymore. Unfortunately, that's what most professionals will try to plug you into.

It confuses me as to why people pay so much in fees just for that,[335] but so many do![336]

If you do choose to work with a financial advisor, you'll need to find one who understands the flaws of Modern Portfolio Theory.

☐ Understands MPTs Flaws

This will be someone who doesn't simply rely on summary statistics. They'll use data, research, and logic to help you understand why they're recommending what they are.

Now, let's make sure your prospective advisor actually understands the investment strategies that would best help you ...

## Uneducated Professionals

Many advisors don't understand some of the options available to them and their clients.[337] One example of this is the general ignorance when it comes to alternative investments.[338] Most advisors and investors don't even understand how these investments work, let alone how they could benefit a diversified portfolio.

A 2012 Morningstar study showed that 48% of advisors and investors admit to and blame a lack of understanding for their hesitation to invest in alternatives. So, if an advisor hasn't talked to you about alternative investments,[339] there is a chance he doesn't really understand them. And, whether or not you decide it

---

335  If a stock-and-bond-only portfolio is all you want, hit up Vanguard or one of those other low-cost robo-advisor options. But first, go back and read Myths 1–10 ... make sure you understand the risks there!

336  They don't seem to be helping people overcome the behavior gap, so I don't really know why else you would. ... See the end of Myth 6, and 7 & 8.

337  You'll see some of those alternative investing solutions in Myths 15 & 16.

338  We'll talk more about alternatives in Myth 16 and how they've significantly boosted the returns of several university endowments over the last 20 years.

339  Traditionally, alternative investments tend to make more sense for clients with a higher net worth. So, there is also a chance that your assets are just not yet high enough to warrant a conversation about alternatives.

makes sense to include alternatives in your portfolio, wouldn't you want your advisor to at least be aware of how all your options work?

☐ Understands All Your Investment Options

Seek advice from an informed professional.
Next stop: Does experience really matter?

## Inexperienced Advisors

It's important that the person you're going to trust with your hard-earned money has experience.[340]

You don't want someone who is straight out of college. Even a fresh designation is not necessarily a sign that they know what they're doing yet. Remember, Modern Portfolio Theory is what's taught in schools and in certification programs. So, if you're trying to overcome the flaws detailed in Myths 1–10, you'll need someone who has learned these truths on their own. If all their time has been in a book (with the exception of this one, of course!) their limited experience is not going to be able to help you here.

☐ Experienced

Now, don't get me wrong. I'm not trying to discourage young people from entering the field. That wouldn't make sense; it's not about age—it's about wisdom gleaned from real-world experience. Honestly, I think young people should start by apprenticing or interning for different advisors. They should ask questions until they find a practicing professional that can satisfactorily field and answer their questions and concerns.

They should learn as much as they can from that person before even considering offering financial advice on their own.

> "True intuitive expertise is learned from prolonged experience with good feedback on mistakes."
> **—Daniel Kahneman**

---

340 Honestly, this one is hard for me—I feel bad saying it, but I think it's true. In the same way that you wouldn't let a child of the same age babysit your child, you don't want someone with no real experience managing your money.

### Advisor Checklist

After applying all these filters, sadly, there aren't many options left. So many financial professionals are influenced by sales incentives. The vast majority of the rest get away with charging you a fee for merely plugging you into a simple stock-and-bond-only model. Almost none of them understand the flaws with that traditional investment paradigm.

If you already employ an advisor or representative, did she make the cut? Or are you left with a concern or two ...?

If you end up looking for an advisor to help you overcome these problems, here's that checklist:

- ☐ Not a Commission-Based Sales Rep
- ☐ Fiduciary
- ☐ Independent
- ☐ Aligned Incentives
- ☐ Understands MPT's Flaws
- ☐ Understands All Your Investment Options
- ☐ Experienced

As we've seen, there are so many examples of when the true cost[341] of a financial professional is not justified by their service ...

When, then, would that fee ever be worth it?

## So, Is It Ever Worth It?

Do you remember that question from Myth 2? At that point we were exploring the real and sometimes rather significant impact an advisor's fees can have on your future. That was half of our equation. The other half is understanding the actual value they provide.

If, for you, the value provided is greater than that true cost, then sure, it could be worth it. It's that easy! So ...

- If they're incentivized to recommend certain product solutions over others ... What are you paying for?
- If they only have access to one company's products and you can thus never be sure you're actually getting the best for your unique situation, what are you paying for?

---

341 Explored in Myth 2.

- If they're just plugging you into a buy-and-hold strategy, what are you paying for? We saw in Myth 8 that advisors don't appear to have a great track record of guiding people away from "the edge"—helping them to not get out of the market at the "wrong time."
- If they don't understand Modern Portfolio Theory's flaws, they obviously can't help you navigate them in order to best prepare for your long-term goals. So, what are you paying for?
- If they have no real industry experience, what are you paying for? Especially when you could probably find someone with decades more experience charging a similar fee.

You get the idea. You have to ask yourself, "What exactly am I paying for to justify this small percentage of a fee that really adds up over time?" Do not just go along with a fee because it doesn't feel like that much and seems pretty "standard!" For that relatively standard fee,[342] the difference between the value offered from one advisor to another can be significant.

In that same vein, don't just disregard an advisor because their fee is higher than others. What they are offering may indeed be able to justify that difference. You have to consider both sides of the equation in order to make an informed decision.

If you can find a financial professional who understands the concerns we've explored thus far, who's legally bound to act in your best interest, whose incentives align with yours, who has sufficient industry knowledge and experience, who you believe can help you realize above market returns over the long run … then yeah, they can be *well worth* their fee.

So, what should you look for—what are some of the things a financial professional could help you with that might actually add value to your financial life? And how much are each of those things worth to you?

## Investment Management

Although I consider the services provided by those aforementioned plug-and-play practitioners and their ilk to not be worth their ongoing fee, that doesn't mean I think investment management in general is a waste. I do believe there can be significant long-term value realized by utilizing an advisor who

---

342 That is, advisory fees tend to be sub-3%.

employs strategies specifically designed to overcome those major flaws uncovered in the preceding myths. Of course, you'll still need to understand what it is that they're actually doing for you. **Active management is not easy, but strategies designed to limit your investments' downside while still capturing much of the market's upside can lead to significant long-term outperformance.** We'll talk more about specific market strategies in Myth 16.

## The Financial Planning Model

As alluded to earlier, many financial advisors will also position themselves as financial planners. That is, they will work with you to help you understand and optimize your current money situation while guiding you along the best path toward your financial goals.

The financial planning process begins with a thorough evaluation of the individual's current financial state and future expectations.

☐ Goal Setting

Being aware of your financial position and setting goals can be easy when you're first starting out in life. At that point, this value may not be worth that much to you. But, as your assets and liabilities grow and life becomes more complex, it's increasingly difficult to keep up with all the financial opportunities available to you. Having a professional help you get to the bottom of your long-term goals and understand what is possible given various financial strategies can be extremely valuable—the more complex your financial life, the more an experienced professional's guidance could be worth.

This is especially helpful when they're good at pairing your goals with every other aspect of financial planning ...

☐ Planning Modules

Financial planning is becoming increasingly complex. Every year there are changes to laws and tax codes on the federal, state, and local levels affecting multiple aspects of your financial life. Having a professional or team of professionals by your side to guide you through some or all of the following is absolutely worth something ...

- Optimized Debt Elimination
- Ongoing Debt Management
- Cash Flow Planning

- Tax Planning
- Estate Planning
- Retirement Planning
- Insurance Planning
- College Education Planning
- Social Security Optimization
- Real Estate Portfolio Planning
- Business and Passive Income Strategy[343]

The list goes on. Depending upon what you're looking for or might need, expert insights and coaching on some of these various planning aspects might be worth more to you than others.

Now of course, just because a financial planner promises on his website that he'll be able to help you with these things, that doesn't necessarily mean he'll be able to provide you with the best advice in these respective areas. What is his actual level of expertise? Is he a Certified Financial Planner™? If you need tax advice as well, is he a CPA or does his firm have one on their team? Do they have actual lawyers providing that estate planning advice? As with anything, advice from some professionals will be worth more than advice from others …

- Advice from the best tax planning professionals could result in hundreds of thousands of dollars of additional savings over your lifetime.
- Advice from the best estate planning professionals could save you from hundreds of thousands of dollars in unnecessary future expenses.
- Advice from the best investment management professionals could help you build a portfolio with hundreds of thousands of dollars more in retirement.
- And so on …

Obviously, real professional advice like this could absolutely justify those ongoing fees outlined in Myth 2.

---

343 These latter two are rare, but I personally believe them to be extremely important (as you'll see in Myth 15). Especially for those individuals who are interested in these areas—real estate, business, passive income—having your financial planner/advisor as an asset and resource to help you build those out in concert with every other aspect of your financial life can be invaluable!

Even if you don't have a complex financial situation and we're not talking about hundreds of thousands or millions of dollars here, there can be value in a professional taking things off your plate.

- You know there are things you can and should do to optimize your future tax situation, you just haven't had time to get around to it ... for the last five years!
- You know you need to get that will (and maybe a trust?) in place, but you just haven't googled it yet ... so you continue to put it off.

Even just having a financial professional you can trust to quarterback these types of life concerns, that *is* worth something. I can't tell you exactly how much it would be worth for your unique situation, but the resultant stress reduction absolutely has value. It'll be on you to determine how much that actually is.

If paying an advisory fee gets you access to a professional or team of professionals qualified to help you with one or all of these areas, I hope you can see where such a fee could be more than justified.

## Sounding Board

Finally, sometimes it's just nice to have someone to talk to! Having a financial professional you know you can trust because you sincerely vetted them previously can be a valuable resource throughout your life as you are subjected to the financial noise that increasingly surrounds us.[344] When all the cool kids are talking about a particular stock on their YouTube channels, it's beneficial to have someone you can trust to talk you through it; that can be nice.

There are other things financial professionals will identify as services performed for their clients. Your challenge will be to assign each of those things a value: What is it worth to you? And then, compare that to the fee they charge.

---

344 Like Odysseus trying to avoid the dangers of listening to the Sirens, your trusted and vetted professional could be your mast.

## Fees Explained

So, the commission-based guy who is offering to manage your investments—he's out, right? His fees are going to be higher. He's likely just plugging you into a buy-and-hold strategy. And he's likely using the high-fee mutual funds his firm incentivizes him to use. So, you'll potentially end up paying way more than any fee-based advisor might have charged you *and* you're not really getting any unique investment value, so ... he's out? Great.

## Fee-Only

You could go the so-called fee-only route. Those are the advisors that have effectively sworn an oath[345] to never sell another insurance product. That sounds pretty good. It removes that massive conflict of interest.

These advisors will charge you a fee based on the assets they're managing for you. Some will charge you a financial planning fee to boot. But they absolutely will not sell you anything upon which they might receive any sort of commission ...

This creates an environment that allows for a more honest relationship not marred by any fear of your agent acting solely to score a higher commission. **There are many great financial advisors and planners[346] in this category.**[347]

## Fee-Based

In between the commission-based and the fee-only is the hybrid: the so-called fee-based advisor. They can charge you those same fees for managing

---

345  Exaggeration ... but yeah, they can't sell insurance.

346  This is also where you will find many Plug-and-Play Practitioners, Investment Outsourcers, Uneducated Professionals, and so on ...

347  My only problem with this "fee-only" model is that it often leads to an "off-loading" of any sort of planning regarding the structure and details of any insurance recommendations that are warranted for some clients. And there are some incredibly useful things you can do with smart insurance planning. So, I personally hate the idea of off-loading that to someone else (... an insurance salesman at that!). Personally, as an advisor, I want to be in control of any insurance policy's structure, if for no other reason to ensure that as little as possible goes to any sort of commissions.

your assets and for creating your custom financial plan. But they can also still sell you a product that might have a commission tied to it.

You have to be careful with this bunch. They can charge an upfront planning fee—creating that environment of trust I described previously—and then potentially strike with their commission-riddled recommendations. Double dipping right out of your pockets![348]

## Avoiding Conflicts

Although not common in the industry, there are ways to avoid these obvious conflicts of interest.

For example, a firm could entirely offset a client's planning fee by any insurance commission on a dollar-for-dollar basis. This aligns the client's and the planner's incentives. The planner has no incentive to bump her commission from the insurance sale—she will be compensated the same regardless. So, that only leaves her with the incentive of making her client happy by doing what is in his absolute best interest. The client, on the other hand, knows his insurance is being structured by the planner he trusts. And, if there ends up being a commission,[349] he knows it will have been as small as possible and will end up offsetting his financial planning fee anyway.

In fact, there's no reason fee-based planner-advisors couldn't do that same thing for the fee collected from the investment assets under management. That same logic could be applied to the fee-only planners as well. Do they really need to double dip? Collecting a planning fee and also collecting another fee on the investments they manage creates an incentive for them to push every extra dollar of yours into those assets, thus increasing their total fees collected. When this advisory fee directly (on a dollar-for-dollar basis) offsets the planning fee, there is much less of an incentive to recommend such a move unless it absolutely makes sense for the client. If they'd be better off investing in real estate or in their business, no problem!

There is no reason a fee cannot be set to ensure the planner-advisor is adequately compensated for their holistic planning services. Then, any solutions put into place which pay any sort of fee back to the advisor can directly offset the

---

348  In the past, I've called them "wolves in sheep's clothing."
349  As is often unavoidable with some insurance products. That being said, there are more and more **commission-free insurance solutions** being created. Just another reason to be with an advisor you can trust whose incentives are aligned with yours.

client's planning fee. The planner is adequately compensated and in a position to do the absolute best job for the client. And the client doesn't have to worry nearly as much about all those conflicts of interest so rife within the financial industry.

## What's Worth It?

In the end, if you can find that advisor who understands these concerns, is legally bound ***and*** *incentivized* to work in your best interest, has sufficient industry knowledge and experience, then yeah … she can be well worth her fee.

It can be difficult to find one like that: who satisfies all those requirements and meets all your criteria—who can help you with all the unique circumstances of your life. But, once you do, and have experienced the ongoing value they can add—the money they can save you, the general resource they can be, the financial stress they can alleviate from your life—you could begin to see your financial life improve in ways you never imagined possible!

---

**MYTH:** "Financial Advice Is All the Same."

**REALITY:** Not all advisors are created equal. The industry is rife with conflict of interest. **Although the right advisor can be well worth their fee, it will likely take some work on your part to identify them.**

---

Don't lose hope: there absolutely are planners and advisors out there who can give you quality, customized advice. Use the checklist and other relevant observations in this myth along with the general knowledge you're picking up from this book to guide you in your search, and you'll be fine!

In that search, however, you will inevitably discover that most financial reps will just plug you into some mainstream recommendations without a second thought ...

# MYTH 13

---

## "The 401(k) Is the Ultimate Tool"

OKAY SO, WHAT AM I SUPPOSED TO DO WITH ALL THESE ACCOUNTS I HAVE AVAILABLE TO ME?

## Origins

Let's explore some of the mainstream recommendations when it comes to saving for retirement. A discussion of the best ways to take advantage of the tools we have today will prove more fruitful after first developing an understanding of how those tools—and our entire concept of "retirement," for that matter—came about.

### Ancient History

The concept of receiving funds to support your lifestyle for the rest of your life is not new. The first records we have of this come from the Roman Empire, where, during the first century AD, they began to pay their soldiers pensions. All you had to do was put in 25 years of service for the Roman army and still be alive ... Good luck!

Thus, the idea of retirement was born. It continued for the most part to only be for military personnel until the 19th century.

You see, the idea of retirement as we view it today is relatively new. What's more, the retirement reality we face today—those entering retirement now and who will be entering retirement in the coming decades—is very different than generations before. You'll see what I mean as we explore the timeline of key events that bring us to today.

### Modern Era

In the mid-1800s in the United States, larger cities began offering retirement income benefits to police and firefighters. That started a trend that would expand over time to include most public sector workers.

In 1881, Otto von Bismarck, the conservative Minister President of Prussia, proposed a governmental pension for "older" workers.

A decade later, Prussia created a form of social security that began at age 70. In 1908, England followed suit with the Old-Age Pensions Act, which also created a form of social security beginning at age 70.

For reference, in 1900, life expectancy in the United States was less than 50 years old. [350] Also at that time, roughly 75% of all males over age 65 were working. If a man over 65 was not gainfully employed, it was likely due to a disability. [351]

## Corporate Pensions

The first private pension plan in the United States was created by the American Express Company in 1875. This plan only applied to workers who had been with the company for at least 20 years, had reached the age of 60, had been recommended by a manager for retirement, and had been approved by a committee along with the Board of Directors. They would then receive half their annual salary, up to $500 per year, for the rest of their lives.[352]

The Internal Revenue Act of 1921 helped spur the growth of these plans by exempting corporate contributions to employee pension plans from the federal corporate income tax.

By 1926, approximately 200 private pensions had been established by larger employers in the United States. Most of these early pensions were not designed to fully replace a final income. They merely paid out a relatively low percentage of an employee's pay at the time of retirement.

In 1935, the United States government jumped into the game with Social Security. When it was first enacted, it was done so under the assumption that most workers would not live for an extended period of time after their retirement and thus would receive minimal actual payments. An actuarial study commissioned by the committee on economic security—the committee in charge of drafting the Social Security legislation—showed that "using age 65 produced a manageable system that could easily be made self-sustaining with only modest levels of payroll taxation."[353]

---

350  https://www.statista.com/statistics/1040079/life-expectancy-united-states-all-time/. So, that'd be like our Social Security full retirement age today being 98! 20 years above our current average life expectancy.

351  Steven A. Sass, The Promise of Private Pensions, The First Hundred Years, (1997).

352  Steven McCourt, Defined Benefit and Defined Contribution Plans: A History, Market Overview and Comparative Analysis, 43 Benefits and Compensation Digest (2006).

353  Social Security Online, History, FAQ: The Origins of the Retirement Age in Social Security, http://www.ssa.gov/history/age65.html.

Note: at this point in history, life expectancy in the United States was still only 60 years from birth[354]—as in, on average, people were expected to die a full five years before they'd become eligible for any retirement benefits. Also note: in 1939, only 6% of the population paid income taxes.

It wasn't until the economic boom decades following World War II that the idea that employees *should* have some kind of defined benefit in retirement gained popularity and support. It became a part of most large corporate recruitment and retention efforts.

Starting in the 1940s, labor unions began to push for increased benefits. For companies to remain competitive, many complied—promising to replace more and more of an employee's average pay. As a result, company loyalty was strong; it was not uncommon to see employees work their entire lives for the same corporation.

The rapid adoption and growth of pension programs is likely attributable to employers' desire to attract and retain talent while also allowing companies to "more [humanely] remove older, less productive employees."[355]

Employees loved these so-called defined-benefit plans. For them, they greatly reduced one of the major risks anyone faces today upon retirement: longevity risk, or the risk of outliving your income. If a retired employee lived for an extraordinarily long time … they were still covered.

On top of that, these plans placed both the investment decision-making responsibility and the investment risk associated with market volatility on the company, instead of the worker. Thus, everything associated with Myths 1–10 would have been the concern of the corporation, not the individuals. In fact, Harry Markowitz's initial observations from around this time that led to Modern Portfolio Theory make much more sense in this context—businesses have much longer time horizons than the life expectancy of an individual employee. As such, they're in a much better position to handle long-term fluctuations in the market. Not to mention the fact that a corporation is much more likely to have access to competent long-term money managers than the average individual.

---

354 William Wiatrowski, Changing retirement age: ups and downs—laws and research, United States—Statistical Data Included, Monthly Labor Review (April 2001). http://www.bls.gov/opub/mlr/2001/04/art1full.pdf.

355 Joanna Short, Economic History of Retirement in the United States, EH.NET Encyclopedia (Robert Whaples, ed. 2002).

These defined-benefit pension plans were so popular that by 1970, about half of all private sector employees were covered by one in some way.[356]

## Beginning of the End

One concern that began to surface with these traditional plans was the lack of flexibility for the workers—the corporations controlled the contributions and the investments. For an employee to make more from them in retirement, they would have to work longer, make a higher salary, or live longer ...

After a few plans failed, the government "came to the rescue" and enacted the Employee Retirement Income Security Act (ERISA) of 1974. This new legislation dramatically increased the regulatory complexity involved with maintaining a defined-benefit pension plan. Over the decades that followed, Congress continued to pass more and more legislation of this nature.

Section 401(k) was born when Congress passed the Revenue Act of 1978, paving the way for the so-called defined-contribution plan. Initially intended to allow high-income earners an additional way to save, employees could now contribute to their retirement efforts in a tax-advantaged way.

Although these defined-contribution plans were initially designed to *supplement* the defined-benefit plans, as people began to live longer and regulatory complexity increased, more and more corporations had to leave their old-school pension plans behind.

Now, instead of a corporation being on the hook for a guaranteed monthly or annual benefit to be paid out for an indeterminate amount of time ... the corporation could just match fixed sums contributed to employees' 401(k)s. This not only shifted the investment risk associated with long-term planning away from the corporations, but it also alleviated them of much of the management responsibility and costs. Over time, different types of plans were created to serve different types of workers: 401(k)s for the private sector, 403(b)s for nonprofit and public education, 457 for states and municipalities, and Thrift Savings Plans for federal employees.

Over the years, the government passed more and more legislation increasing the regulatory complexity for a corporation to maintain a pension plan. These laws brought with them the unintended consequence of encouraging corporations to abandon their pension initiatives altogether ...

---

356 Employee Benefits Research Institute, History of Pension Plans (1998).

After all, the longevity risk to companies still offering defined-benefit pension plans was increasing. Today, life expectancy in the US is more than 78 years from birth—18 years *longer* than when the Social Security retirement age was set at 65! And those who make it to 65 are now expected to live another 18 to 21 years.

It became increasingly easier for corporations to just opt for the much-less-risky-to-them defined-contribution plans.

## The Changing Landscape

As a society, we've gone from planning to work our entire lives, to trying to get out of working as soon as humanly possible. I'm assuming *you* too want to stop working at some point? Okay, there's nothing wrong with that.

### Corporations

As it turns out, the corporate pension was a noble pursuit. I know it's difficult for most of us still working today to imagine working for the same company our entire lives.[357] But that definitely would have provided us with a straightforward path to accomplishing this retirement goal. I mean, just look at the original terms from The American Express Company. They simply asked that you at least put in 20 years and then, if you'd done a good job, they'd kick you out when you were 60 and keep paying you for *as long as you lived*. That's not a bad deal at all!

But in reality, this pursuit proved more difficult than simple math might have initially suggested to the sophisticated executives structuring these plans. There were just too many variables. People started living longer. The market didn't always perform how it had in the past (even though a company has a way longer time horizon than you do). **Even with their expensive expert investment advisors, companies began to fail to meet their obligations to fund their employees' retirements.**

Perhaps what's even more indicative of how difficult it was for these companies to manage a promise like *your lifetime income*, is how quickly they jumped ship. As soon as the government and financial industry were able to sell the public on another viable option—the 401(k)—corporations sprinted for the exits ...

---

357 According to the U.S. Bureau of Labor Statistics, in 2014, the average employee tenure was 4.6 years.

### Figure 22

## Percentage of Private-Sector Workers Participating in Various Employment-Based Retirement Plans

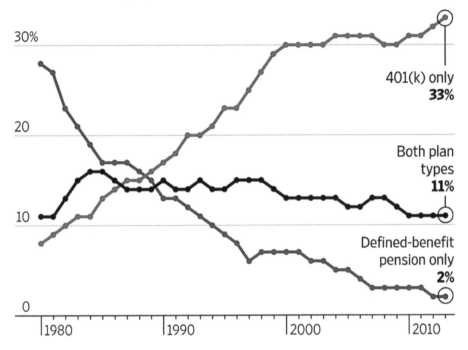

Source: Wall Street Journal; U.S. Department of Labor (participation).

Just as you do today, corporations had all the research behind Modern Portfolio Theory at their disposal. For each of their employees, they were effectively trying to build up a nest egg large enough to support them during retirement (no matter how long that may have ended up being). **Except their job here was actually easier than yours is today.** You see, they had the law of large numbers on their side. Remember this quote from Roger Lowenstein's *When Genius Fails*, cited in Myth 10:

> The beauty of cards is that the universe is known; there are 52 cards in a deck, and only 52. Life insurance is a bit different: since new people are always being added to the universe, actuaries rely on samplings. They aren't perfect, but they work, because the sample of people is very large and mortality rates change only very slowly. But in markets, we are never sure that the sample is complete.

Well, the risk to corporations is more like that of an insurance company than the individual trying to tackle the market alone, as the corporation is able to "pool" all that risk. The companies were also in a position to make regular adjustments to their contributions to account for variable changes throughout your lifetime—even while you were no longer working, the company still was.

You, on the other hand, do not have any of those luxuries. You might be the one who lives "too long." You might be the one who retires right as the market begins to crash. Corporations were able to diversify those risks. Yet—despite all those advantages over the individual—**many were failing and almost all wanted out!**

They were more than happy to alleviate themselves of all that investment risk and the ever-worsening variable of longevity risk. They gladly replaced all that with a generous offer to make a tax-deductible contribution to your 401(k), should you decide to do so yourself. As it turns out, this is far cheaper for them than making all the contributions themselves and being responsible for whether or not there's actually enough in there to provide you with that promised lifetime income. Now, when their employees retire, the company's obligations to them are done. **Just like that, they were able to shed the onerous burden of trying to figure out how to fund your retirement.**

And for the most part, most of those few companies still offering a defined-benefit plan are in heavily unionized industries (think: airline and auto sectors) and have been fighting to either reduce or eliminate their plans.

## Governments

Unlike corporations—which have to remain financially viable in order to stay in business—the government is stuck between a rock and a hard place as it struggles to continue to fund its employees' pensions.

For example, in the public sector from 2009 through 2013 alone, 48 states amended their public plans: 34 added or increased their employees' mandatory contributions; 30 reduced their cost-of-living adjustments (COLAs—an adjustment meant to account for and protect against inflation).

The federal Social Security program is facing similar longevity pressures, but as with our national debt discussion in Myth 10, it would be political suicide to make any long-term sustainable changes there. So, we're likely to continue to see patches in the future as the government tries to find ways to kick that proverbial can further down the road.

Consider the language the Social Security Administration (SSA) is putting on every benefits statement sent this year: "By 2034, the payroll taxes collected will be enough to pay only about 77 percent of scheduled benefits."

The sources that many are depending upon are in a precarious state. And now, this task of building up a nest egg to fund your retirement—a task that was so clearly challenging for some of the savviest business operations in the world and with which the government is quite obviously struggling—is left to you. And, perhaps most frustrating of all, it's presented as though the solution is so easy and obvious.[358]

## Government to the Rescue

Remember, the government created the 401(k) as a way for high-income earners to avoid more taxes. It was initially meant to supplement the existing defined-benefit pension plans. It definitely was not intended for the everyday worker to be able to fully fund their own retirement.

*That'd be ludicrous! Individuals being able to fully fund something as variable as that, especially considering the struggles that large sophisticated institutions have had with it, ha, the thought ...*

Oh wait, so now that is what we're expected to use?[359] Okay ...

### Traditional 401(k)

I guess we need to become familiar with this tool that has been given us. How exactly does a 401(k) work?

---

358 And hey, if you're lucky enough to hit on all those good investment return years at all the right times—referring to the potentially devastating impact of sequence risk during early retirement withdrawal periods as outlined in Myth 4—then sure, it will probably feel easy to you. I suppose the path you take here just depends on how much you like to gamble ...

359 This won't be an exhaustive list detailing every single option you have available to you, just the most common. I don't want to distract from the main points of this book. So sure, along the way you may think of a strategy or two that you've heard of that could help a little with your retirement. For example: yes, some people should take advantage of HSAs (health savings accounts), and although we help our clients with this and countless other mainstream strategies, the benefit of doing them is relatively negligible compared to the risk of a reader getting distracted by the minutia and missing the more important points of this book. Instead, there are a few key strategies and mindset shifts here that can change your life. My goal, more than anything else, is to do everything in my power to help you walk away with those by the end of this text.

- An employee can make contributions up to limits set by the Internal Revenue Service (IRS).
- An employer will often match an employee's contribution, sometimes on a dollar-for-dollar basis up to a certain percentage of income, sometimes less.
- Contributions are tax-deductible, meaning they are deducted from an employee's income and thus not taxed today.
- The employee is responsible for choosing the 401(k)'s underlying investments from the often-very-limited list of funds offered by their employer.
- Any growth realized on the money inside the 401(k) will not be taxed until it is withdrawn. This is known as tax-deferred growth.
- Unless you meet certain hardship criteria as spelled out by the IRS,[360] you must be at least age 59½ to begin making withdrawals without incurring a penalty.[361]
- In general, withdrawals before this age come with an additional 10% early-distribution penalty tax on top of the other taxes you might owe.
- After age 72, you must withdraw at least the IRS-required percentage from your plan each year.[362] These are known as required minimum distributions, or RMDs.

**With a traditional 401(k): your contributions are tax-deductible; your account grows tax-deferred; your withdrawals are entirely taxed as ordinary income.**

### Traditional IRA

Individual retirement accounts (IRAs) have been around for even longer.[363] From a tax perspective, these accounts behave in the same way as the traditional

---

360  Such as being totally and permanently disabled.
361  As with pretty much everything created by the government, there are a few additional exceptions to this rule, like the Rule of 55, for example, which for some can allow for earlier penalty-free access.
362  If you're still working at that time for the company where your 401(k) is held, however, you may not have to take the RMDs.
363  They were established in a 1974 legislation and first became available that following year.

401(k): tax-deductible contributions, tax-deferred growth, and taxed fully as ordinary income upon withdrawal.[364]

The main difference here is that you can open one of these accounts yourself as opposed to your employer having to provide it as an option.

With both of these account types, you're postponing the payment of any taxes. Think about what future tax brackets will look like. Obviously, no one knows exactly what they'll be, but considering how high the national debt is and that the national deficit still continues to grow each year, it's hard for me to believe that we won't have higher taxes in the future.

But, even if you think that there's a possibility for lower taxes or for taxes to stay the same and that you'll drop into a lower tax bracket, surely you would like to remove the variable. I know I would! I like the idea of removing as many variables from my retirement equation as possible. In this case, we're talking about the tax variable.

So, if you think there's a chance that taxes may be higher in the future, does postponing paying those taxes really make sense? Unfortunately, that's what most people feel is their only option when planning for retirement.

Here's an over-exaggerated metaphor to put into perspective these retirement accounts that everyone is encouraged to rely so heavily upon ...

Your uncle approaches you with a business proposition:

- You front the money.
- You take all the risk.
- You manage that business every single year.
- And 30 years from now, your uncle will show back up and tell you how much you owe him!

Would you want to go into business with your uncle on those terms? Of course not!

But how different is this scenario than the terms of a 401(k) and a traditional IRA?

This is not to suggest that traditional IRAs and 401(k)s are not some of the best options we have to save for retirement ... as sad as that may be. Instead, I'm

---

364 There are limits to the amount that an individual can put into their IRAs in a given year. There are also income restrictions depending upon how you file your taxes—once you earn over a certain income, you can no longer make additional contributions.

suggesting that perhaps they're not as great as what we've been sold. They're not a panacea. If we really want to hit the lofty goal most of us have, we are going to have to do more.

Enter: Congress, to the rescue once again ...

## Roth IRA

Roth IRAs were introduced in legislation sponsored by the late Senator William Roth Jr.[365] in 1997. Their tax treatment is effectively the opposite that of traditional IRAs. Contributions to Roth IRAs are made with after-tax dollars, so they're not deductible. But, with Roths, that's the last time that money will be taxed. It'll still grow tax-deferred. And then, the withdrawals will be entirely tax-free.[366]

Whether you believe a Roth or traditional account will make more sense for you will depend on your current tax bracket, your expected tax rate when you retire, and just how strongly you feel about removing as many variables from the equation as possible.

## Roth 401(k)s

To round out our brief overview of the most prominent tax-favored retirement vehicles we'll need to visit legislation passed in 2001. The Economic Growth and Tax Relief Reconciliation Act created the Roth 401(k). Since 2006, employers have been allowed to change their 401(k) plan documents to allow employees to elect for Roth-IRA-type tax treatment for some or all of their retirement contributions.

For those who have access to it, this can be a big deal. An opportunity to remove the tax variable from a much larger chunk of retirement savings than ever before. Although Roth 401(k)s are still subject to the RMD requirements (and steep penalties for failing them) and contribution limitations, they are not subject to any income limitations to participate.

So, after corporations bailed, these—along with an underfunded Social Security—are the main tools with which the government has provided you to fund your retirement.

---

365  R-Delaware.
366  As with traditional IRAs, Roth IRAs are subject to contributions limits and income restrictions.

## Experts to the Rescue

What can you do to right this ship? The one who used to be captain has since jumped overboard and now they're telling you that you're in charge. Well, don't worry: there's no shortage of "experts" willing to tell you what to do …

They'll make the path you're supposed to follow sound easy and obvious. You're probably already familiar with that traditional advice since it's all the same and so frequently parroted. A quick google search for "how to save for retirement" will bring up a page filled with many prominent financial voices singing the same song.

Take this opening blurb from NerdWallet, for example:

> The best way to save for retirement is in a retirement savings account. We're not trying to be cheeky. Just super literal. There are lots of different types of investment accounts, but retirement accounts like IRAs and 401(k)s were created specifically to give people incentives to save for retirement.

Here's the basic pattern they all follow:
- If one is available to you, take advantage of your employer's match.
- Then, max out your Roth IRA.
- Then, go back to your 401(k) (or its equivalent provided by your employer) and max that out.
- Once you've hit your limits on all those, open a brokerage account and pump more in there.
- Invest all of these in low-cost, broad-market-based ETFs with a stock-and-bond allocation that is suitable for your age.
- Don't touch any of it until you're ready to retire … so long as that is after 59½.[367]

Okay. Easy enough. So, you've got this, right? The financial professionals of the last couple of decades have been able to put their heads together and come up with foolproof strategies. Right? Since every "expert" is saying the same thing, there can't be more to it, right? This is a no-brainer?

Since all this is so obvious and in-your-face now, I'm sure this has made it to where more people than ever before are actually prepared for retirement … right?

---

367  To avoid the penalties of all those qualified accounts (the IRAs and 401(k)s).

It would definitely stand to reason for this to be the case if these strategies are in fact the ultimate solutions they're made out to be.

However, according to Boston College's Center for Retirement Research ...

- Despite all the various tools incentivized us by the government,
- Despite no shortage of finance gurus so clearly dumbing this all down for us,
- And despite decades of trying to understand the markets and figured this all out,

People are actually less prepared today than ever before. Their research suggests that 52% of US households are at risk of running low on money during retirement.[368] That figure is up from 31% of households in 1983.

I guess that's what happens when you—a mere mortal—assume all the risks and continue to try to use the same strategies that weren't working for some of the largest and most savvy corporations in the world.

> "Insanity is doing the same thing over and over again and expecting different results."
> **—Most often misattributed to Albert Einstein[369]**

Perhaps, this failing is due in part to the fact that in 1983 many of those entering retirement had pension plans to supplement their lifetime income needs? Or perhaps, it's because people are living longer today and healthcare is more expensive? Probably a combination of many things. But once again, we're hit with the realization that even more of our retirement variables are subject to change ...

Everyday savers are less prepared for their long-term goals than ever before despite all these so-called qualified plans, despite all the very loud pundits, and despite Modern Portfolio Theory. The problem is not that people haven't heard these mainstream suggestions—with the internet, social media, and YouTube, they're undeniably more in your face than ever before.

---

368 Based on projections of assets, home prices, debt levels, and Social Security income.
369 Fun fact: the first actual documentation of this quote came from an attendee of a 1981 Al-Anon meeting ... much less authoritative than Einstein.

So, either the traditional investment paradigm is not working or people are getting more stupid.

I tend to believe the former: **traditional investment advice is fundamentally flawed on multiple fronts.**

Wait, so what's wrong? Why is this not working?

### Change of Tune

Many of the original proponents of the 401(k) back in the late 1970s and early 1980s are now regretting the push they made for congressional and industry adoption. Ted Benna, referred to by some in the industry as the father of the 401(k), was a benefits consultant with the Johnson companies. He was one of the first to publicly make that push. Mr. Benna told the Wall Street Journal[370] that he's since realized that now "individual savers have too many opportunities to make mistakes." He went on to say that "he doubts 'any system currently in existence' will be effectual for the majority of Americans."

Another staunch advocate for Section 401(k) was Economist Teresa Ghilarducci.[371] She sold the idea to unions and before Congress by assuring the concerned audience that with this new defined-contribution plan employees would have enough to retire …

Ms. Ghilarducci has since changed her tune and is fighting for change once again. In fact, **she'd like to abandon the 401(k) altogether** saying that she now realizes that the math she used to gain support for it in the 1980s no longer works.

So, what are some of their concerns? What are these experts now seeing that is causing individuals to be even less prepared? Why the change of tune?

## Problems

### Limited Options

If you follow that mainstream advice, the vast majority of your investment dollars are being directed into your 401(k).[372] Now, you—a lay investor—are

---

370  https://www.wsj.com/articles/the-champions-of-the-401-k-lament-the-revolution-they-started-1483382348.

371  Director of the Schwartz Center for Economic Policy Analysis.

372  Either traditional or Roth.

supposed to choose your underlying investments. Often, however, the options you have within these plans are relatively limited. Investopedia warns:

> In terms of retirement plan design, the conventional wisdom in the 401(k) plan investment industry is that 'less is more' ... to streamline your investment decision-making responsibilities to minimize the complexity of your investment choices.

Because most of the individuals making these decisions are non-investors, the 401(k) industry is kindly limiting your options. And, when most of your funds are being funneled into a vehicle with very few diversification options, it's easy to become even more dangerously exposed to the vicissitudes of the market.

## High Fees

Qualified 401(k) plans are an expensive employee benefit. They involve numerous compliance concerns and thus have to be monitored and serviced constantly. There are also several supplemental services that must be available to plan participants. Employees often end up impacted by these mandates through participant fees, itemized charges for various 401(k)-related services, higher fund expenses, and other more discrete costs.[373]

Plans can be even more expensive for participants at smaller companies where they cannot bring the same economies of scale to the 401(k) provider.

A 2012 Demos[374] study[375] concluded that "over a lifetime, 401(k) fees can cost a median-income two-earner family nearly $155,000 and consume nearly one-third of their investment returns."

## Complex Tax Implications

Not paying any taxes today sounds like a great deal—you'll have more money growing for you on a tax-deferred basis. That's all true. But it's a little more complicated than just that. You see, after paying ordinary income tax on money invested in a non-qualified account, you might only owe long-term capital gains

---

373  U.S. Department of Labor. "A Look at 401(k) Plan Fees." https://www.dol.gov/sites/dolgov/files/ebsa/about-ebsa/our-activities/resource-center/publications/a-look-at-401k-plan-fees.pdf.
374  A nonpartisan public policy research and advocacy organization.
375  https://www.demos.org/sites/default/files/publications/TheRetirementSavingsDrain-Final.pdf.

tax on any future gains incurred (that would be the case for any investment held for more than one year). Historically, long-term capital gains rates are less than ordinary income rates.

Your ultimate withdrawals from your traditional 401(k) and IRA will be taxed as ordinary income. If taxes never change, you would still come out ahead by delaying those taxes and opting for the higher ordinary income tax rate. But, if you're decades from being able to utilize these funds that you're locking away, you can be sure that taxes will change in some way over that time, not to mention the fact that you very well may be in a different tax bracket, at which point the math may not end up working out in your favor. It's just not quite as cut and dry as it is often initially presented.

## Illiquidity

While your money is growing inside your 401(k) you have limited access to it. You are often allowed to take out a loan against your total value up to a certain amount.[376] But, if you ever decide to completely withdraw any amount before that magical age of 59½—say for example, to fund another investment—in addition to increasing your ordinary income tax due that year, you will be subject to the additional tax penalty of 10%.

So, if your plan is (as those experts advise) to put all your savings—at least as much as the government will allow—into these qualified accounts, then you'll need to prepare yourself for the lack of financial flexibility that comes with that decision.

## Tiny Windows; Steep Penalties

Then, you only have that weird, relatively small window in which you can access your money without fear of additional penalties. Every single dollar that you withdraw during that period will of course still be counted as additional ordinary income come tax time but at least there won't be penalties ...

But then, just over 12 years into your peaceful retirement, well ... *the government wants them taxes!* At age 72, whether you've touched your traditional

---

376 Here is the 401k loan limit rule as it's written today on the IRS's site: "The maximum amount that the plan can permit as a loan is (1) the greater of $10,000 or 50% of your vested account balance, or (2) $50,000, whichever is less."

qualified account funds or not, you are forced to take taxable withdrawals. And if you miss? Oh, don't worry: it's just a ... *50% tax penalty!*

## Alternate Recommendations

These are just some of the concerns with the mainstream retirement planning advice. There are more and we could have gone into more detail, but I hope they inspire you to be open to better ways even if they end up requiring a little research and work on your part.

So, what should we do with these mainstream investment vehicles?

### Consider This

As I will repeat in the coming sections: everyone is a little different. So, although I will try my best to provide you with some actionable advice, I only do so with a disclaimer that some variation of all this might be even better for your unique set of circumstances and goals. By continuing to read, you are agreeing to these terms of service ...![377]

Although everyone's circumstances are unique, here are some common, baseline recommendations that will apply to many.

- **Contribution Total:** At no point would I recommend sending every single long-term investment dollar into qualified plans only or any single location. Initially, I'd recommend setting up a savings account—something separate from your main checking account—to contribute some portion of your total savings each month. Yes, even if you're not maxing out on your company match quite yet ...

- **Emergency Fund:** Do this until you have a sum that provides you and your loved ones with peace of mind. That sum is going to vary by individual—for some, it'll only be three or six months' worth of essential living expenses; for others, maybe a year; others still may prefer the comfort of a $100,000 lump sum; and so on.[378] Be prepared to turn those regular contributions back on should this account be reduced in the future.

---

377 Just kidding! But really... I hope, if anything, this book helps you critically think about all things financial planning and investment related. I hope it leaves you with a better mindset as to what you can do to make all your goals a comfortable reality!

378 Once they understand all the details, many of our clients will consider various emergency-fund alternatives allowing them to feel comfortable with even less just sitting in their

- **Company Match:** If your company is offering a match, I'd take advantage of that. I know it's in a 401(k)-type vehicle and entirely tied up in the market and none of that is ideal, but a match is still a great deal. There aren't many investments you can find where you can be sure to double (or bump by 50% or whatever your match is) on Day 1.
- **Roth IRA:** There are very few ways to entirely remove the annoying variable that is taxes. So, I generally recommend that clients max out their Roth IRA contributions for themselves and their spouses (if married). If your income is too high to qualify for a Roth IRA contribution via the traditional means, you might consider using[379] the "backdoor Roth"[380] to get tax-free funds socked away.[381]
- **Roth 401(k):** After that, I often recommend investments outside these qualified options in spite of the advice from industry 'experts' to the contrary. One of the few reasons that I would circle back around to your company's qualified plan is if it offers a Roth version. This is becoming increasingly common for employers and I do believe it can be a great option given the opportunity to remove the tax variable all together. But I wouldn't go too crazy with it. As you work to max out contributions here, I generally recommend directing a larger and larger percentage of total contributions toward other diversification efforts— efforts designed to remove other variables and risks from your long-term financial equation.[382]

## Why Not More 401(k)?

As with everything I do for myself and my clients, I try to look at the full picture. The 401(k) is sold to us as a way to avoid taxes today. Great! It absolutely accomplishes that.

But how much is that worth to you? I know I've asked you to consider that same question a lot throughout these last few myths, but this is one that we

---

savings account earning next to nothing. These might include but are not limited to, understanding how a 401(k) loan works, having access to a HELOC, and so on.

379  At least for now, at the time of this writing.

380  A **backdoor Roth** IRA is where you convert a traditional IRA into a Roth even if your income is too high.

381  Don't forget the first point here though: at no point would I recommend sending every single long-term investment dollar into only qualified plans or any single location.

382  Detailed in the coming myths.

can actually quantify in a way so that you can see the impact and significance of the financial planning considerations I'm talking about here. Let's compare a $10,000 investment into both a 401(k) and a non-qualified account (i.e., not an IRA or employer-sponsored plan). We'll make the following assumptions to help us isolate the true impact of this tax advantage:

- Ordinary Income Tax Rate: 30%
- Long-term Capital Gains Tax Rate: 15%
- Annualized Rate of Return: 8%

On Day 1, that 401(k), untouched as of yet by Uncle Sam, will have $10,000 in it. Our non-qualified account, on the other hand, after paying the upfront tax bill, will have only $7,000. After 10 years, the investment in our 401(k) will be worth $21,589. Withdrawing that to help fund our retirement would increase our taxable income that year by that full amount. Assuming taxes were still the same for us, that would leave us with $15,112.

After cashing out of our non-qualified investment after 10 years and paying the long-term capital gains tax on the gains, we'd be left with $13,896. With this scenario of fixed tax and return assumptions, the 401(k) will always win.

So, how about those assumptions? We've already discussed the stress that should come with too much of your retirement-earmarked funds being 100% subject to ordinary income taxes.

But what about our other variable here? The assumed annualized rate of return. What if we found investment solutions—unavailable to us through our 401(k)'s limited options—which we felt provided us with the potential for higher returns?

How much greater of a return would we need to realize in order to entirely offset that tax savings—that difference between the 401(k)'s $15,000 and the non-qualified account's $14,000?

What do you think: 5%, 3%, 2%? Surely we couldn't entirely offset that tax savings with a meager additional 1% annualized return over those 10 short years in our non-qualified investment ... could we?

In fact, we can. By changing our projected annualized rate of return for our non-qualified account from 8% to 9%, after accounting for those additional long-term gains taxes that would be due, we're left with $15,136. That was it: a 1% greater rate of return was all it took.

Given a longer time period that non-qualified account in our scenario just keeps looking better and better than its 401(k) counterpart. And of course, bumping that return assumption further would result in an even quicker turn-around.

### What's Right for You?

So now, when you're making your decision as to whether or not more savings should be pumped into your 401(k), you should consider both sides of this: what options you have available to you within your plan and how those compare to your options elsewhere.

Some people have a lot of options available to them; some don't. Some people have exorbitant fees to consider; some don't. Some people are even allowed what is called a brokerage window, which gives them the option to control the investments for some or all of their 401(k) funds via a brokerage platform—it's effectively a self-directed 401(k),[383] opening them up to many other investment securities. You see, people's options within their company's plan can vary greatly.

Outside of an employer-sponsored plan, however, the investment world is your oyster. Depending upon your circle of competence, you very well may be able to find opportunities where you feel more than confident in a much higher annualized return than you could realize within your 401(k). At which point, if the math works out, why wouldn't you take advantage of that non-qualified opportunity instead of just blindly making extra 401(k) contributions as almost everyone recommends? Not only could that put you ahead over the long run, but you'd also get the benefit of avoiding all the byzantine rules and regulations that accompany qualified plans.

In the remaining myths we'll explore some of those investment strategies that might make more sense for you. Again, this is not blanket advice. For some, additional 401(k) contributions might be your best option. But I hope it's becoming more clear to you how *not* cut-and-dry these issues are while at the same time equipping you with the logic needed to assess your own situation.

---

383 Self-directed IRAs come up in Myth 15.

---

**MYTH:** "The 401(k) Is the Ultimate Tool."

**REALITY:** It's certainly one of the better tools the government has given us, but blindly making additional contributions above a company match is **far from the best way** to prepare for your financial future.

---

So many people have a large portion of their retirement savings in their 401(k). Unfortunately, this blanket advice that continues to be promulgated throughout our mainstream investment world, leaves investors exposed to significant risks.

# MYTH 14

---

## "You Need to Focus on Your 'Retirement Number'"

## What Are You Even Doing?

What are you working towards anyway? Before you can make an adequate financial plan—or find the right person or people to help you, for that matter—you need to know what your end goals are.

> "If you don't know where you are going, you'll end up someplace else."
>
> **—Yogi Berra**

For some reason, our concept of "working so that we can someday retire" has become oddly distorted over time.

I JUST NEED TO FIGURE OUT MY "NUMBER," RIGHT?

THE AMOUNT OF MONEY I'LL NEED IN MY "NEST EGG" TO BE ABLE TO RETIRE...

### Your "Number"

An ING ad campaign from a decade ago would ask, "Do you know your number?"[384] as a way of determining whether you're ready to retire. Today, the FIRE (Financial Independence, Retire Early) movement has an army of people working toward achieving their "number" so that they can retire. In fact, if you sit down with representatives from many financial services firms, they'd be more than happy to help you calculate your unique "number."

Your "number" is supposedly what will allow you to achieve your retirement goals. It's the size of the nest egg you would need in order to support your lifestyle without working or running out of money. Think: the safe withdrawal rate concept explored in Myth 9. Calculating your "number" will require you to make several assumptions: at what age you plan to retire, how much money you'll spend each month, how your investments will perform, what tax rates will be, and at what age you'll die. The output of this calculation is the lump sum dollar amount—nest egg—you would need in order to be in a position where you could retire at your desired age.

---

384  https://vimeo.com/15284991.

For some reason, our collective idea of preparing for the long term, has morphed into just shoving as much money as one can into the market trying to build up an account large enough to satisfy this numeric goal, and then hoping for the best.

## Retirement Dream

But what does your dream retirement actually look like?

- You own your small house a few blocks away from your children. It has a large yard in which your grandchildren can play. You and your spouse can sit on your rocking chairs on a large porch overlooking the scene. You know you have more than enough coming in each month to cover your needs leaving you with little stress allowing you to enjoy those peaceful moments.
- You own your dream cottage just outside of town on several acres of land. You have everything you need to live happily and cherish the most important things in life to you for the rest of your days.
- You're able to travel the world visiting all the beautiful sandy beaches, sipping piña coladas, staying in the world's most luxurious resorts, and crossing off bucket list items you never knew you had.

So, what's your goal? What are you working toward?

Is it a large lump sum of money all tied to investments over which you are only vaguely familiar and have very little control?

No!

Ha, at least I hope not. For most, that nest egg concept is just a means to an end. But is it really the best way for you to bring your idyllic retirement vision into fruition?

What one really needs to facilitate all those retirement dreams, is a stable source of predictable lifetime income. Income that is, ideally, being generated from multiple sources and—to the extent possible—from sources that you actually understand. Now of course, you would need different amounts of monthly income coming in to facilitate those differing visions of retirement: those world travelers funding adventure after luxurious adventure would require a much greater flow of cash than the couple with the downtown home. But both would be far better served by focusing on building up their stable lifetime income to the point that would allow them to realize their respective dreams as opposed to simply focusing on their market-based "number."

Unfortunately, the financial industry tends to promote the latter.[385] Market-based investments absolutely have proven to produce good returns in the past. As we've seen that's no guarantee for the future, but that doesn't mean it's a bad idea to include it as a piece of this puzzle. *But it should not be the entire puzzle!*

In reality, when you study all the risks to which this "number" focus leaves you exposed, you discover that it's actually a relatively inefficient way to reach that long-term goal of yours. **This traditional concept of building up one's nest egg can require a lot of finger crossing at times.**

## What Could Get in Your Way?

Although I can't (within this text) speak to all your specific and unique goals, for the most part, people do want to at some point have the flexibility to stop working (read: achieve true financial freedom). They want to be comfortable and secure. So, for the remainder of our conversation here, that will be the contextual focal point—figuring out how to best overcome risks associated with that end goal. The alternative focus I propose at the end of this myth will also conveniently provide adherents with greater flexibility for other goals you may have along the way.

So, let's first explore those risks you will need to overcome.[386]

### Market Risk

We beat this one to death in Myths 1–10. There is no guarantee for how your market-based investments will perform—they may perform better than average throughout your retirement or they may grossly underperform, or anywhere in between.

Throw in sequence risk—specifically the risk that the first couple of years of your retirement turn out to be particularly terrible—and it becomes clear that if at all possible, we don't want all of our investment dollars exposed to this risk.

---

385 Easier to collect more in asset management and fund fees that way …

386 This is not an exhaustive list of every obstacle that could impede your progress on a financial plan. The risks we're discussing here are those variables that could be avoided or minimized by better investment management strategies.

## Tax Risk

Nobody knows what future tax rates will be. Will the highest tax bracket ever surpass its previous peak of 94%? For four decades, that highest rate never dipped below 70%. Today, it's only around 40%.[387]

Depending on the tax treatment of your various sources of future funds, dramatic changes to federal, state, and local tax rates could impair your ability to achieve your goals.

## Inflation Risk

As that milk, bread, and peanut butter become more expensive, traditional assets may not get you as far as they used to.

## Healthcare Risk

The cost of healthcare in the United States has risen faster than the median annual income. Some prescription drugs are becoming prohibitively expensive. People are living longer. All of these factors have contributed to retirees' rising healthcare costs. According to Fidelity Investments' Retiree Health Care Cost Estimate,[388] the average 65-year-old couple retiring in 2020 could expect to spend $295,000 on all their health-related expenses throughout retirement.

Remember: this is an average. Some people end up having to spend way more than this on healthcare alone in retirement. And this figure excludes the very real risk of needing to fund a long-term care event …

Consider this:

- A 65-year-old today has about a 70% chance of requiring some type of long-term care (LTC) during their lifetime.
- On average, women need care longer than men (3.7 vs 2.2 years).
- Roughly 30% of 65-year-olds today will likely never need LTC support, but about 20% will likely require it for *more than 5 years*.[389]
- The estimated lifetime cost of care for a dementia patient is more than $350,000.[390]

---

387 https://fred.stlouisfed.org/series/IITTRHB.
388 https://www.fidelity.com/viewpoints/personal-finance/plan-for-rising-health-care-costs.
389 https://longtermcare.acl.gov/.
390 https://www.alz.org/alzheimers-dementia/facts-figures.

- The median annual cost for a private room in a nursing home is more than $100,000.[391]

## Longevity Risk

A lot of people don't realize how big of a concern this is until they near retirement. For example, on average, for a 65-year-old couple, at least one will live to age 93. Additionally, 25% of 65-year-old males will live to 93 and females to 95.[392] If your financial plan is only projecting out to age 90—as our good friend John's was in Myth 1 and as mainstream advice will often suggest— is that enough?

We are living longer now than generations before. For the most part, that's a good thing. But of course, if you run out of money, that would definitely put a damper on any retirement fun you were having.

## Public Policy Risk

As I've mentioned, it would be political suicide to try to reduce entitlement benefits from Social Security or Medicare. But it would also be naive to entirely depend upon them as a reliable source of income and support. As the government's obligations swell, there will be increasing pressure to fix this problem—they may reduce benefits or just decide to tax more of the benefit you end up receiving.[393]

As with all these risks: only time will tell what the reality will be for you.

# Risk-Filled Reality

Being exposed to all these variables throughout our financial planning lives is inevitable. By understanding them, we can take intentional steps to limit and diversify away our exposure to each as much as possible.

For most people, their largest account at retirement is their 401(k), followed by IRAs. As explored in our previous myth, that's where conventional wisdom

---

391 https://www.genworth.com/aging-and-you/finances/cost-of-care.html.

392 Based on Society of Actuaries RP-2014 Mortality Table projected with Mortality Improvement Scale MP-2017 as of 2018. https://www.ssa.gov/OACT/population/longevity. html.

393 Benefits are already taxed today. For example, if you're married filing jointly and reporting over $32,000 of income, you can be taxed on up to 50% of your benefit. If your taxable income is over $44,000 (single, $34,000), up to 85% can be taxed as ordinary income. https://www.ssa.gov/benefits/retirement/planner/taxes.html.

instructs you to put pretty much all your retirement savings. Yet these accounts leave you almost entirely exposed to all of these risks ...

## Back to John and Mary

Think back to John and Mary and the seven-figure sum they were planning to responsibly save starting in their 20s so that they could comfortably retire in their 60s. In addition to all the concerns presented in Myths 1–10, consider to how many obstacles the industry's stereotypical recommendations[394] leave them exposed.

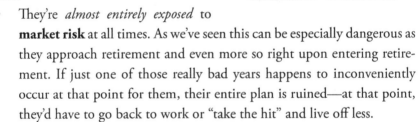

Let's see, following this mainstream advice...

- They're *almost entirely exposed* to **market risk** at all times. As we've seen this can be especially dangerous as they approach retirement and even more so right upon entering retirement. If just one of those really bad years happens to inconveniently occur at that point for them, their entire plan is ruined—at that point, they'd have to go back to work or "take the hit" and live off less.

- With most of their assets in their 401(k), they have significant **tax risk** given their exposure to the unpredictability of future rates. Just think about how much it would throw off their plans if all tax rates were up by 10% as they enter retirement.

- When you couple this risk with **healthcare risk**, the damage is amplified—as John and Mary spend more than their previous "normal" to cover their rising cost of health and long-term care needs, they're having to pull more than expected out of their 401(k). Since all those additional withdrawals are taxed as ordinary income at that point, it can easily push them into higher tax brackets.

- With four decades before they plan to retire, there are so many changes that could take place that might affect the treatment of assets within all these government-created vehicles. The only pension-type asset they plan to have is the government-controlled Social Security. And the main

---

394  Explored in Myth 13 along with some alternate suggestions.

help they're counting on to offset all those potential rising healthcare costs is government-funded Medicare. This leaves John and Mary very exposed to **public policy risk**.

- If all goes according to plan, they will have this big seven-figure lump sum at the time they plan to retire. So, that's good! But once they get to that point, what if John and Mary are extremely healthy and realize they have no idea how long they may live? It might occur to them that all their projections have been based on *average* life expectancies from decades prior.

So, as they start to spend down their nest egg, that concern—the concern of outliving their money, of **longevity risk**—would remain in the back of their minds. As their account balances dwindle, they'd likely stress and need to "pinch pennies" not knowing for how long they'll need it to last ...

Sounds stressful. I know. I've worked with enough people in these scenarios to know that **these stresses are a reality for most—*even when everything has gone as projected and planned!***

They may not have realized it in their 30s, 40s, or even 50s as they were diligently socking away savings to hit their goals. But once they were finally in retirement, the reality of those risks—those variables with devastating potential—is all around them.

- They have family members attempting to navigate the exorbitant costs of long-term care.
- More and more of their friends and associates are experiencing the increasing costs of their own healthcare.
- They start to pay more attention to how frequently changes in public policy that would adversely affect them are discussed by lawmakers.

You get the idea. Risks and variables are much harder to conceptualize the further you are away from them. That does not, however, make them any less real and dangerous. And there's no better time to start preparing for them than now.

## Self-Assessment

Think about your situation. Where are all your assets invested? To which of these risks are you or will you be exposed?

Think about your life in retirement. Try to mentally put yourself there as you consider each of these variables and how they would impact your quality of life. If you're just following the traditional advice, you'll end up doomed to the same risk exposure that John and Mary were. And that's if you're lucky—if all goes "as planned!"

# A Better Mindset

We got distracted and confused somewhere along the way. The goal was never to build up this large lump sum of money—this nest egg. The goal is to fund our dreams in a stress-free way. Part of that, for most, involves getting to a point where you can support the lifestyle you want without having to work. That sounds more like creating a lifelong income than a single lump sum. Perhaps that's where we should focus …

As we explore some potential better alternatives in the coming myths, to best help you, you'll need to shed this dream of building a large-enough nest egg. Or at least, you should make it secondary to the idea of creating income stability.

## Income Stability

You see, the real return reality is even more varied than discussed at the end of Myth 4, when we examined those charts reframing your market expectations.[395] That was assuming level contributions and withdrawals. Ours are often not, which makes future values even more unpredictable.

Income stability can bring predictability to your long-term plans. It's the idea of knowing where your next paycheck is coming from. Most people only think about that during their working years: how stable is your income and your ability to earn a paycheck? But, come retirement age, that's not what's talked about anymore. Now, it's all about the size of your nest egg …

People tend to associate income stability with working and since they don't plan to work in retirement, why would it concern them? But it is possible to

---

395 When we discussed Sequence of Returns Risk during periods of contributions and withdrawals.

create reliable income streams not tied to active work. This is the sort of income stability we should seek for our retirement.

When working with clients, for example, we'll illustrate their "probability of retirement success" just like most financial advisors (like the examples from T. Rowe Price at the end of Myth 9). But we're also evaluating how much of their projected monthly retirement needs and wants will be funded via ongoing income sources. When we first organize this information for a brand-new client, it's not uncommon for us to uncover an income stability score of 20%—that is, 20% of the monthly cash flow they want for their retirement is coming from relatively stable streams of income. They know from month to month that regardless of what the market does, this is a sum of money upon which they can more reliably depend.

Your goal as you plan and prepare for retirement should be to get this number up. It's impossible to quantify the psychological value of knowing you have a steady source of income to meet your bare essential needs. Consider the planning benefits as well. How much easier would it be for you to comfortably invest the rest of your money when you've built up that kind of "floor"? Think about how much less stress those other investments would now incite for you. Remember that emotional exercise we did in Myth 6—where you imagined your investment dollars rapidly shrinking. When did you break? When your account was down 30%? 50%? Never?

Regardless, think about how much less stressful a fall like that would be if via other investments (i.e., those not tied to the stock market[396]) you knew you already had an 80% income stability for life!

You could also afford to take more risks with some of your money. Most people aren't willing to do that (nor should they) when all of their investment dollars are tied to this magical nest egg figure that they can't be entirely sure will be enough to support them for however long they may end up living …

**Income stability brings flexibility and peace of mind.**

Honestly, there's no reason this figure even has to stop at 100%. Obviously, your goals are going to change as you begin to realize that level of predictability and stability for your long-term financial plans. But just imagine if in your 50s you were able to reach a 120% income stability score for the goals you set for

---

396 We'll explore several in Myth 15.

yourself when you started planning in your mid-30s. How much better would this feel than having a seven-figure investment account at retirement?

I know they would both feel pretty good, but be honest with yourself here.

- A seven-figure account tied to the market that you'll be pulling from to cover all your expenses for however long you end up living, or …
- Assets that are indefinitely providing you with a monthly income that is more than what you need.

When you consider all the concerns highlighted thus far throughout this book, and you honestly think about how you'd like to *feel* during retirement (as in, confident and not stressed about money), the second option wins by a landslide.

## Diversified Income Stability

Ideally, on the whole across all your accounts, you should be diversifying those stable income sources as much as possible. [397]

Consider the 20% income stability of our average brand-new client from earlier. That percentage is being generated by Social Security and nothing else. If this were the case for you—as it is with most—100% of your income stability would be subject to public policy risk. Put another way: a single change in public policy (one that would impact Social Security payouts in this case) could impact *all* of your lifetime income.

Ideally, instead, you should build out multiple sources of stable lifetime income to support your long-term dreams.

---

397 That can be difficult in some account types, like the 401(k), for example. Where IRAs can be "self-directed" and thus provide you with a lot of flexibility as to how the money within is invested, 401(k)s can be much more limiting.

**MYTH:** "You Need to Focus on Your 'Retirement Number.'"

**REALITY:** Making your "number" your primary focus, leaves you exposed to a plethora of risks and related stress. **A focus on building sources of stable lifetime income would serve you far better.**

# MYTH 15

---

## "The Stock Market Is the Only Meaningful Way for You to Invest"

> "Don't find fault, find a remedy; anybody can complain."
> **—Henry Ford**

## Disclaimer

The more I began to understand these problems, the more stress I felt. The issues were becoming blatantly obvious; the solutions, however, eluded me. I could captivate a colleague by helping them understand the validity behind the flaws with Modern Portfolio Theory. Yet, when that same colleague would ask how they could help their clients overcome these flaws and I had no solution ... understandably, they would leave in frustration.

> "Where ignorance is bliss, 'tis folly to be wise."
> **—Thomas Gray, Ode on a Distant Prospect of Eton College (1742)**

Naturally, this frustrated me as well. As the problems became clearer, it became increasingly difficult to serve my clients. After leaving the firm where I started my career, much of my time over the following years was consumed by trying to wrap my head around that elusive "better way"—digging for existing strategies, researching new ones, trying them out on my own accounts, stress testing them throughout various scenarios, and optimizing the ways they could all work together to best help people.

These days, although I have viable solutions through which I guide my clients, I hesitate to mention them here. Not because I'm worried about giving up trade secrets or anything like that, but rather because the plans we create for clients are custom to them and their unique situation. Meaning, the exact strategy you should pursue to best overcome these obvious flaws with the way everyone is telling you to invest will differ from your neighbor and your coworker. It should be unique to you.

So, the best you can do in that situation—now that you understand the problems—is seek to understand the potential alternative solutions *and* to understand yourself: your situation, your goals, your dreams, your opportunities. Then, you can begin to intelligently optimize and piece together your financial picture.

Or you could seek help, [398] which is the other side of my concern here …

You see, I share with you the strategies that I've been able to successfully implement with my clients. My hesitation comes from that fact that many of these strategies are difficult to implement on your own. [399] And some of them, impossible. If they were things people could do on their own, I would have created a different business model: one where I just educate people (as inexpensively as possible for them) on how to do it all. [400]

But, as frustrating as this will be for some readers, the reality is: there are some elements that require a professional's help. Obviously, the solutions I've found are the ones I implement for my clients—as I find new ones, or if I ever find better ones (I'll never stop searching), I'll implement those as well.

But despite those concerns, I know that if I just left you hanging—with a solid understanding of the problems but nothing to do about it … with no hope—I suspect you'd walk away frustrated, just as my colleagues used to. So, you'll see in this part that, where applicable, I do my best to provide you with enough information for you to understand how and why each of these strategies work. [401]

This book is not intended as a sales piece. Its primary purpose is to bring the information from these myths—especially Myths 1–10—into the mainstream dialogue. Professionals should not continue to brush it aside.

Now that you understand where I'm coming from, if reading these proposed solutions will take away from the significance of this book's message thus far, then you might want to stop here. Feel free to skip ahead to the conclusion. All that being said, I obviously don't want to just leave you hanging …

---

398 Myth 12.

399 Remember my warning from the introduction: these potential solutions are not as "easy" at the traditional buy-and-hold strategy.

400 To the extent that is possible, we do just that—that's why you've seen so many links to gain free access to our courses and other resources throughout this text. In fact, don't forget to check out all the companion resources we created for readers of this book at **SpicerCapital. com/Go.**

401 If you do end up needing help with the implementation of some of these strategies, you can use the knowledge and insights you gain from these last two myths to vet the professionals you plan to potentially solicit for help. As I stated in Myth 12, from my experience, most practitioners do not understand the issues. Understandably, then, even fewer know how to overcome them. So, be careful.

So, with that warning/disclaimer in mind, the following are some of the alternative ways we help people invest their hard-earned money outside of the stock market.[402]

## Start with Yourself

There are several ways you could invest to make this concept of income stability a reality. The challenge is that most of them will take time to understand and execute properly. To that end, the first place people should consider investing is in themselves.

### Your Career

This advice is more applicable to younger readers than those currently in or about to enter retirement.[403] If you have time on your side, you're lucky! Let's make the most of it.

This clichéd advice of investing in oneself is often not taken too seriously by the investing public. In actuality, there are times when no better investment could be made. And I'm not just talking about feeling good about making the most of your talents. I mean it can be the best investment from a long-term financial perspective.

Consider this: John's making $50,000 per year early on in his career. There's an industry certification that would dramatically increase his compensation, but it requires an investment of $10,000 and years of study to obtain.

---

402 Mine is not the only financial planning firm offering solutions. In fact, now that you understand the problems, perhaps you'll be able to uncover some solutions of your own that I fail to mention in this book—I'd love to hear about them!

403 If you fall into that latter category, the end of this chapter—about the "lazy man's" path to a stable lifetime income—and the next chapter—about market investment with better downside protection—will likely be the most relevant to you.

What if, instead of blindly plugging into the mainstream advice, John and Mary directed some of their savings here? By investing in John's credentials, they miss out on some of those coveted early years of compound interest growth within their qualified accounts—a big no-no according to conventional financial wisdom. But, after making that sacrifice, John's income leaps to $90,000 per year—a level of income he wouldn't have otherwise reached for more than 15 years. With his new skills, credentials, and income trajectory, he and Mary will now conservatively be able to realize more than 50% in additional earnings over his working life for the same amount of work.[404] No other investment could have provided them with as high—let alone, secure—of a return on investment.

WHERE SHOULD WE INVEST THIS $10,000?

Everyone's situation is different. There won't always be something like this available to you. But, if there is a way for you to increase your earnings potential within your chosen career path—even if it does require time and money—that may be your best long-term investment option.

## Your Financial Education

Most people would also be well-served by investing in their financial education. Understanding the best strategies to eliminate and manage your debt could save you tens of thousands over the long run. Knowing how to best navigate your cash flow each month could have a similar long-term result. There is so much free information available on these subjects that, for the most part, they simply require an investment of time.[405]

---

404  Roughly $6MM in lifetime income ($90,000 over 37 years with 3% raises) compared to roughly $3.8MM ($50,000 over 40 years with 3% raises).

405  These two examples—debt elimination planning and cash flow planning—are beyond the scope of this text. For those of you who are interested, **owners of this book receive free access to our comprehensive course exploring these subjects**. Find the details among the companion resources at https://SpicerCapital.com/Go.

> "The time it takes just to figure out your budget—which nobody does—the time it takes just to analyze your spending habits, you can get a better return, and you'll end up with more cash than trying to fight ... these guys who have hundreds of analysts working for them."
> **—Mark Cuban**

For some clients, getting their debt and cash flow under control results in hundreds and sometimes thousands of dollars being freed up each month. Clearly, prudently investing some of this money each month over the remainder of your working life can more than justify the time you'll have invested.

Time and money invested in helping you better understand how to capitalize on the money you have can produce some of the most enriching returns.

## Your Skills

When it comes to putting that money into various opportunities, you should always make sure each investment is one in which you have interest and actually understand. That last part is important. A lot of people get burned when they try to invest in something they don't understand, even when the idea itself has strong potential.

As we briefly touch on some of these specific income-producing investments over the coming pages, if any speak to you, make a note. If you're not very familiar with them, spend some time—maybe even some money—to understand them as well as you can. Don't dive in headfirst without truly knowing what you're doing. That is a recipe for disaster.

Most people will see the value of incorporating these strategies into their holistic financial plans but not want to invest the time it would take to fully understand them. Most people won't be motivated enough to deeply familiarize themselves with something unless they're truly interested in it. Or maybe, they're just not that interesting to you. That's okay; that's normal.

At that point, if you still want to find a way to work them into your overarching strategy, you may want to find someone you can trust to help—one of those vetted professionals from our checklist in Myth 12. As with many things in life, there is often a time/money tradeoff option ...

- You can mow your lawn, or you can pay the neighbor kid to mow for you.
- You can spend the time to figure out how to properly file your taxes, or you can pay a professional to file for you.
- You can invest your time to understand some or all of these strategies, or you could pay a firm to guide you.

## Stable Lifetime Income Strategies

This is not an exhaustive list of all the ways you could generate stable lifetime income for yourself. These are just the most common and some of the most advantageous. My goal here is not to teach you how to best implement each of these strategies—that would be impossible without first knowing more about you. Rather, my goal is to help you continue this evolution of the way you think about how you invest your hard-earned money.

In this section, we'll start with the easiest for one to learn and apply on their own and increase the difficulty from there.

### Dividend Stocks

Many large established companies pay regular dividends to their shareholders. That means, you just have to buy a share—becoming part owner in the company—and you're well on your way to a relatively-stable passive income.

Dividend stocks historically perform better than the rest of the market during crashes. As long as the company is healthy, and thus will be more likely to be able to continue paying their dividend, they are looked upon as a sort of safe haven. During crashes, investors view healthy dividends as additional downside protection. As such, you'll see a lot of scared growth-stock investors shift into these dividend payers. This helps the stock of these companies not fall quite as fast as the rest of the market.

These income-producing stocks also have an underlying value that tends to move with the rest of the market. By investing in healthy, dividend-paying companies, you're still able to capitalize on some market returns, while also protecting your portfolio a little from major downswings. And, even if there is some long and drawn-out crash in our future, you could still potentially have an income source from the dividends.

## Aristocrats and Kings

Look for the stocks of large companies[406] that have paid and increased their dividends without interruption for decades. These tend to be mature, established businesses which means their underlying stock price tends to be less volatile. In fact, these types of companies tend to be thought of as recession-proof, enjoying stable profits in both good times and bad.

A company that has raised its dividend consistently for the past 25 or more consecutive years is considered a dividend aristocrat. There are usually less than 100 at any given point in time. A dividend king is an S&P 500–listed company that has increased its dividend payout for more than 50 consecutive years.[407]

Of course, this status, as with anything, is no guarantee of future performance, but it can be a great place for a novice investor seeking stable lifetime income to begin. In general, when you're investing in individual stocks, you should understand the company's business model. It should be clear to you what they do and how they make money. Also, try to imagine it still being around and profitable 30 years from now (or whatever your long-term timeframe is). If you struggle to see how it might be able to compete and survive, you probably shouldn't invest.

> "The worst thing you can do is invest in companies you know nothing about. Unfortunately, buying stocks on ignorance is still a popular American pastime."
> **—Peter Lynch**

## Risks

You are investing in individual companies here. Sure, these tend to be well-established companies that have been very stable for a long time, but still … an investment in any company brings with it individual business risk. So, if this is a strategy you choose, you should definitely look to pick up a basket of them as opposed to just one or two. No matter how long the company has been around, that is still not a guarantee that it can't come crashing down.

---

406  Companies that are listed in the S&P 500.
407  In 2020, there were 64 dividend aristocrats listed among the S&P 500. There were only 29 dividend kings.

If you go into this strategy for the stable passive income that comes with many of these dividend aristocrats—in other words, you're not banking on an increase in the prices of their respective stocks (like a traditional stock investor)—then you'll probably be pretty happy with the results you'll realize here no matter what potential chaos may wreck the market as a whole.

## Real Estate

I purchased my first real estate investment house during my sophomore year of college. Although I was studying the stock market, I was attracted to real estate's promise of diversification and passive income. Since that day, I've continued to buy, rent, and sell real estate on the side, but my process has evolved. Here's a glimpse inside that process today ...

## Our Process

When my team and I are looking for real estate investment opportunities, either for ourselves or for a client, we're able to scour listings across the United States. We're looking for real estate markets with the ideal coupling of rental rates and home prices. Not all markets are the same and no one market will *always* be hot. When we find a market where home prices are below average but rental rates are above average, we know we'll be able to discover opportunities with the perfect variables to ensure our projects come out with a significant return on investment (ROI).[408]

With how connected the world is today, we're able to vet agents and property managers in that area to find a few with which we're comfortable. We work with them to find rental properties that will produce comfortably positive cash flows. That means that after the mortgage payment and conservatively projected expenses and vacancies are accounted for, there is still a comfortable surplus each month.

You should evaluate your market and know how to project a property's ROI before jumping in. And, if you're not interested in keeping up with potentially nagging tenants, you'll want to be sure you have access to quality property managers. Before we explore some of the major risks, consider these advantages of owning investment real estate ...

---

408 Honestly, I got lucky: I just so happened to start in one of those ideal real estate markets ...

## Passive Income

When done improperly—ongoing expenses too high, major repairs needed, high vacancy rates—rentals can be a massive drain on your finances. So, this isn't something to jump into lightly. Study real estate investing first to learn what you're looking for or find someone you can trust to help. Because when done right, real estate can give you the opportunity to have a steady stream of income flowing into your account each month. With good property managers and the right properties, that money could be flowing in with relatively little effort on your part.

## High ROI Potential

If you have access to good financing options, it's possible to realize some pretty incredible returns on your investment. I'm not talking about overleveraging yourself (taking on a dangerous amount of debt); I'm talking about using prudent negotiation and being patient. As a simple example: you could have the seller give you a check at closing for repairs. If that check is larger than the down payment that you owe to the bank, you can effectively realize an infinite ROI[409] since you'll be immediately recouping your entire initial investment. You could then tackle any needed repairs with the ongoing positive cash flows each month. Of course, that won't be a possibility for every good opportunity, but it is a possibility that is unique to real estate.

## Reduced Exposure to Market Risk

During the Great Recession, residential real estate prices fell alongside everything else. But that was a statistical anomaly. Usually, they're pretty uncorrelated. In 14 of the 15 previous US equity bear markets,[410] home prices rose. And, in that lone bear market prior to 2007 in which home prices did fall, they did so by just 0.4%.

So, owning residential real estate can not only provide you with rental income even during a market crash, but it can also insulate you from capital depreciation.

---

409 It wouldn't technically be infinite, in that you would have to have some money available to make that initial purchase, so although you might recoup it a day later when you deposit that check, there was some money utilized even if for an incredibly short period of time. The ROI would technically then just be extremely, extremely high ... ah, technicalities.

410 From 1956–2006.

## Inflation Protection

As the cost of your milk, bread, and peanut butter are increasing in the store, so are the prices of land. As Mark Twain observed, "buy land, they ain't making any more of it." Inflation risk can be difficult to invest away. As more money is printed by central banks, the risk of real inflation increases. Real estate offers you a way to hold an income-producing asset that should rise in price right alongside everything else.

## Appreciation

Which brings up another great advantage of owning positive-cash-flowing real estate: you still have this underlying asset that is increasing in value. For me, the appreciation aspect of real estate is far less exciting than the prospect of building up a larger and larger stable lifetime income. But it is absolutely there and extremely valuable! It's especially valuable when you consider the fact that your tenants are effectively paying your mortgage for you each month. This reduces the remaining principal you owe on the property. As in, when you finally decide to sell, not only should the property's value have increased, but the amount you owe back to the bank will have decreased—you're increasing your net worth from both sides of that deal!

When we're working with ambitious younger clients, they're often blown away by the return possibilities here. As a quick example, here's the simplified version of a strategy we often find ourselves explaining ...

- Many lenders are willing to offer conventional loans on a primary residence with a 5% (sometimes less) down payment as long as you live there for at least a year.
- On a $200,000 home, 5% would entail a $10,000 investment.[411]
- After your required year of living there you could purchase a new primary residence, securing similar lending terms.
- Now, you can rent out that first home in the way we've outlined above: with a comfortably positive cash flow each month—all considerations and research that should have been done before the initial purchase.

411  This is for illustrative purposes only. Obviously, there would be more involved in this calculation—closing costs, for example, not to mention your ongoing mortgage payments during that first year while you don't have a tenant paying the mortgage down for you, all of which should be considered as part of your investment into this property—but the overarching point being made here is still valid.

- As a result, you've created an income stream that with proper mainte-nance could be secured for life.
- You're also realizing an ongoing return on your initial investment, which will vary depending on the market in which you live.[412]

This is all great! If a young couple rinsed and repeated this strategy for a decade or so before finally settling down, they could easily be the proud owners of ten comfortably cash flowing rentals by their mid-30s.

But now, here's that delicious cherry on top. Let's stay with that first home. Consider the value of your equity in that home and how that compares to your initial investment. If in a given year, your property appreciated in value by 3%, what was your return on investment for that aspect of this deal?

The answer is not 3%. No, in fact, it's way more than that. Remember, your initial investment wasn't $200,000; it was $10,000. So, a 3% increase in the value of a $200,000 property—$6,000—actually comes out to a 60% return on your initial investment in a single year.[413]

Bottom line here: even though I view appreciation as a secondary return consideration when I make my own real estate investment decisions, it can definitely add significant long-term value.

## Control

Investors in real estate also have more control over their assets. With a stock, you have to worry about management and a number of other factors that are very disconnected from your world. With real estate, you're the one making the decisions; you're the CEO.

There are more advantages, but I'm sure you can already see why building out a cash-flowing real estate portfolio would help you mitigate the risks to which Modern Portfolio Theory and mainstream investment wisdom leaves you exposed.

---

412 This strategy isn't advisable in every city—it won't work as well in real estate markets where home prices are high but rents are relatively low.

413 And this didn't include the fact that the mortgage payments you're making each month—which, after Year 1, are being funded by your tenants—are reducing the amount you owe the bank for that mortgage. That increases your equity by even more, which in turn of course increases your ROI by even more. But you get the point!

> "Let every man divide his money into three parts, and invest a third in land, a third in business, and a third let him keep in reserve."
> **—Talmud**

## Risks

Investing in real estate brings with it its own set of variables and risks. No matter how careful you are, unpredictable things can and will happen. I've had a house ruined by flood.[414] I've had tenants move out without telling me but not after opening "their" home to squatters who proceeded to punch holes in walls and let their dogs use one of the bedrooms as a toilet. ...[415] Bad things can happen even if you're taking all the right precautions.

If you only want to own one rental, I'd probably caution against it or at least make very clear your risk. At that point, the lifetime income you're building with it is less "stable." It'd be like owning a single stock. Even if the company is really good, that's still not the best strategy. Bad and unpredictable things can and do happen.

But, if you do your due diligence and work up to a half a dozen or more, when that inevitable "something bad" does happen to one of them, you can still come out ahead.

## Property Manager

And, if you are investing out of town or you just don't want to be responsible for the day-to-day of managing a rental, you need a good property manager. They can make all the difference in the world. Make sure the real estate markets in which you're investing have several to choose from and don't shortcut your due diligence here either.

After my first property manager moved away, I was living in a different state and desperate to fill the role. I went with the first recommendation I received. About a year later, he fallaciously claimed to have fallen off the roof of one of my properties and proceeded to sued me. As the case dragged out over the following three years, more and more issues surfaced. Turns out, he had been stealing

---

414 Insurance more than covered that one, so we actually came out way ahead ...
415 That one was bad. Very upsetting!

money from my tenants and from me. I set myself back a few years due to that mistake. Do not underestimate the importance of due diligence when dealing with real estate.

### Peace of Mind

All in all, having a solid real estate portfolio can give you peace of mind. Aside from boosting my stable lifetime income, it offers me even greater protection and flexibility without sacrificing growth, no matter what happens in the stock market.

But I have to admit: I did get lucky. I just so happened to start in one of those markets where the unique combination of low home prices relative to high rental rates allowed for incredible ROIs. At first, I thought this was all just super easy. I wondered why others in my new city weren't getting the same returns on their properties as I was back in my hometown. That's when I realized how fortunate I had been. And even my hometown market has changed since that time. This was the impetus for helping our financial planning clients—no matter where they're from—find the best opportunities. And, with a little know-how and some intentionality, you too can benefit from all that an investment real estate portfolio has to offer.

## Monetize Your Passion and Expertise

This category of stable lifetime income strategies definitely won't be for everyone. It tends to appeal more to a younger generation, more comfortable and familiar with the social media world in which we live. Although, I do believe older generations, often armed with greater wisdom, could benefit from them just as much.

There is no shortage of so-called passive income strategies out there. I'm not a fan of anything gimmicky or salesy. What I help clients consider—what I'd encourage you to consider—is ...

- Do you have some unique value to share with the world?
- Is there something that you're known for among those closest to you?
- Everyone who knows you seeks your advice when they have questions about ... what?

Whatever that thing is: if you're passionate about it—you just enjoy talking and sharing on the subject in general—you can profit from that passion and expertise. If you know what you're doing, you can use it to create a stable passive income.

Now, this would be a long-term play. These strategies take people a very long time to monetize and many are unsuccessful at that. This is why it's so vitally important to do something you enjoy. That way, whether you're able to profit from it long term or not, you still feel good about what you're doing.

Getting started could be as easy as just sharing that general knowledge with the world. You could do that via a blog, a podcast, YouTube, or any other social media platform. As your expertise is recognized, you'll gain loyal followers. That may take time, but as long as you're talking about something you love and are independently knowledgeable about anyway … that's okay, right? As you gain true fans—superfans, as passive income expert Pat Flynn[416] calls them—you'll have the opportunity to turn your passion and valuable insights into a passive income stream.

The internet and social media have made it possible for us to put ourselves out there into the world and get connected with those who are actually sincerely interested in and will *benefit* from your passion and expertise.

As your influence grows:

- You could offer a little bit more of your time through a paid membership. Your best fans would love to see you more, and many would be happy to pay that fee as a way of giving back.
- You could run advertisements.
- You could have paid sponsors.
- You could see if your favorite products or services offer a residual-paying affiliate program just for sharing them with your fans.
- You could put that unique value of yours into an online course, ebook, or other digital resource that even those who discover your content for years to come might be interested in purchasing.

---

416 Founder of Smart Passive Income and a great resource if the idea of generating passive income in this way is something about which you want to learn more.

Again, this isn't a strategy that will appeal to everyone. My wife, for example, is an expert in a lot of things[417]—people seek her out for her wisdom—but she has zero interest in putting herself on the interwebs …

There are others out there, however, for whom this is the perfect strategy for them to supplement their stable lifetime income.

## Business

When I have a client who is interested in starting or growing a business, I am thrilled at the prospect. Not only because I love helping and watching a business grow, but because I know what a successful business can do for your holistic financial plan.

### Risks

There are *so many* risks involved with trying to start a business. *So many fail.* So many people lose so much money in their attempts. So, it's definitely not something that should be taken lightly. It is not a strategy I would *push* on anyone. As such, we won't spend too much time on the subject.

### The Big Play

That being said, we love the opportunity to work with someone who has an incredible idea, passion, motivation, drive … you know, all the things one needs to be successful here. It can be even more exciting to help our clients through the growth stage of their businesses. A successful business can be a boon to one's financial plan unlike anything else.

Think about it: if you're able to grow a truly profitable business, you can effectively create your own pension plan! That's exciting.

## Self-Directed IRAs

The government will even allow you to implement some of these strategies inside your IRAs. Did you know that? By getting your Roth or traditional IRA qualified as a "self-directed IRA," you gain much more freedom as to where the funds are ultimately invested. That means, you can invest in a business or some real estate all inside a tax-advantaged account! Pretty cool, right?

---

417 She really is brilliant—an industrial engineer and mathematician who I'm lucky enough to have actually want to homeschool our children!

Go back to that list of risks to which people following the traditional invest-ment paradigm are exposed. Think about how many of those you could diversify away by incorporating a smart real estate portfolio and/or passive income busi-ness strategy inside your self-directed Roth IRA.[418]

## Don't Over Diversify

Just because I mentioned something here that doesn't mean you need to do it. A strategy can be an ideal solution for one person and a potential disaster for another. There is no magic pill that will work perfectly for everyone. **You should invest in what you know ... and you should know in what you invest!**

> "Know your circle of competence, and stick within it. The size of that circle is not very important; knowing its boundaries, however, is vital."
> **—Warren Buffett**

As mentioned in the beginning of this section, time—and yes, even money—spent on expanding your circle of competence may be your absolute best invest-ment option at some points in your life.

## Redefining the Game

You can use all, some, one, or even a different strategy along these same lines to create a stable lifetime income for yourself. You can redefine the "retirement savings game" you're now playing. While everyone else is keeping score based on how large they're able to get their nest egg, you're focused on what really matters: how high you can build your stable lifetime income.

Once you get it above the cost of your necessities each month—that's a big deal—throw a party![419]

And then, once it surpasses what you'll need each month to be able to do whatever you want, well ... you might as well start doing that now! Start doing what you want. Start checking off those bucket list items. Is this retirement?

---

418  I know there wasn't actually a question here, but ... the answer is: almost all of them (except maybe healthcare and long-term care risks, which would be better mitigated via insurance).
419  For real! It's a big accomplishment—your life will never be the same! I hope you tell me all about it. I might even send a celebratory gift your way!

## The Lazy Man's Way

All these strategies take time. Some (probably now frustrated) readers don't have the luxury of time. Others, even after implementing some of these strategies, will still have a monthly income gap they'd prefer to fill. Other readers still will have absolutely no interest at all in dedicating any amount of time to any of the above strategies.[420]

Maybe upon reaching your target retirement age, you find yourself sitting on a few million in savings, a little stressed about how real longevity risk now is to you, and not sure the best way to proceed. Well, lucky for you, like paying the neighbor boy to mow your lawn, there is a pay-your-way-out option for this as well.

Enter: the annuity.

## Annuities

Annuities get a bad rap, and I totally get it. In fact, I don't disagree. Their reputation has been tarnished over the last several decades by slimy salesmen pushing high-commission products taking advantage of innocent boomers ...

### The Good

An annuity is designed with the express purpose of providing you with a guaranteed monthly income for life. It's effectively an insurance policy designed to protect you from longevity risk. It can be like your very own pension plan.

Especially if you're healthy, the idea of securing a lifelong income stream becomes all the more valuable to your financial health and overall stress levels. When you have reason to believe that you might live longer than those averages explored in our last myth, the potential benefit for you relative to the cost is even greater.

### The Bad

Annuities do cost money; the fees don't have to be ridiculous though. In fact, today there are even commission-free annuities. That doesn't mean they are without cost. Obviously, to provide those sorts of guarantees—similar to every other type of insurance—a company would need to pool money from all participants in order to continue paying benefits to those who do indeed end up living lon-

---

420 Perhaps just reading that previous section stressed you out ...

ger than average. But "commission-free" does mean you wouldn't have to worry about prospective commissions influencing the solution being recommended.

At the same time, this doesn't necessarily mean that every annuity that does charge a commission is bad. As with everything here, it's important to understand all the associated costs and compare those to the value being added to your life.

Freaking out about a reasonable fee associated with an annuity is like stressing over the $50 you paid that neighbor kid to cut your grass. Sure, if you hadn't paid him to mow the lawn, you'd be $50 richer. But then … either you have to invest your own time into mowing your yard or it just keeps growing until the city gives you a citation!

### The Ugly

That being said, annuities are complex financial vehicles. They are difficult even for some professionals to understand.[421] Some unsavory salespeople like to capitalize on their complexity to rake in massive commissions often at the expense of the elderly.

Become familiar with the cumulative cost before making your decision. Yes, obviously the ability to turn a part of your ugly lump sum of money into a beautiful stream of guaranteed income for life should cost something. It's on you to determine exactly how much that is worth to you and to do your due diligence to ensure you're not getting taken advantage of. This is yet another example of where it would be nice to know that your planner understands all your options and is not incentivized by anything other than your best interests.[422]

The takeaway: know that there is a way to pay for the comfort that comes with a guaranteed lifetime stream of income without having to put in all the work and time involved with the strategies from the last several pages. But, as with almost everything in the complex world of finance, without proper due diligence, you could lose a lot …

---

421 My goal here once again is to introduce you to the concept; I want you to know that this is an option. To provide you with all the information you'd need to make an educated decision as to: 1) which of the many ways of structuring an annuity will make the most sense for you, 2) which of the many providers have the best track records, and 3) when it would make the most sense for you to open one, if at all … would require chapters of additional information. To that end, **owners of this book can gain free access to our course** designed to guide those of you who are interested in considering this route. You'll find all the information among the companion resources at **SpicerCapital.com/Go**.

422 As explored in Myth 12.

## Social Security

While we're on the topic of annuity payments, we should touch on the government's annuity: Social Security. Optimizing one's Social Security payments is not as easy as it would seem on the surface. There are hundreds of different Social Security filing strategies you'd need to test in order to identify the optimal benefit for your unique retirement needs and goals.

On the surface, as most financial advisors will tell you, waiting appears to make the most sense. In today's environment, for example, payments taken at age 70 will be 32% higher than if you began just a few years earlier.

But the reality of what might make the most sense for you is more complicated.

- From an investment perspective, if you have a sound strategy in which you're confident, then you may be better off over the long run taking and then investing those payments as soon as possible.

- From a tax perspective, taking earlier distributions will increase your taxable income during those years and interfere with any income distribution plans designed to minimize the taxes you pay throughout your retirement.[423]

- From a longevity perspective, if you're in poor health, then yeah, it would probably make the most sense for you to just take the money as soon as you can. The inverse of that, for those in good health, may also be true.

- Or, if you're skeptical about Uncle Sam with his massive and rapidly rising debt load being able to flawlessly keep all his promises ... then sure, I understand you wanting to take that money while you know you can!

## Reverse Mortgage

Another dirty term in the world of finance; I know. So many people have been taken advantage of. And you know what: this would never be my first choice. But this is kind of "the lazy man with very little savings" way to gain income stability. If ...

---

423 Everyone's a little different as to when applying for benefits would make the most sense. This is another one of those planning elements through which a good financial professional should be able to guide you. For some, these considerations can make **a six—often even seven—figure difference** in the amount of money you have available to you throughout your retirement. If you're recently in or approaching retirement, **see how much of a difference these decisions could make for you here: SpicerCapital.com/Retirement.**

- You didn't invest the time and energy into building out enough stable lifetime income.
- You don't have enough in savings to make an annuity work for you.
- You're concerned about the potential of outliving your income.
- And you own your home.

… this could be the best option you have. Retirees with few other income sources may find a reverse mortgage to be a helpful source of money. Like a home equity loan or line of credit, a reverse mortgage allows you to tap into the equity you've built up in your home.

But, similar to annuities, they can come wrapped in a lot of fees. Be sure you understand whether you're getting a lump sum, a line of credit, or a lifetime income. Get familiar with the true cost of all the fees[424] and see if it's worth it for you.

**MYTH:** "The Stock Market Is the Only Meaningly Way for You to Invest."

**REALITY: It is one of several viable options.** Most people would greatly benefit from taking the time to learn and understand some others that appeal to them.

---

424  Although reverse mortgages are now federally regulated, it's a good idea to apply with several companies to compare rates and fees.

# MYTH 16

---

## "The Stock Market Is Too Risky and Should Be Avoided"

## Alternative Investing

Professional money managers in charge of large endowments and pensions have long known the importance of finding ways to diversify beyond just stocks and bonds. For example, if you had invested $1,000,000 in a 60/40 stock/bond portfolio at the beginning of 1997, it would have been worth $3,756,000 at the end of 2016. If you had been able to invest that money in Princeton's endowment, it would have been worth $10,078,000—**168% more!**

The biggest difference? Princeton has over 70% of their portfolio allocated to alternative investments. The term "alternative investment" (or just "alts") is generally used to refer to any asset that is not one of the conventional investment types, such as stocks, bonds, or cash. That could be real estate (as discussed in the previous myth), private equity, hedge funds, commodities ... the list goes on. University endowments make up some of the largest pools of invested assets, and since they have to publicly disclose their returns and allocations, they provide us with some amazing insights.

Four of the five largest endowment funds have embraced an alternative investment strategy. Over the past couple of decades, each shifted their portfolio from an allocation very close to the traditional 60/40 paradigm to an alternative focus.

Those four university endowments are:
- Harvard ($32.7B)
- Yale ($23.9B)
- Stanford ($21.4B)
- Princeton ($20.7B)


The performance of these portfolios over the long run has been nothing less than impressive. Over the last 20 years, Harvard averaged a 10.4% return; Yale, 12.6%; Stanford, 10.7%, and Princeton, 12.3%. It's worth noting that these endowment returns are *after* accounting for the endowment managers' hefty fees.

Over that same period, the S&P 500 Index averaged 7.7% per annum, while the Barclay's Bond Index averaged 5.3%. These are the indices most often used to benchmark that traditional stock-and-bond portfolio recommended to the retail investor. Thus, the traditional 60/40 portfolio had an annualized 6.8% return over this same 20-year period (*and that's without accounting for any fees*).

**Figure 23**

University Endowment Investment Performance

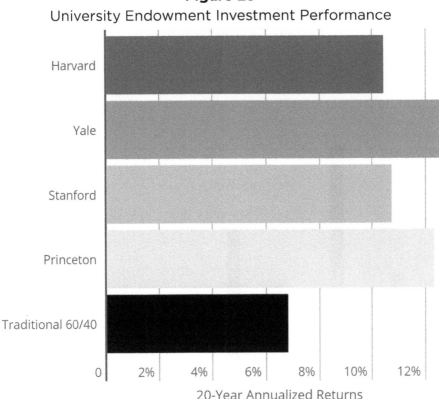

20-Year Annualized Returns

It's no coincidence that each of the endowments embracing alternative investments substantially outperformed the traditional portfolio benchmark. Consider their asset allocation and how it differs from the traditional stock/bond split advisors recommend. These endowments' outsized allotment to alternative investments have clearly contributed to their long-term outperformance.

## Figure 24
### University Endowment Asset Allocation—
### Where Do the Best Invest?

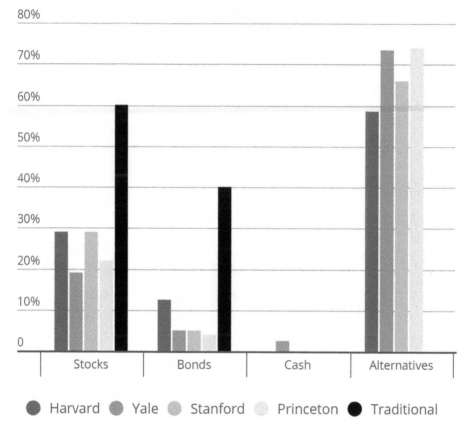

● Harvard ● Yale ● Stanford ● Princeton ● Traditional

These four universities are not alone. Here are the average allocations to alternatives for different types of investors.

- The average pension fund invests 30% of its portfolio in alts. [425]
- The average endowment invests 52% of its portfolio in alts. [426]
- The average individual invests only 5% of her portfolio in alts. [427]

---

425 Willis Towers Watson, "Global Pension Assets Study," 2019.
426 National Association of College and University Business Officers, "TIAA Study of Endowments," 2018.
427 Money Management Institute, "Retail Distribution of Alternative Investments," 2017. Averages provided are dollar weighted.

Alternatives, as an investment category, tend to be thought of as only being accessible to high-net-worth individuals—there absolutely are some that are

exclusively available to those who can claim the so-called accredited investor[428] status. But the concepts employed by these successful endowments do not have to be exclusive to the ultra-wealthy. The main idea behind alternatives is finding good investments that are uncorrelated with stocks and bonds. You can accomplish this same thing by investing in some of the strategies explored in our previous myth.

There are also ways to achieve that endowment style—high return, low correlation—diversification using the stock market …

## What about Stocks?

After Myth 15, you now know some of the best and most popular ways to design your stable lifetime income. Focusing there as opposed to stressing about stocks your entire life will make that life so much more enjoyable.

Does that mean we should ignore the stock market all together?

No, absolutely not! Stocks are not inherently bad. I love the stock market. I still think it's one of the best places to invest—just not with all of your money—and *definitely* not according to Modern Portfolio Theory. If you want to be confident in your stock market investments, you need to focus on downside protection. That being said, I still actively seek strategies that will allow me and my clients to benefit from the significant upside potential the market brings while limiting that inevitable downside as much as possible.

With stocks, as with any investment, you're much more likely to find lasting success when you understand why you're invested the way that you are. As with all the lifetime income strategies, if you're sincerely interested in putting in the time and research it will take to get to that point … then sure, personally build-

---

428  In the United States, the SEC defines an **accredited investor** as a person worth more than $1MM or who is consistently earning more than $200,000 ($300,000 for joint income) per year. Some investments require this status before you're allowed to take part.

ing and keeping up with a stock portfolio can be a valuable part of your overarching investment plan.[429] But that's not how most investors do it.

Just think about how people are with their 401(k) investments, for example. They select some funds—often arbitrarily—from an already limited list. They almost never have any idea what underlying stocks the funds actually hold. As in, most people have no clue in what they're actually invested ... That's madness! It's so disconnected. That's not investing. When you want to profitably invest in something, you buy things that for one reason or another you *expect* to go up in value.

By not understanding where your money is ultimately invested, are you really investing? Do you have any reason to believe that "investment" should go up in value ... other than the fact that everyone tells you it should?

That all certainly sounds more like gambling ... just "hoping for a desired result."

So, how can you avoid gambling in the stock market? And how can you use the stock market to intelligently diversify your overarching portfolio similar to those aforementioned endowments?

## Value Investing

Value investing is the idea of only betting on stocks that you've determined to be currently trading for less than their true, or intrinsic, value. Value investors believe that the market tends to overreact to news and other inconsequential information, causing some stock prices to not correspond with a company's underlying fundamentals.[430]

Warren Buffett is likely the best-known value investor of our time, but there are many others. I'm a big fan of Peter Lynch (from Myth 5) and Joel Greenblatt[431]—both very successful value investors. These investors will study companies inside and out. They'll review their financial statements. They'll evaluate the effectiveness of management. They'll compare prospects to industry competitors. After gleaning as much as they can from all that publicly available information,

---

429 Note: even when you understand them well, they should still just be a part—not the whole.

430 Investopedia defines **fundamentals** as, "the basic qualitative and quantitative information that contributes to the financial or economic well-being of a company, security, or currency, and their subsequent financial valuation."

431 If you're truly interested in learning to become a value investor, check out Lynch's book One Up on Wall Street and Greenblatt's book You Can Be a Stock Market Genius.

they're able to determine what they believe the company should be worth. If that perceived fair value is far enough above the stock's current price in the market—that is to say, there is a large enough "margin of safety" to make the bet—they may buy shares in that company.

When your research is sound and you always invest with a large enough margin of safety, you will inherently be building some downside protection into your own portfolio: as the market falls, your already undervalued stocks should fall by less.

Now remember: just because you find a company that you like or that has a good story, that doesn't make it a good investment! For example, just because you see an infomercial for a really nice blender, that doesn't mean it'll make a good investment for you. You need more information. You have to determine what you think that blender is actually worth *and compare that to its asking price.* If you can buy the blender for less than what you believe it's worth (the value it'll bring to your life, in this metaphor), then absolutely go for it! Only then can you know that it's a good investment.

This is a common problem among the YouTube investment gurus of our era. They find a stock they love for what are often very legitimate reasons. But they fail to figure out what those things they love about the company are actually worth. Without that information, true value investing is impossible. You're investing blind—be careful!

Also, an undervalued stock is not the only thing for which successful value investors are looking. The best investors seek a catalyst as well. Just because a company may be undervalued, that does not mean its value *will* go up at any point in the near future. The market too would have to recognize that fact after you've taken your position. Is there anything coming up that makes you believe the market might finally acknowledge this reality you've discovered? Remember, there is some reason it's priced the way it is today. You need to figure out why that is. Without a catalyst, it might take a decade before the market wakes up to the fair value you're seeing in a particular company!

There are a lot of smart people who control a lot of money in the stock market. They have teams of analysts working for them scouring financial statements looking for these same things you are. **It is possible to do this successfully, but it is definitely not easy to out sleuth them …**

To be effective long term here, you really should be doing it full-time. Warren Buffett makes value investing look easy. It is not. Think about the amount of time he spends dedicated to his craft. For example, he spends five to six hours every day reading five different newspapers and 500 or more pages of financial statements and corporate reports. Are you interested in that level of dedication that it's taken for Buffett to be successful? Very few people are.

> ### "I just sit in my office and read all day."
> **—Warren Buffett**

For many who are inspired by Buffett himself, their venture into "value investing" quickly becomes just hoping and praying. So, for the average investor, not interested in constantly reading corporate financial statements, a methodical approach could prove more appealing ...

## Technical Investing

Investopedia defines technical analysis as "a trading discipline employed to evaluate investments and identify trading opportunities by analyzing statistical trends gathered from trading activity, such as price movement and volume."

Technical analysis is often thought of as the antithesis of fundamental analysis, as flying in the face of value investing. But I believe they both have merit. And a familiarity with both can benefit anyone who wants to participate in the stock market.

Those who invest based on technicals study the movements of a stock's or the entire market's price. They're watching how quickly and by how much the prices are moving up or down. They're taking note of the volume behind those price changes—i.e., the number of investors involved causing those movements. They believe this provides a more revealing window into investor psychology than anything else. They study this same information from historical charts, identifying historically based probabilities of certain movements given various criteria. As in, when prices are moving in a certain way over a certain period of time, history suggests that the investing masses are more likely to push that price even further in one direction than the other.

In short, the technical school of thought holds that prices tend to move in trends and that history tends to repeat itself.

One of the most successful track records of a disciplined technical trader is a man by the name of Ed Seykota.[432] After his interview in *Market Wizards*, Jack Schwager observed that his "achievements must certainly rank him as one of the best traders of our time." From 1990 through 2000, Seykota averaged returns of nearly 60% per year net of fees![433] No one has a better public track record than he does—not even Warren Buffett.[434]

Seykota found a system based on historical technical indicators that worked for him. He's not the only one. If you begin to explore this side of the market, you'll discover that there are actually numerous successful investors who primarily adhere to technically driven strategies. The mainstream financial media (CNBC, Bloomberg) doesn't like to give credence to or even talk about these strategies and their adherents. Perhaps then viewers might conclude that the "news" they share is now just a waste of time …?

So, how could we use technical strategies to provide downside protection so as to promote greater growth long term?

What if you knew that for the last hundred plus years, when the price of the stock market moved in a certain precise pattern, that 70% of the time, the market fell by 20% or more before going back up? Would you want your money to "sit on the sidelines" for a bit before getting back in the market? If seven times out of ten that would save you from a 20% or greater loss—even if you did miss out on some upside during those three times it proceeded upward—mathematically, you would still come out way ahead. So, what do you think? Wouldn't you rather temporarily remove your exposure to the asset that has a historically based 70% probability of declining by at least 20% in the very near future? Most people would, especially when they understand exactly when they should get back into the market by studying similar technically based data.

Of course, as we know, history is not a perfect indicator of exactly what will happen in the future. Those percentages very well may change over time. But in this example scenario we're not talking about making a bet based on

---

432  His career is explored in detail in Trend Following by Michael Covel.
433  Daniel P. Collins, Long-Term Technical Trend-Following Method for Managed Futures Programs. Futures, Vol 30, No. 14, November 2001.
      If you're interested in learning more from Ed … you're going to want to check out this gem: https://youtu.be/LiE1VgWdcQM. You're welcome!
434  To be fair, Buffett is managing way more money than Seykota ever tried to. The more money you're investing, the more difficult it is to realize higher returns.

this probability data. On the contrary, we're talking about taking money off the table—de-risking ourselves because the data are so greatly stacked against us. For the most part, for myself and my clients, we use this data to inform our decisions to take money out of the market when there are higher historical probabilities that prices will fall.

This means that even if we end up being wrong much of the time and on the sidelines missing a percentage point or two of growth each year, when those big crashes do come—as they always do—we stand to lose way less than the market. If you remember the math from Myth 1 demonstrating how much more important it is to avoid losses, you know how significant this could be for your long-term returns ... not to mention your nerves! Imagine being on the sidelines during the Dotcom crash in 2000 or the entire terrible investing year that was 2008. **Over your investing life, reducing the impact on your portfolio of the market's drawdowns would result in** *substantially* **greater returns.**

Opponents of strategies like this will say, "But you risk missing the absolute best days in the market." After all, "Time in the market, not timing the market" is the Modern Portfolio Theory practitioners' mantra. To push their buy-and-hold agenda, advisors like to point to those statistics that say, "If you miss the best 25 days of the market since 1970, your return would have dropped from 6.7% a year to a measly 3.4%." [435]

While using those technical indicators, sure, sometimes you may end up missing some of the best days in the market. That is absolutely a possibility. You could even call it a "risk" of these technical strategies. But you tell me, knowing what you know now from Myth 1, what's more important for your long-term returns: being in the market for a 50% gain or being out of the market during a 50% crash?

The problem with this manipulative observation about missing the best days is that it's only one side of the story. If you were to just miss the 25 worst days, for example, your return over that same period would have jumped from that 6.7% average to almost 11%.

Or, what if you were only able to miss both the 25 best and the 25 worst days over that same time period? Ideally, a technical investing strategy like this that is

435 Batnick, M. How missing out on 25 days in the stock market over 45 years costs you dearly. MarketWatch. February 17, 2016. https://www.marketwatch.com/story/how-missing-out-on-25-days-in-the-stock-market-over-45-years-costs-you-dearly-2016-01-25.

worth pursuing should be able to perform better than that, but even then, your average annual return would go up from 6.7% to 7.5%—all while having your investment portfolio out of the market during its most chaotic times. This is a more realistic, conservative goal for one of these technical strategies …

1. Long-term outperformance even when compared to that traditional buy-and-hold.
2. To be on the sidelines during many of those chaotic periods when the market is in a freefall.

As explored in Myths 5–8, it's because Modern Portfolio Theory doesn't offer downside protection like this that practitioners consistently underperform even that 6.7% average mentioned in this example. When done right, these technical strategies can be a way for you to overcome that significant flaw in mainstream dogma.

## Artificial Intelligence

Technical investing strategies can work. Yes. And they can be learned. Sure. There is no shortage of YouTube wizards trying to guide you through it all and get you plugged into their technical indication services … for a monthly fee.

But honestly, of all the strategies we've talked about in this book, why would you try to learn this one?

Consider the evolution of artificial intelligence (AI):

- **1994**: Chinook, developed by the University of Alberta, becomes the **checkers** world champion.
- **1997**: IBM's Deep Blue was able to beat the reigning world **chess** champion Garry Kasparov.
- **2011**: IBM's Watson beat **Jeopardy!** champions Ken Jennings and Brad Rutter.
- **2016**: Google's AlphaGo AI was able to beat **Go** champion Lee Sedol. For those unfamiliar with the game, Go has more possible moves than there are atoms in the universe, making it extremely difficult to compute and "outthink" a human.

The study of technical analysis will have you watching charts and measuring various variables in an effort to identify any one of a number of patterns in the way the data present. With how capable computers are today, do you really hope to be able to notice these indicative patterns before they can? Not to mention how the sheer volume of data points and speed at which computers can analyze everything would make an individual's efforts seem entirely futile.

This is why trading floors at large brokerage houses are becoming a thing of the past. Where they used to employ hundreds of traders studying the markets, looking for technical opportunities, they now have computers. Turns out, computers are less expensive and way better at their job—both in speed and accuracy.

Regarding what all this means for the future of the investing industry in general, consider this excerpt from an article by Larry Cao, CFA in the *Enterprising Investor.*[436]

> Given AI's superior brain power and lack of emotions ... the market will eventually be dominated by a small number of AI programs, maybe even a single one. Case in point: The Man Group, a hedge fund, had an AI program manage a small portion of the assets in one of its largest funds. By 2015, the AI accounted for roughly half the profits.
>
> AI also has support in academic circles. Campbell R. Harvey of Duke University believes AI will assume a major role in investment decision making and that the proliferation of AI and big data will result in '15 to 25 investment management superpowers that can harvest all the data.'
>
> So the big question is when—not if—AI will supplant human investment managers.

Hedge funds and other institutional investors appear to have been making this transition over the last decade. As has always been the case throughout history, as profitable shifts happen in the investment industry, the retail trader (that's you!) is always the last to the party. Everyday investors are gradually starting to have access to strategies like these via professional money managers who offer their services through RIA firms.[437]

---

436 Cao, L. Portfolio Managers, Artificial Intelligence Is Coming for Your Jobs. CFA Institute. March 9, 2018. https://blogs.cfainstitute.org/investor/2018/03/09/portfolio-managers-artificial-intelligence-is-coming-for-your-jobs/.
437 As of this writing, I have yet to find a reliable way for individuals to do this on their own (these money managers tend to only work through RIAs), but if I ever do, I'll let you know!

## Rules-Based Investing

Another way some tactical investors attempt to capitalize on a stock's or a market's momentum[438] is through a strategy known as rules-based investing. These disciplined investors will follow self-imposed investment "rules" to remove emotion from their investing process in order to optimize their portfolios. The basic idea is …

- First, select a universe in which to invest (only S&P 500 stocks, for example).
- Then, create criteria by which you'll select your stocks (i.e., the stocks with the lowest price-to-earnings ratios).
- Finally, determine how often you'll reassess and update your holdings (weekly, monthly, annually, etc.).

When my team and I are doing this, we research how various combinations of criteria would have performed in the past. When we discover one that would have realized significantly higher returns with much less risk than the market, we study it further. Of course, as discussed at length in Myth 10, past performance does not guarantee future results. But, when done right, strategies like this can provide you with a systematic way to detect and capitalize on an investment's trend—providing you with rules to help you know when to get in and out. So, when our team can identify a logical reason for the same pattern to continue into the future, we might add it to our investment repertoire as one of a diversified set of similar models that we employ.

Here's a simple example:

- You only consider the **30 stocks of the Dow Jones Industrial Average**.
- You invest equally across the **top ten** stocks when sorted by **free cash flow yield**.[439]
- You review your holdings at the same time **every quarter** and only sell your positions if they've fallen out of the top 20. When that happens, you buy the next stock in line according to that sorted list.

---

438 Read: trend.
439 **Free cash flow** yield is one of many fundamental indicators used to help investors determine the relative value of a company. It can be calculated by dividing a company's free cash flow by its enterprise value.

If you had followed these rules over the last 20 years, you would have realized an annualized return of more than **12%**,[440] compared to the S&P 500's less than 8%.

Here's another, more complex, example:

- You only consider companies in the **S&P 1500** that do not violate certain so-called faith-based principles (such as being involved with tobacco, pornography, gambling, etc.).
- You invest equally across the **top ten** stocks when sorted by a **liquidity ratio**.[441]
- You review your holdings at the same time **every quarter** and only sell your positions if they've fallen out of the top 20. When that happens, you buy the next stock in line according to that sorted list.

These rules, over the last 20 years, would have realized an annualized return of almost **28%**![442]

There are absolutely tactical and rules-based strategies you could implement yourself. There are firms out there that specialize in this kind of research. There are also tools you could use to run these analyses yourself. If you go that "do it yourself" route, you should make sure the data you're using span at least one major crash or bear market. You should also study the worst historic draw-

---

440 Historical performance does not guarantee future results. Also, these examples just represent what would have happened had you been able to buy into each of the stocks at the prices they were at each specified point in time (i.e., at that same time every quarter). These returns do not represent an actual trading account. There may have been material economic or market factors not reflected here—such as potential liquidity issues—that could have impacted actual returns. These returns reflect a retroactive application of these rules designed with the full benefit of hindsight.

441 In this particular example, for the returns I'm about to share, we're using the Amihud Liquidity Ratio, a fundamental measure of a stock's liquidity. The more liquid a stock is the easier it is to buy and sell without incurring high transaction costs and without substantially impacting the stock's price.

442 Again, historical performance does not guarantee future results. Also, these examples just represent what would have happened had you been able to buy into each of the stocks at the prices they were at each specified point in time (i.e., at that same time every quarter). These returns do not represent an actual trading account. There may have been material economic or market factors not reflected here—such as potential liquidity issues—that could have impacted actual returns. These returns reflect a retroactive application of these rules designed with the full benefit of hindsight.

down[443] that would have occurred within a portfolio adhering to this strategy—given that people struggle to stay in the market as it is, you most likely shouldn't try to follow a rules-based model that will bring with it even more downside volatility than the market itself. As you discover strategies you like—that make logical sense to you, that would have realized a higher return than the market, and that would have come with less risk than the market—you could attempt to manually adhere to them on your own. Again, if that all sounds like something you're interested in, learning more about these strategies could be a valuable use of your time.

For most, however, that's not what I'd recommend—it can be difficult to be that disciplined.[444] But I do believe that for some, with enough time and dedication, it is possible to experience long-term success and overcome Modern Portfolio Theory's flaws.

## Bottom Line

The buy-and-hold, stock-and-bond-only portfolio has significant flaws as thoroughly explored throughout Myths 1–10. But that doesn't mean you should abandon the stock market altogether. **The solution to overcoming these flaws is to find strategies like these—that make sense to you— that can reduce your downside risk without sacrificing your upside potential.**

IT'S LIKE THERE'S A WHOLE 'NOTHER WORLD OF STOCK INVESTING OUT THERE...

---

443  Need a refresher on what drawdown is? Here's the footnote definition from Myth 5: Drawdown is a peak-to-trough (high-point-to-low-point) drop in value during a specific period for an investment, trading account, or fund. It's usually quoted as a percentage—derived from the total drop divided by the previous peak (high point). For example, if your investment account had $100,000 in it, and the funds drop to $80,000 before moving back above $100,000, then your account realized a 20% drawdown = ((100,000-80,000)/100,000).

444  This is another area where, for most people interested in this strategy, having a competent, qualified professional do the research, run the analyses, and manage the day-to-day buying and selling of securities could be worth a reasonable management fee.

MYTH: "The Stock Market Is Too Risky and Should Be Avoided."

REALITY: There are several ways to **limit your exposure to the market's downside risk** while still being able to capitalize on its upside potential.

# Conclusion

The stock market is an incredible way for people to invest their hard-earned money. It presents an amazing opportunity to take part in the growth of industry. It can positively impact your wealth in a big way.

But the traditional investment paradigm taught in schools, preached by professionals, and regurgitated by almost every financial personality out there leaves individual investors exposed to potentially devastating, life-altering flaws. If the past is any indication, many will probably get lucky and everything will work out just fine for them. But even then—even in a scenario where market returns aren't worse than ever before ... even then—with the odds of a roll of the die, people still get *screwed over by this easy advice*. **The mainstream investment paradigm is flawed in ways that could leave you financially devastated.**

**The good news is that these flaws can be overcome. It is absolutely possible realize better returns without being exposed to those risks.** Most of the potential solutions explored here are not new; they just might require a little extra effort on your part or some outside help. And that's not advice that most people want to hear—it doesn't sell quite as easily as the clichéd message of buy-and-hold and set-it-and-forget-it. I hope you see that now. And I hope you see the potentially life-altering importance of finding a better way to protect and grow your life savings.

## What To Do Next?

So that this can actually be the start of your journey to making a meaningful difference for your financial future, I've created free resources for those of you who made it through the book. You'll find all your actionable bonus material at **SpicerCapital.com/Go.**

I mentioned many of them throughout the footnotes of the book, and we're regularly creating more. You'll find information on how to access some of our comprehensive courses for free and guides to help you get started no matter where you happen to be right now.

Don't wait. Don't let this be just another one of those "good books you read but were unsure how to put it into action." At the very least, check out the site and see what's there …

*SpicerCapital.com/Go*

I hope you now have an idea of where you should begin your unique financial journey. I'd love to hear about it—my personal email is <u>Stephen@SpicerCapital.com</u>—please, reach out. Let me know how you plan to put yourself in a less stressful financial position.

I look forward to helping however I can.

I sincerely wish you all the best. Take care!

# Acknowledgments

More than anyone, I want to thank my amazing wife, Jessica. When I told her I was unsatisfied with and wanted to leave my well-paying job with a major financial institution, she was encouraging and incredibly supportive. Her patience has allowed me to build my business in a way I know will positively impact more people (versus making more money faster). Of the many lessons she's taught me, one of the most valuable has been to have the courage to challenge the traditional paradigms when something doesn't make sense. Honestly, if it weren't for that critical concept, my business would not be what it is today: finding the absolute best ways to help people invest and plan their financial future. Instead, it would probably be just another cookie-cutter financial firm. Jessica, I cannot imagine life without you. You make me a better person. Thank you!

If it weren't for my amazing team, I'd never have had the time to get my thoughts collected and out in the world like this. My talented property manager and resident real estate expert, Phillip Bentz, works more than full-time to keep my real estate interests thriving. My lead planner and cash flow expert, Brody Boston's, commitment to doing what is in our clients absolute best interest is inspiring. A big thanks to you both and all of Spicer Capital's growing team!

What we're building here would have taken much longer to achieve, if at all, without the help of my business partner, Edward Pritchett. Every time I've told him that we'll forgo recommending a certain product or investment because doing so is the right thing to do for our clients (even though it might have made our firm more money), he has always been 100% supportive. He shares our long-term vision of relentlessly finding and providing the absolute best there is. For that, I am extremely grateful!

David Hancock and the whole Morgan James Publishing team helped make this process a breeze. I feel unbelievably lucky to have the opportunity to work with them.

The talented Jillian Farnsworth has always been willing to lend a helping hand. Her skill with the camera is undeniable (jillianfarnsworth.com). I appreciate your love and support. I'm also very grateful for my illustrator, Damroe, who skillfully brought to life the characters in my head.

One more thing … is it weird to thank my children? As I write these acknowledgements, Grey, Lyle, Cass, and Rosie are only 8, 6, 3, and 0, yet they inspire me more than anyone to create resources of which I'm proud—resources that have the power to help anyone (especially them, if something were to happen to me) better care for themselves and their families financially. Thank you, kiddos! I am sure that over the years you will continue to bring out the best in me.

# About the Author

After operating under the umbrella of a large brokerage firm, Stephen came to realize that his personal investment strategy was incongruent with what he was supposed to, or even allowed to, recommend.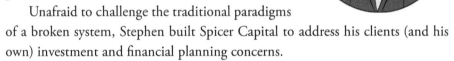

He grew increasingly uncomfortable with the prescribed advice.

Unafraid to challenge the traditional paradigms of a broken system, Stephen built Spicer Capital to address his clients (and his own) investment and financial planning concerns.

His goal is to guide concerned investors and savers to their own educated decisions. That process may take longer and require a little extra mental energy than does following mainstream advice blindly, but their understanding and conviction will be much stronger. They will be prepared, come what may!

Anyone who knows him well will confirm: Stephen is driven by his growing family. He married his brilliant high school sweetheart, and they have four beautiful children. His search for a better way to invest was initially inspired by his desire to care for them.

He hopes to be a resource for all who feel the same. To learn more about Stephen and Spicer Capital, visit: SpicerCapital.com/About.

# A free ebook edition is available with the purchase of this book.

**To claim your free ebook edition:**

1. Visit MorganJamesBOGO.com
2. Sign your name CLEARLY in the space
3. Complete the form and submit a photo of the entire copyright page
4. You or your friend can download the ebook to your preferred device

Morgan James **BOGO**™

A **FREE** ebook edition is available for you or a friend with the purchase of this print book.

CLEARLY SIGN YOUR NAME ABOVE

**Instructions to claim your free ebook edition:**
1. Visit MorganJamesBOGO.com
2. Sign your name CLEARLY in the space above
3. Complete the form and submit a photo of this entire page
4. You or your friend can download the ebook to your preferred device

## Print & Digital Together Forever.

Snap a photo

Free ebook

Read anywhere

Lightning Source UK Ltd.
Milton Keynes UK
UKHW011348250422
402024UK00011B/162